Flying Fingers

Master the Tools of Learning
Through the Joy of Writing

Dedication

I dedicate this book to anybody who likes reading, writing and believing in children, especially to my family and all the people who have influenced me and helped me along the path of writing and learning.

ISBN-13: 978-1-888045-19-12

ISBN-10: 1-888045-19-1

Library of Congress Control Number: 2007920903

Printed in the United States of America
10 9 8 7 6 5 4 3 2

For information concerning quantity discounts for educators, writing groups and home school organizations contact the publisher at:

Action Publishing, LLC
PO Box 391, Glendale, California 91209
(800) 644-2665 Fax: (323) 478-1767
www.actionpublishing.com

For information about Adora Svitak, visit www.adorasvitak.com

Book cover and typesetting by Visualscope Studios
www.visualscope.com

Flying Fingers

Master the Tools of Learning
Through the Joy of Writing

" I want my readers to be inspired by me to read and write more. "

Adora Svitak and Joyce Svitak

Action Publishing

If You Are a Parent
Who Desires to Better
Your Child's Chance to Be Happy and Succeed in Life
If You Are an Educator
Who Strives to Be More Innovative and Effective
If You Are Somebody
Who Enjoys the Innocence and Magic of
Imagination and Fantasy
This Book Is For You

Contents

Foreword
Our Philosophy and Approach
Q & A
How to Use This Book

Part I: The Joy of Writing

Part II: Learning Through Writing

Part III: Master The Tools Of Learning

Part IV: Best For Last

Foreword

What Adora has achieved is fascinating, but what interests parents more is how she is able to do it. Parents are eager to gain some insight from the mother who has witnessed the whole process. I am happy to share some insights with you, hoping that you will be inspired and encouraged to help your child achieve success and happiness in writing and learning.

I'd be lying if I denied being overjoyed with my children's achievements. However, my overwhelming sense of awe and pride in their accomplishments is sparked by their innate desire to learn, their passion for seeking knowledge and wisdom, their impulse to better themselves through self evaluation, their openness to constructive criticism, and their hard work.

Similar to the impressive but still humble beginning of Adora's writing journey, I started my odyssey to help Adora without much knowledge and guidance. I knew I needed to support and encourage her. I also knew I had to be able to give her concrete suggestions. I have an intuitive idea of a good story when I read one, but in the beginning I didn't have the exact language I needed to analyze Adora's stories and demonstrate how she could improve them. I read every writing book I could find at the library, but discovered that books about teaching children to write were scarce. The books I did find seemed to set their sights pretty low. Adora was already excelling beyond the levels of proficiency the authors touted as impressive. As luck would have it, it turned out I already had a writing teacher in the house—Adora herself.

I studied Adora's learning process by watching her write everyday. I observed which activities worked and which didn't. When Adora's writing began to really take off (and by that I mean when we realized she had written 250,000 words in one year and that most of it was entertaining and even profound), we set up a writing workshop to see if the same principles of teaching would work with other children. I observed the students in our writing workshop and learned triggers for breakthroughs. A lot of my studying was a process of trial and error. I offer you a shortcut to becoming your child's passionate audience and coach.

Your most important role in helping your child's writing is to become his/her loyal and enthusiastic listener. Showing absolute genuine interest and faith in your child's writing endeavor makes your child feel comfortable and motivated to show you their ideas and actual writing. Children feel insecurity just like adults—it is a big risk to their ego to expose their writing to you. It is crucial to be sensitive about your criticism. Instead of voicing your dissatisfaction directly, be curious and inquisitive. Your child will feel encouraged to discuss his/her work and think further with you.

Our Philosophy and Approach

You help your child's writing by showing interest, by encouraging reading, by using an inquisitive approach, coupled with the advantage of technology, and, finally, by nurturing writing as a form of entertainment, of play!

W — With Interest
R — Reading
I — Inquisitive approach
T — Technology
E — Entertainment

Showing your interest in your child's work is the first step towards becoming an effective writing coach. Most, if not all, children are eager to demonstrate their skills. It's your job to show them you are deeply interested in their work. This means taking the time to actually read every word they have written. Your interest means a great deal to them. It encourages them to continue even when the going gets rough.

Children who write read with a more critical eye. Consciously or unconsciously, they pay closer attention to sentence structure, word choice, and other key components of writing. This awareness then feeds back into their writing. Adora is aware of the tendency to write something that too closely resembles another writer's work she has read, but it is clear that the tone and style of the book she is currently reading often influences her writing style that day. I don't see this as a negative thing. Children's early learning depends heavily on imitation of various sources. Even if they can't verbalize abstract tenets of style, their natural inclination to mimic what they are reading will enhance their range as writers. It is essential to provide your child with a diverse selection of quality reading materials.

Because most children lack extensive life experience, in order for them to write with any depth they must be exposed to other people's experiences in their reading. A child's emotional connection to reading cannot be underestimated. When asked to write about something that made them sad, many students in our writing workshop wrote about things that had happened in their favorite books. Adora wrote that she feels so connected with the characters she reads about that when something sad or terrible happens to a character, she sometimes makes up new endings to stories in her head. No one wants their children to be sad, but it is important that they begin to develop understanding of people and events outside the scope of their own lives, which may be relatively comfortable.

An inquisitive approach toward your children's writing is more effective than direct, straightforward criticism. When you put your reaction toward the writing in the question format, more like a discussion or an offer of help, your child is more likely to open up to you and be less timid about sharing his or her work and more willing to consider other alternatives. Most problems in writing are not necessarily 'wrong', just things that can be improved. Ask your child 'What would make this better?' Most children/students have desire to improve themselves when the environment you create is conducive to exploring possibilities.

Utilizing the versatility of technology is essential to making your child's writing experiences less frustrating and more fun. Children declare their achievement with a sparkle in their eyes and excitement in their voice. With Microsoft Office/Word program, they can easily count the words they have written and feel proud of their accomplishment instantly. The result of their effort is tangible. The sense of instant success motivates them to go on and add one more sentence, one more paragraph and one more story to their portfolio. Children who write on computers are no longer limited by their inability to spell every word correctly or required to already know the exact definition of the words they want to use. The spell check and look up function can free them from fear and limitations, unleashing their creativity and building their confidence and love of writing.

One of our writing workshop's (www.seedsoflearning.com) proudest moments was when the mother of a student told us she had overheard her daughter encouraging a playmate to write as a playtime activity. One of our most reluctant students had become an activist, urging other children to explore and learn. Just a few weeks spent in our writing workshop changed her completely. From painfully dragging a few words out at a time to typing sentence after sentence without pause, a smile on her face, her eyes intent, she has discovered in writing a passion and form of entertainment.

When children realize that writing is one place where the sky is the limit and they are free to create whatever they want, they begin to turn to writing as a source of fun. Children have a natural love of 'make believe', and when you make them aware that writing is just another form of 'let's pretend,' it will lose the 'boring' association that sometimes accrues from the kinds of writing assignments given in school.

We have never imposed upon Adora's creativity by telling her how or what to write. However, most people will agree that there are certain basic factors that divide good writing from poor writing. Adora's intuitive understanding of many of these rules is cultivated by the tremendous number of books she reads. It has been our goal to encourage her to discover the rest of them on her own with some guidance from her parents and educators. The joy of discovery is tangible and a vital factor in a child's growth as a writer.

We hope that the story of Adora and the stories she has written will inspire and encourage you and your child to explore your own immense potential as writers.

Q and A with Joyce

In the following excerpts from interviews with other parents, Joyce answers a wide range of questions on how to encourage a child's interest in writing while simultaneously teaching basic and more advanced writing skills.

Julia's dad: My daughter loves to read and she has read many books. I would imagine that she could write pretty well and enjoy writing since she has read so many books.

Joyce: Enjoying reading doesn't automatically transfer to love for writing, but fortunately your daughter already has the basic building blocks needed to complete the foundation that supports becoming a good and passionate writer. Writing takes more effort, courage, and patience than reading. Writing involves complex thinking and constant practice. It's time consuming, and it leaves us open to criticism. It may not offer the instant gratification that reading offers.

In order to help your daughter transfer her passion to writing, you need to help her start practicing writing and begin to associate writing with the same kind of joy she derives from reading. When she sees your excitement and pride as you read her writing, she'll begin to realize that she has the power to entertain and inspire, and that this can be just as satisfying as being entertained and inspired. Reading and writing go hand-in-hand, but when she writes frequently, she will fully appreciate the beauty she encounters in her reading.

Bob's Mom: My son's handwriting is so messy and he hates to write. He makes so many grammar mistakes and spelling errors that he gets frustrated with his mistakes and his inability to write a decent assignment.

Joyce: Don't let the mechanics of writing block his creativity and passion. Providing him with a computer (a laptop is preferred) and teaching him basic typing skills will give him the freedom to change and correct his own work, using spell check and other helpful functions. After he learns how much fun writing can be, you can begin giving him creative assignments so that he can practice his handwriting. Once he has the creative bug, I guarantee he will be much less resistant.

Sarah's mom: My child shows a natural inclination towards writing, but I don't feel that I am equipped to evaluate her writing and give appropriate suggestions. I am afraid that I will make mistakes guiding her.

Joyce: As a parent it's paramount for you to become familiar with the subject you want to coach. In order to establish the credibility you need to gain the respect and confidence of your child, read as much as you can about the subject first. Read through this book and other writing books to develop some teaching techniques and skills.

Johnny's Mom: My child is really struggling with school writing assignments, such as book reports.

Joyce: When the school assignment becomes the symbol of fear and unpleasant memories, your child will do anything to avoid it or will turn out mediocre work in order to get the job done with quickly. The most effective method to help your child get out of this situation is not to directly tackle the problem; instead, set the assignment aside and work on something different.

For example, you can start to tell tall tales to each other as a family pastime. To release your child's inhibitions about creating stories, you can ask your child to recommend a book for you to read. Ask them why they think you would like the book. Thinking of reasons that you might want to read the book will awaken the same descriptive skills and reasoning that he'll need to write a good book report in the future.

Then, when he sits down to write his next book report, remind him of what a good job he did convincing you to read the book he liked. Explain that writing a book report is pretty much exactly the same thing, only this time he has the opportunity to create an even more convincing argument because he has more time.

Another strategy is to take Johnny to a bookstore and let him choose a book to buy. But before he can buy it, tell him he has to elaborate reasons for buying the book. You can structure your questions to get him thinking about what makes a book good. Learning to think this way will be useful to him when he sits down to write a book report in the future. When your child feels that he can easily describe stories and come up with answers about books, writing book reports will not be as daunting as before.

Ava's Dad: My child seems to enjoy writing and has a pretty impressive output. However, when I read her writing, it seems that it lacks themes. The story is boring and the plot doesn't make much sense.

Joyce: Congratulations! You have won half of the battle. Her interest in writing will motivate her to examine and evaluate the quality of her writing. At this juncture, learning to self-revise and edit will take her writing to the next level. In order to ensure that the process doesn't become tedious and tiresome, using a computer to perform such tasks is highly recommended. You can go over her writing with her and show her that adding a few words or sentences here or there is easy and can add so much to a story. When the plot seems unclear, ask her questions. Encourage her to make revisions in a fun way. Appeal to her interests. Propose your questions like a puzzle. How can you show me what you mean? What can you have your character do to help me understand this about their life or personality? Your child will find it so easy and quick to transform long but ordinary writing into a polished and sophisticated product that she will feel proud of her work.

Jessica's Mom: My child is in a gifted program. They have many academic writing assignments. She used to love creative writing when she was younger. Now, it seems to me that she just wants to get her assignment done, instead of spending time and effort to put more details and better organization into her writing.

Joyce: It's not uncommon that smart children turn in mediocre assignments. I think that it's very important not to kill your child's love for creative writing as they face more academic writing. If the demands of academic writing are stifling and preventing your child from using her imagination and creativity, you should find an opportunity to shift her attention to continuing her creative writing. The reason that your child doesn't find inspiration and motivation to write a book report may well be that she doesn't find any purpose in such writing, other than to fulfill a requirement. When the task we are required to perform has no meaning to us, we have neither stake nor pride in the end result, and therefore, the writing tends to be mediocre. It's time to reignite the joy she once felt about writing when she was younger. Children love to create their imaginary world through writing stories, and the freedom they have in story writing empowers their sense of self and pride.

Judy's mom: My child likes to write okay, but I wish that there was some way that I could devote more time to help her to write better. Where do I start and how do I start when I don't know how to encourage her to write more and give her productive and concrete suggestions?

Joyce: Schedule a workable time schedule to read your child's writing. To motivate her to write every day, express your eagerness to read the next chapter of her story. Give positive and concrete comments about her writing before raising questions to steer her to think about areas that need improvement.

Mike's mom: My son doesn't like to read, and I don't think that you can get him to write at all. What can I do to help him?

Joyce: The ability to read and write correlate with each other. The first step to get him interested in writing is to get him to read first. It will require a substantial investment of time and effort from parents to undo his old habits and establish the new and healthy habit of spending time reading as a pastime. Reduce other distracting activities such as watching television and playing video games and make books available instead. Find what interests him and get books that nurture his interest. Most kids like to tell jokes and be humorous. Get some kids' joke books to read and laugh together. Help your son to associate happy family time with reading together. Meantime, let him tell some stories or draw some cartoons with story lines. It may take some time, but the payoff will be his lifetime of love for reading and writing.

How to use this book

There are four parts to this book. The first part is comprised of nine stories, each followed by a writing lesson. At the beginning of every story, we include definitions to help your child with difficult vocabulary. Each story illustrates one component of good writing. At the end of each story we include an accompanying essay for parents or educators—tips which include questions to ask your child to enhance their learning followed by Adora's own tips and insights on writing, and a fun exercise to help your child make the connection between the abstract and the concrete.

Adora's stories serve four purposes. Her stories are here to inspire kids and parents to think beyond the boundaries of age. Adora's earlier stories are impressive in terms of length, but they are only exceptionally extraordinary when we limit our imagination by thinking that sophisticated writing is the province of adults and that children have no place in this arena. Her stories are a testament to what kids can accomplish when we, as their mentors, learn that age should not define how much they are capable of achieving.

On the contrary, as the role of technology continues to grow, more and more children will discover the ease and freedom that it can bring to their creative process. We hope that more children will come to share excitement and confidence in making use of technology.

Adora's stories are also helpful to novice writers because she uses an extensive vocabulary throughout her stories so reading them is a great way to pick up new words. Each story contains vocabulary in bold and the corresponding definitions. Reading Adora's stories will provide your child with proof that even kids can make big words sound easy and natural.

Adora's stories further provide excellent illustrations of basic writing principles. The stories provide you with a good base of examples of principles that can be applied to your child's own writing.

After your child reads one of Adora's stories, flip to the learning section. Though our suggested questions are simple in the larger context of Adora's interviews and the exercises, they are probably the single most important component to teaching your child to think for his or her self. Once your child has learned the patterns of questioning and thought that lead to new discoveries, they will be able to apply these same questions and patterns to other aspects of academics, creativity, and life.

After you have worked through the questions, read Adora's interviews and tips with your child. Ranging from funny to surprisingly mature, they provide unique insight into a child writer's creative process. They also convey a lot of Adora's personality, giving your student a down-to-earth guide that he/she can relate to.

We end each segment with a creative activity Adora enjoys. These are designed to awaken a child's joy in the creative process, and to encourage them to make the connection between that joy and creativity and more abstract concepts.

The second part of this book is devoted to "Learning Through Writing." We focus on the building blocks of writing (grammar, spelling, sentence structure, etc.) by demonstrating that the best way to learn fundamental aspects of writing is through writing itself. This segment also includes tips, interviews with Adora, and exercises.

The third part of this book focuses on using writing as a tool to teach other subjects. We present Adora's various styles of writing to show you ways that writing can be used to enhance or showcase a student's understanding of other subjects.

You will find a fascinating interview with Adora with topics ranging from serious to delightful in the fourth part of the book. We also selected a few poems from Adora's large collection of poetry.

Perhaps, most importantly, this book is designed to help you to encourage your child to write, write, and write. Your encouragement and enthusiasm are more important than rules. Wait until your child has written several stories before you begin correcting technicalities or asking him/her to think too abstractly. When your child is confident and excited about writing, you begin to encourage him/her to stretch and grow and explore.

Part I

The Joy of Writing

I am so occupied with my own writing that
I do not see much of the world around me.

Adora Svitak

Make Believe is Child's Play

"If you were given a choice of story writing or book reports, which one would you choose?" I asked one of my students from our writing workshop.

"I would choose stories," Sarah answered.

"Why?" I kept inquiring.

"Because I can make up anything I want when I write stories," Sarah replied, a smile on her face.

Most kids love to play games of make believe. When you give children an opportunity to create their stories without many restrictions or rules, their fear and inhibition will evaporate and they will enjoy themselves.

I once asked Adora about how she feels when she is writing her stories. These are her own words: "I feel as if I am in the story myself, a spectator high above the sky watching my characters. Sometimes I feel as if I am a character myself, and I feel their losses and their happiness. I do not pay attention to anything else but my own story. I am so occupied with my own writing that I do not see much of the world around me." When we truly enjoy ourselves, the rest of the world seems to disappear.

Her favorite posture when she is really into her writing is with her feet dangling from a tall chair, swinging back and forth, her head limply rested on her shoulder. The only sound you hear is the sound of the keyboard. The joy she feels when she writes is so overwhelming. It's hard to pull her away from her writing sometimes.

We have selected nine stories she has written in recent months. They vary in styles and types. They are arranged chronologically to show her progression as a writer.

All nine stories were edited only slightly in order to protect their original meaning and preserve her voice. Adora listened to suggestions and typed the corrections (including syntax and grammar) herself. Certain details may seem incongruous or illogical, but we think that they offer insight into the way a child's mind works and perhaps convey some of the spontaneity and joy Adora feels when she is writing. Though these stories have hardly been altered from their original form, Adora is militant about correct syntax and grammar, and you can use her stories to help explain writing guidelines to your child.

One of Adora's funniest stories, *The Realm of Possibility*, which Adora wrote in April of 2005, is the story of a headstrong and adventurous young girl named Gwen who exposes a plot against her father's kingdom. Unlike Adora's later stories, which have stronger plots and more evident themes, *The Realm of Possibility* is episodic. Some of Gwen's adventures are nonsensical, but they are also lively and wonderfully described. We included this story to give you a clear sense of her development and progress in comparison to her most recent work. We hope that it will give you a clear idea of how much you can help your child advance by following the same simple tenets and exercises that Adora finds helpful.

Conversely, *The Journal of a Pre-Teen* is chatty and contemporary. The nine-year-old protagonist is irritated when her mother decides she should keep a journal, but as the months progress she begins to use the journal as an outlet for her feelings about her older sister and the new baby her parents adopt from China. The main character's breezy tone and comedic asides make this insightful look at sibling rivalry hard to put down.

Returning to medieval times, *The Triumph of Love* is the story of a bookworm named Rotrind who takes to the battlefield when she discovers she is about to be married off for political reasons. This story showcases many of Adora's favorite things to write about: plucky protagonists who like to joust and read, children triumphing over boorish adult antagonists, and political hypocrisy from the view of a seven-year-old.

Set in ancient Egypt, *Agymah and the Amulet* is a great example of one of Adora's favorite tricks: mining ancient history for settings and plot lines. At the heart of this tale of palace intrigue is the growing friendship between a noble girl and the slave who is sent to care for her and her brothers. Some of our favorite bits: magic amulets, bizarre curses, and a particularly memorable crocodile hunt.

The first of Adora's stories to clearly illustrate a theme, *The Rebel's Reward* emphasizes the importance of having the will to go against the grain and do what you love. At an academy designed to turn its students into model wives, Kathryn is the only girl who bothers to learn to read and write. Instead of praising her, the teachers scold her for her messy appearance and her rebellious activities, which include sneaking off to learn how to fence. When a visiting nobleman is charmed by Kathryn's intelligence and spunk, her classmates are shocked to realize that sometimes learning can win you a good man, where etiquette alone won't.

As you may have noticed, most of Adora's stories feature a spunky and interesting protagonist that fascinates children. *The Danger Ship* is no exception. When Amber's parents die, she is sent to live on her uncle's ship, where a series of incidents (mutiny, a visit to a Louisiana plantation, and a fight with pirates) change her haughty attitude.

One of Adora's best stories, *The Tools of the Trade*, centers on the complex relationship between a master painter and his apprentice. Set in 15th C. Italy, this insightful coming-of-age story is rich with historical detail.

In *The Spoiled Prince*, a group of disgusted fairies kidnap pampered Prince Garrick and force him into situations where he learns lessons about patience, humility, compassion and other qualities he will need in order to be a good leader.

Showcasing the many things Adora learned the year she was seven, *Uncontrollable Magic* has a strong theme, snappy dialogue, an imaginative fantasy setting and memorable characters. While Adora was writing this, she told us that she was "really taking the time to let the relationship between Rowena and Anders deepen." It shows. Perhaps Adora's most emotionally mature work, *Uncontrollable Magic* contrasts dramatically with the author's work earlier in the year.

Adora writes with tremendous vigor, amusement and joy. We hope that her entertaining stories will bring delightful chuckles and loud laughter, a sense of wonder and childlike innocence to you when you read them. We also hope that you will enjoy reading these stories as much as Adora has enjoyed writing them.

The Triumph of Love

Rotrind sighed, rubbed her eyes, and slowly repeated the Ten Commandments. She was dreaming that she was with her favorite tutor, Master Hurston.

"Rotrind! Come back to your senses! You are supposed to recite the sentence about Plato!" Rotrind's other tutor, Master Verrick, exclaimed, adjusting his spectacles.

"Yes, Master Verrick," Rotrind said, half-awake.

"Now, we begin with the sentence about Plato, shall we?" Master Verrick asked. It was more of a command than a question.

"Yes, Master Verrick," Rotrind murmured obediently, though she had barely heard what Verrick had said.

"Good. Now…" Master Verrick began the sentence with Rotrind until the end of the lesson, when he was sure that Rotrind had it fully memorized.

"Remember, do this sentence, write an essay about the quest of Sir Galahad, write another paragraph chronicling the story of Sir Lancelot, research a bit about the theories of Aristotle, and remember not to sleep during the lesson…" Rotrind fled before Master Verrick could finish his sentence.

In her room Rotrind found **solace** by her tall window, and knelt down to pray to Saint Bede, patron saint of scholars. As she clutched the gold crucifix that hung around her neck, she prayed that she would learn and be intelligent. A few minutes later, a knock came at the door. A train of maids entered as Rotrind opened the door.

VOCABULARY LIST

solace - a source of comfort
petticoats - under dresses
kirtle - a long dress worn from the Middle Ages until the 17th C.
spherical - rounded like a ball
oubliette - a dungeon that can only be accessed through a trap door in the roof
virginal - in this case, a small legless harpsichord
feigned - pretended or faked
duchy - the territory ruled by a duke or duchess
amiable - friendly, easygoing
intently - with fixed attention
hastening - hurrying
haughtily - with air of being superior
ornate - highly decorated
antechamber - lobby or waiting room near the entrance
consent - permission
quintain - a medieval knight's target for jousting practice
devoured - eaten or consumed

5

"Your grandmother, Madame Sterling, wishes for us to help you dress for the main meal," the tallest, Lydia, said.

"Is it not rather early for the main meal to be served?" Rotrind inquired.

"Yes, milady, but Madame Sterling wishes it."

"Yes, then, Lydia, all of you, come in," Rotrind said.

First Rotrind was bathed in rosemary water. Then her long reddish-brown hair was brushed one hundred strokes, curled, and piled into a tight, painful hairstyle on top of her head. She was then dressed in three uncomfortable white **petticoats** and attired in a green velvet **kirtle**. Lydia tied the corset so tight that Rotrind could hardly breathe, and the white stockings that she pulled on just seemed too stiff. Last of all her feet were squeezed into a pair of tight silk slippers.

"You look gorgeous, milady!" Lydia cried with amazement.

"Escort me to the Main Hall," Rotrind commanded.

"Yes, milady," Lydia said softly. She and another maid took Rotrind's arms and escorted her downstairs to the Hall. Barons, counts, dukes (such as Rotrind's father), noblewomen, noblemen, knights, jesters, dancing dwarves, and servants stood chatting, exchanging friendly gossip, and commenting about the food. At the very head of the long table the king sat, looking on at the commotion and devouring an unusually large portion of spiced beef. His daughter, Princess Eleanor, sat at the foot at the table. She was queen in all but name.

"Announcing the arrival of Lady Rotrind, daughter of Sir Richard, son of the Duke of Cornwall and Aragon!" Rotrind felt her cheeks grow warm as two trumpeters played a loud fanfare to announce her arrival. The noblewomen moved away so that there would be room for Rotrind to sit down on the wooden bench.

"Did you hear that Madame Sterling might marry? For the fourth time?" Gossip spread easily around the court. Rotrind's ears perked up.

"What is that about Madame Sterling?" another noblewoman said.

"She might marry again! And to the Duke Tomas Fitzgerald!" the first noblewoman said.

"Madame Sterling is going to marry again—and to the Duke Tomas Fitzgerald?" Rotrind asked, amazed.

"She might! But that old codger Fitzgerald would make Madame

Sterling look beautiful—although Madame Sterling's beauty is limited." The noblewoman just then realized that she had been speaking to Madame Sterling's granddaughter, and hastily said, "No, I mean, er, well, I think actually Madame Sterling is very beautiful —"

Rotrind cut the noblewoman off and cried, "I will inform my father, Sir Richard, of this!"

The noblewoman looked frightened and said, "My dear, let's just smooth it all over and—"

"All of your efforts to flatter me will be for naught," Rotrind said coldly. The noblewoman said no more after that and after eating a generous helping of peas, cornbread, and some delicious salmon that had been caught by one of the King's huntsmen, Rotrind retired to her room, undid her hair, allowing it to hang in a cascade down on her shoulders and to her hip, took off her corset, flung her petticoats in the laundry basket, and changed into a plain white gown with black lace trimming the low neckline. Then she put on a black hooded cape and set off for her father's chambers, which were on the other side of the castle. Making sure that nobody was watching, Rotrind ran up to her father's door, knocked three times, and when the door was opened, threw off her hood.

"Father, I have something to speak to you about," Rotrind said quickly.

"Come in, Rotrind, my beauty," Sir Richard said. He was wearing a shirt of chain mail—obviously he had been practicing a few sword strokes with his close friend, the Duke Laurence, who was seated in the only chair in the room.

"Hello, Rotrind," Duke Laurence said. Rotrind nodded and curtsied, but she did not reply. She did not like Duke Laurence's pointed nose, his black, bushy eyebrows that almost covered his eyes, or his short black hair.

"What is it that you want to tell me? And should we have a bit of privacy…no offense, Laurence."

"Duke Laurence may stay if he wishes," Rotrind said, "however I do not believe this subject will be of much interest to him."

"Well put, Rotrind. However I will stay. Perhaps there will be a grain of interest in your story," Duke Laurence said in his cold voice.

Rotrind began, ignoring Duke Laurence and shifting her attention to Sir Richard, saying, "I have heard a certain noblewoman who was sitting next to me insult Grandmother Sterling."

"Who was that person?" Sir Richard exclaimed, jumping up and waving his sword, roaring, "I shall banish that woman off to some faraway place or else smite off her head!"

"I think I can help you," Duke Laurence said, his slow, cold voice cutting into Rotrind's thoughts, "I have a vast knowledge of noblewomen in this court due to my many marriages. If Rotrind can give me a proper description, I will be off and return promptly with the cursed woman."

"Thank you, my friend. Rotrind, what was the woman like?" Sir Richard asked.

"She was rather…**spherical**. She wore a heavily powdered wig. There was much rouge on her cheeks and she wore a black dress."

"Ah, I know who you are talking about. The name is Countess Armaine. She hangs around and listens to what should be kept private for other ears," Duke Laurence said.

"Summon her here immediately," Sir Richard said, "she has insulted my mother, and I do not want a woman who has insulted her mistress in this court."

"Yes, my friend," Duke Laurence said. Soon he returned with the countess, who looked frightened and was cursing.

"You will be sorry for this!" she shrieked as Duke Laurence held her tightly.

"Countess Armaine, you will be stripped of your title and banished to the far west," Sir Richard said majestically.

"Not the far west!" Countess Armaine looked terrified.

After pondering a bit, Sir Richard said, "For the sake of your husband, the Count, you will be sent to a convent that is not far from here. You will leave all of your personal belongings and dresses and jewelry here."

The Countess Armaine exclaimed, "Surely you can not be condemning me to this kind of cruelty! I am quite sure that there is no other duke crueler than yourself."

"My dear lady," Duke Laurence said coldly, "there is no duke more just than Sir Richard. And if it were not for his wishes, your head would be off by my sword in a matter of minutes."

"That may be," the Countess Armaine said, "but—"

"OUT!" Sir Richard suddenly bellowed. Countess Armaine fled for her life, but two knights pursued her, intent on claiming a reward from Sir Richard.

"If you insure that this woman is taken to the convent of Saint Veronica, this woman's trinkets and gems will go to your family," Sir Richard said. The two knights were off at once, and soon returned, saying that everything had gone smoothly.

"Thank you, Rotrind, for informing me of the Countess Armaine's insult to your grandmother," Sir Richard said to Rotrind after everyone had gone away from his apartments.

"You're welcome, Father," Rotrind said. Sir Richard looked outside at the darkening sky and remarked,

"You should be in your room now. I will escort you."

"Thank you, Father," she took his hand.

As they exited the room and stepped onto the dewy grass, Sir Richard exclaimed, "Rotrind, do you know who that is?"

"Who?" Rotrind asked.

"Him," Sir Richard said.

Rotrind looked ahead and saw a dark, sinister figure approaching them. Sir Richard drew out his sword from its glinting scabbard and said, "Rotrind, go quickly to the castle. Alert the king and his knights. If they do not believe you, here is my written note." Sir Richard took a piece of paper from his breast pocket and in his untidy scrawl, wrote,

Come quickly - unknown man approaching. Be on your guard.

Rotrind ran into the castle and alerted the king and the knights. The king called Rotrind "a little cherub" for alerting them. The knights, in full chain mail and armed with swords, lances, and shields came marching out smartly.

"Halt, unknown traveler!" the king commanded.

"I am a poor pilgrim, with nothing to defend myself except my knife, which would not hurt anybody and is merely made to cut soft bread or perhaps a block of smelly cheese. What do you wish of me?" the man whined.

"Show yourself," the king ordered. As the man flung his hood aside, he drew a sharp dagger from its leather sheath and cried out wildly. He lunged at the king, bringing the dagger down on his helmet. But the knights were ready. They had their swords, and Sir Richard wounded the man badly at the thigh.

When the knights had him finally cornered, he exclaimed, "The vengeance of my successors will be great! You will be sorry you ever treated me this way! They will avenge my death—"

The king complained of an earache and commanded that the man be gagged and imprisoned in the oubliette until an appropriate hangman could be found.

"Yes, majesty," the jailer said, turning away.

"Oh, first, ruffian, tell us your name," the king said.

"I shall tell you villains nothing," was the sullen reply.

One day, a few weeks later, Rotrind was studying Scripture with Master Hurston. Suddenly there was a banging and scraping at the door. Rotrind and Master Hurston leapt up from their chairs. Two squires whom Rotrind knew to serve her father opened the door. They were holding Master Merrtont, who taught Rotrind the lyre and the virginal.

"What is the meaning of this?" Master Hurston sputtered angrily, almost drowning out the sounds of his unusually loud fart.

"Yes, do you not know that you are in the presence of Lady Rotrind, daughter of Sir Richard, son of the Duke of Cornwall and Aragon?" Rotrind demanded angrily, clenching her teeth. She advanced towards the squires, her hand on the gold pommel of her dagger.

"Sir, and fair lady." At this the squires kissed Rotrind's extended hand. "I bring before you this villain, who is accused of plotting murder against fair Lady Rotrind, by poison in Lady Rotrind's wine that was to be put in by one of his associates (who do not reveal their identities) this evening. We hope you excuse us for our unseemly interrupting, but it is our duty to Sir Richard, son of the Duke of Cornwall and Aragon, and our duty to Lady Rotrind, daughter of Sir Richard, to inform you of this."

"Has my father been told of this, my men?" Rotrind asked, although she already knew the answer.

"No. We thought it best to inform you first. You and...er..."

"Master Hurston," Master Hurston said warmly, taking the squires' hands and shaking them firmly.

"Well met, Master Hurston."

"Yes," Master Hurston replied.

"And may I ask, are you sure that this man is the culprit? Or that there is even a plot against me? Do you have proof of this all?" Rotrind asked.

"Well…no. Duke Laurence, who is an honorable man and who would never lie, told us of this. He said that he had seen a message passed between Merrtont and a person whom he believed to be an old castle messenger," one squire, Peter, said.

"Duke Laurence is a shady character and not to be trusted." Rotrind's voice was hard and cold.

"I believe my ears betray me. It sounded like you said that Duke Laurence is not to be trusted?" the squires said in unison.

"I said that you are not to trust Duke Laurence," Rotrind said. Even Master Hurston, who was used to Rotrind's strange ways, was surprised and said,

"Seriously, m'lady Rotrind, you cannot mean what you say. The Duke Laurence is a close friend of your father and he would not lie."

"Yes, m'lady, listen to sense," the squires said.

"Duke Laurence hates Master Merrtont! He would try to frame him for every single thing that goes wrong in the castle. I suspect that Duke Laurence wrote the letter himself and **feigned** that it was written by Master Merrtont. And my father is not to be informed of this. Squires, you are dismissed. And Master Hurston, you also. And…wait! Swear to me you will not breathe a word of this to anyone. And especially not my father."

"As you wish, m'lady," Master Hurston and the squires hastily left the room, leaving Rotrind alone. She felt the desire for some warm drink to soothe her nerves, and rang the bell that summoned Marie, her personal lady-in-waiting.

"What do you desire, m'lady?" Marie asked.

"Bring some tea to me. Make sure that it is hot. And tell the royal hostler to saddle and make ready a horse for me."

"Yes, m'lady," Marie said, curtsying. In a few minutes, Rotrind's tea arrived, steaming hot. Marie tied a rag around the cup so that Rotrind would not burn her fingers when she held it.

"The hostler has made ready a steed?" Rotrind asked.

"Yes, m'lady. The mount is waiting for you to arrive."

"Tell Master Wenner that we will have my riding lessons early and take him to my room."

"Yes, m'lady," Marie said, leaving the room. Rotrind took another sip of tea. Soon Master Wenner arrived. He was a tall, thin man who always wore a waistcoat under his silk doublet, and though many would find him too solemn for their tastes, he had a way of explaining things that made Rotrind feel at ease.

"Welcome, Master Wenner. Please make yourself comfortable," Rotrind said. Master Wenner seated himself in the chair that was across from Rotrind, which was still warm from Master Hurston sitting on it minutes before.

"I have been informed by your lady-in-waiting, Marie, that we are to have our riding lessons earlier than usual today," Master Wenner said.

"Yes. I hope that there is not anything that troubles you with this schedule," Rotrind said.

"No, not at all," Master Wenner said, "I was merely curious, merely curious about this change."

"I wish to ride a horse again," Rotrind said, sipping the last of her tea, "so let us proceed to the field."

"Yes, m'lady," Master Wenner said. Leading the way out to the field, which was not far from the courtyard. At the gate to the field, a graceful dappled mare stood tossing her head and whinnying.

"This mare is not the kind of horse I was hoping for," Master Wenner said, "but it will do."

"I could ask the hostler to make ready another horse," Rotrind said.

"Oh, no, this will do," Master Wenner said, "I do not want to trouble you."

"Alright then," Rotrind said, and easily swung herself onto the saddle.

"Sit up straight. Good! Now hold the reins tight!"

Rotrind jabbed the horse's side with her silver spurs, and galloped off.

"Ride the horse at a gallop two times around the field," Master Wenner commanded. Rotrind obeyed and was soon back to where Master Wenner was standing.

"Now ride three times around the field at a trot," Master Wenner instructed. When Rotrind had finished that, Master Wenner taught her about the different kinds of saddles, and after that the lesson was over and Rotrind was free to do whatever she wanted to until luncheon, which was still an hour away. She went to her room and sat down on her bed. She was about to take a book from the shelf when a knock came at the door. She opened it to see her father's messenger, Fortindo.

"Your father wishes to see you, m'lady," Fortindo said, bowing.

"As you wish," Rotrind said, and allowed Fortindo to lead her to her father's room. After Rotrind was inside, he left.

"Hello, Father. What do you wish me for?" Rotrind asked.

"I have decided who you are to marry," Sir Richard said.

"Who?" Rotrind asked, suddenly alarmed.

"The nobleman Ferdinand Castello. You have seen him before. I decided a few days ago, and I forgot to tell you of my decision." Sir Richard felt guilty about lying to his daughter, but he knew that he could not explain his real reasoning to Rotrind.

"Not Castello!" Rotrind cried. Ferdinand was a short, overly plump man who had hair growing out of his nose, hairy skin, and little piggy eyes. His beard stuck out in places and his breath smelled of ale and moldy blue cheese. Plus he was twenty years older than Rotrind. Nobody wanted to sit next to him at a royal banquet or any other fine occasion because he had terrible table manners and farted at every grand speech. But he was rich and a favorite of the king.

"Yes, Castello," Sir Richard said sternly, astonished that he could sound so unkind to his only daughter.

"But he has the worst table manners and the worst appearance and he has the worst—"

Rotrind was cut off by Sir Richard, who said, "Sometimes you must think of what is best for your family. I couldn't just give you away to some poor serf, could I? Castello is wealthy and a favorite of the king. It may be that you dislike him, but marrying is not meant for love. Soon he will be promoted to the position of Grand Court Lord!" Sir Richard again surprised himself by sounding cold and harsh. Rotrind fought back tears and quivered, "But Father, is there not another man of noble birth that you could choose...just not Castello?"

"Not any who have asked. And you can't just remain unmarried. Not one person in my family will be unmarried if I can help it. You need to make your future. You're a duchess, Rotrind. There's an entire **duchy** counting on you to do what's best for them. And there's your family counting on you to do what's best. You may not agree, but this is what is best for you. I have already arranged with the king's own seamstresses to make your wedding dress and the best chefs in the court to make your wedding cake. And you will not have to see Castello much. He will mostly be away at court conferences." Seeing the horrified look in Rotrind's eyes, he mentally congratulated himself for avoiding telling her until the wedding preparations were already underway.

"But still, Father, it seems as bad as a punishment!" Rotrind said, her eyes growing watery and her voice quivering.

"And perhaps it is. I have heard that you are not doing well in your studies," Sir Richard said coldly. Rotrind, struggling to keep her voice from quaking, implored,

"But how could you say that, Father? You have never been like this to me before."

"You will marry Castello and that is final!" Sir Richard bellowed. "Now out of my room!"

Rotrind dashed away, sobbing uncontrollably, and did not hear anybody else's footsteps except her own. She was disturbed by Fortindo's voice saying, "Is anything wrong, milady?"

"Oh…hello, Fortindo," Rotrind said, wiping her tears away with her sleeve.

"Here, perhaps this might help," Fortindo said, handing Rotrind a pretty damask handkerchief. Rotrind wiped the rest of her tears away and handed the handkerchief back to Fortindo.

"Thank you," Rotrind said.

"Now, as I was asking, is anything wrong?" Fortindo asked.

"Everything is wrong," Rotrind said, her eyes beginning to water up again, "my father has commanded me to marry that horrible pig Ferdinand Castello, and he shouted at me as if he does not love me anymore."

"He has a reason for it, milady."

"What do you mean, Fortindo?"

"Your mother, bless her dear soul, has recently died at the nunnery and your father Sir Richard had not a chance to say his last farewells," Fortindo explained.

Rotrind did not care at all. Her mother had never been a part of her life. "But marrying Castello is the worst!" Rotrind cried, "He is so unattractive and he has the worst table manners…"

"If I may ask, milady, who do you really love?"

"I...I'm not really sure," Rotrind admitted after pondering it for a moment.

"If you permit me to, I will try to find another rich nobleman who is looking for a wife...I am sure that there is another person of your rank or higher, and unmarried. I believe a new noble just arrived yesterday. I could easily find him, if you wish."

"Actually, just stay, please," Rotrind said. "I want you to escort me to my room."

"As you wish, milady," Fortindo said, taking Rotrind's hand and leading her across the dewy field that separated Sir Richard's chambers from Rotrind's room.

"Thank you, Fortindo," Rotrind said, closing the door after him. After Rotrind was sure that he was gone, she tiptoed out and went downstairs to the kitchens. Rotrind was about to step in when a boy who looked to be about two years older than her blocked her way.

"What's your name?" the boy asked, his blue eyes twinkling.

"Lady Rotrind. I am the daughter of Sir Richard, who is the son of the Duke of Cornwall and Aragon," Rotrind said coldly.

"You may pass, then. And I am sorry for any delay I might have caused you. My name is Philip, son of Mark the court cook."

Rotrind, who felt a liking to Philip's friendly blue eyes and his **amiable** way of speaking, asked kindly, "Does your father work on a wedding cake?"

"Ah, yes. It shall be grand! There are to be little castles of brown sugar on the cake and little white sugar swans on the top layer of the cake, for there will be four layers, the bottom layer the biggest and the top layer the smallest," Philip said.

"Who is invited?" Rotrind asked.

"I am not sure," Phil admitted.

"And do you know who this cake is made for?"

"For Lady Rotrind and that aged puppet Ferdinand Castello," Philip said, laughing.

"That is correct. It is not my wish to marry Castello, however. It is for the good of my family," Rotrind said, staring up at the beautifully painted ceiling.

"I thought that. Why in God's name are you visiting the kitchens?" Phil asked.

"I wish to inquire about the food that will be served at my wedding."

"Actually you will choose most of that, and your father, since he is the man who is giving you away to old Castello," Philip said.

"Good. Now bring me to your father so that I can tell him what I want served," Rotrind commanded.

"Yes, milady," he said, leading Rotrind inside the kitchen. A stout man wearing a stained apron was squatting by a fire, watching a stew cauldron **intently**.

"Hello, Father. This is her ladyship Rotrind. She wishes to tell you what she desires to be served on her wedding day," Philip said.

"Ah, yes. Well, milady, just tell me and it shall be prepared exactly as you like," Mark said, bowing.

"I want a salmon dish, with the salmon done just right and sprinkled with herbs, spices, rosewater, and cilantro. Also a chicken roasted to perfection and surrounded by lettuce and cherry tomatoes arranged in an artistic way. Also make sure that there are small cakes that can be put next to the grand wedding cake. The flavors I want for these side cakes are lemon, almond, and vanilla. That is all I wish," Rotrind finished off.

"It shall be made, milady," Mark said, standing up and bowing.

"I will go now," Rotrind said. She walked out of the kitchens to the spiral staircase and went back upstairs to her room.

When she was at her room looking at the grand clock that was across from her window she realized it was already time for luncheon. She rang the bell for Marie and said, "Marie, set up the chair and the table in the luncheon position. I want a bowl of hot pumpkin soup and a salad. Also bring me some bread with oil and vinegar."

"Yes, milady," Marie said, **hastening** away.

About thirty minutes later Rotrind was sitting down in her chair taking dainty spoonfuls of pumpkin soup with cilantro when she heard a cry, a bang, and yelling from all sides.

"IT WAS YOUR FAULT! YOU OLD—"

"NO, IT WAS YOUR FAULT! YOU PACK OF LIES, I—"

"IT WAS HIS FAULT!"

"DASTARD, AS LONG AS I'M ALIVE I'LL NEVER STOP IN MY ATTEMPTS TO GIVE YOU A LESSON ONCE AND FOR ALL!"

Rotrind raced downstairs to see what the trouble was. Ferdinand Castello and some other noblemen who had been shouting with him immediately became silent as Rotrind entered.

"What is the meaning of this unseemly shouting?" Rotrind asked, dangerously advancing closer.

"I had nothing to do with it," Castello said, immediately puffing out his chest and looking at the rest of the noblemen with contempt.

"He is a liar and is a danger to all of us, my ladyship," one nobleman said.

"A danger to all of us! He's a danger to all of us!" Castello mimicked in a high, screechy voice. Rotrind had to bite her lip to keep from laughing and put her hand on the hilt of her sharp knife, which was hidden beneath the folds of her crimson kirtle.

"Just tell me what you have been shouting about," Rotrind said, struggling to keep her voice stern as she loosed the blade in its sheath.

"Oh, it's like this, lady," one nobleman said, "Castello stole something from the castle storerooms—we don't know what the thing he stole is—but whatever he stole, he denied it. He accused us of stealing the object, which of course we haven't."

"Turn your pockets out," Rotrind commanded **haughtily**. Castello grinned and turned his pockets out. A beautiful porcelain doll fell out and shattered on the hard ground.

"Who was this doll supposed to be for?" Rotrind asked sternly, placing her hands on her hips.

"My niece."

Rotrind grabbed onto Castello's leg so that he could not get away.

"I will tell my father about this," Rotrind said, "and you are coming with me." Castello did not seem the least bit afraid. He took her hand and allowed himself to be led to Sir Richard's chambers.

"You are sure that Castello stole this?" Sir Richard asked severely. Rotrind pointed to her father's ornate antechamber.

"I have evidence to prove that lout stole from the castle stores," she said coldly, holding up broken pieces of porcelain. "Is this not the fair make of Anuslin the craftsman? Are these golden locks not the curls of the wigmaker's client?"

"I agree with you, Rotrind," he said wearily. "But nothing can be done."

"Why can you not take action?" Rotrind demanded angrily.

"You are betrothed to him, Rotrind," Sir Richard said wearily, running his hand through his thinning hair. "It would simply not do for you to be married in the oubliette. After you are peacefully married I will warn him that he is not to do such a thing again."

"I refuse to marry such an oaf!" Rotrind shouted, stomping her foot. "Is my consent not the most important part of a prosperous marriage? You will receive no money from Castello if he feels that I am not being a loving wife!" Richard raised his hand for silence.

"Two days only do I grant to you to find a better nobleman," he said slowly. "But if you have not succeeded in your quest by then, you will have to marry Castello."

"Two!" Rotrind fumed with rage, gritting her teeth. "Two is unreasonable."

"Three days only can you search," Sir Richard said. And even without her father's word, Rotrind knew she was dismissed.

One day passed and still Rotrind had not found a suitable nobleman. She canceled all her lessons and spent most of her time searching around the court. She even went so far as to ask the King himself, who merely replied that Ferdinand Castello was a brave and honorable man. On the second day, Rotrind journeyed with her father to the fiefdom of Sir Arthur the Valiant, only to receive a betrothal suggestion about his one year-old son, William.

"That's no good!" Rotrind exclaimed. "My father says I must be married within three days!" Arthur's ambassador shrugged.

"You're actually fortunate to have been asked, your ladyship," he said, tying a few papers into a stack. "I must excuse myself." Rotrind swore under her breath and left the room. Sir Richard awaited her outside the door.

"No luck?" he asked, staring at the dark room. "I didn't think so. There is no choice but to marry Castello."

"There is still one more day!" Rotrind cried desperately.

"Yes, and that day will be spent in riding. We must get back to the castle in time for the grand wedding."

"Are there not any other dukedoms?" Rotrind persisted.

"Lord Elbert of Ainsworth rules a large portion of this land," Richard said doubtfully. "But he is old and ailed with leprosy."

"That is the only other place?" Rotrind asked hopelessly.

"No, I believe the Earl of Wylle has a son," Richard said, turning to Rotrind. "But enough of this. We must make our leave." Rotrind sighed and followed her father.

"Grant me just one more day," she pleaded. "Surely I will be able to find a man then."

"One more day then!" Richard was never that good at opposing his daughter. "But no more!"

As Rotrind mounted her small brown mare, she happened to look back and glimpse a party of horsemen approaching near.

"Father!" she cried, halting. "There are men behind us!" Richard turned sharply and stared at the men.

"They are naught but attendants, my bonnie Rotrind," he said gently, taking her hand. "Let us wait for them on our horses." Rotrind looked at the party again.

"They are approaching now," she pleaded. "Why cannot we just ride on?"

"They are to serve us, Rotrind," Richard said impatiently. "Sir Arthur has given them to us, or so is my guess."

"What if they be in return for me?" Rotrind asked, suddenly afraid. "What if this is to be only a betrothal gift from that empty-headed clod Arthur?"

"Do not speak in such a way of the Valiant One!" Richard exclaimed, turning to face his daughter. "If you are caught on his lands, you will be questioned and imprisoned!"

"I only speak the truth," Rotrind said sullenly, holding up her skirts. "But look, the attendants are approaching." Indeed the men had drawn near, and now Rotrind could see that the party was also composed of four laundresses and two maidservants.

"Halt, good sir, and let this company ride with you," the man in the front said, coming to a stop.

"As you can see, I have already halted," Richard said, a twinkle in his eyes. "And who may you be?"

"I am the Seneschal of the House of Arthur," the steward said proudly, drawing himself up. "I have been sent with a party of twelve squires to attend to you and your daughter. Four laundresses also have you been granted, with two maidservants to accompany your fair daughter."

"I thank you for this enormous gift," Richard said, bowing as well as one could do on a horse. "Are you to ride with us?"

"No, I must return to Sir Arthur," the seneschal said. "But you may take these servants."

"Really, sir, we aren't servants," a squire broke out, making a face. Rotrind stared at him shyly. "The steward just likes to call us that because he doesn't like to bring out the fact that we're of nobler birth than him!" Richard threw back his head and roared with laughter.

"Of nobler birth! Why, my dear squires, in the elder days of mirth and merriment the steward of a high house would often have been of nobler birth than the squires!" he exclaimed, riding towards the squires. "Pages, squires, knights—when you reached the position of knight, you could only then be slightly higher than the seneschal."

"The steward does not even allow us to bear arms!" the squire complained. "How our fathers would protest!"

"You have not yet learned the art of the lance?" Richard asked, raising his eyebrows.

Rotrind frowned. "Yes, we are studying it, but through boring textbooks."

"There is no practice with the **quintain**?" Richard inquired, setting off at a trot.

"No," the squire said, following Richard and Rotrind. "If you wish to know, I am called Walter."

"And the steward is Wendell," another squire chimed in.

"I hate having a name that is like the steward's," Walter said, making a face. "But when are we leaving?"

"Right now," Richard said. Rotrind jerked back to attention and the party set off.

By mid-afternoon the party had reached Darren's Point. It was a flat, empty space with nothing but loose stones and boulders around its rocky cliffs. There was a great ledge jutting out from the cliff wall, on which one could stand and look out onto the crashing waterfall that flowed into the river known as Darfin. Rotrind was awed by it all.

"It's grand, isn't it?" A voice behind Rotrind startled her. She immediately spun around. Walter stood behind her, staring at the great waves.

"Y-yes," Rotrind said, stunned. She looked back at the turquoise-blue waters, then at Walter.

"Why are you looking at me like that?" Walter demanded.

"Errr…I wasn't aware that I was looking at you strangely," Rotrind said, shifting nervously. "Sorry." Walter rolled his eyes and threw a small pebble across the waterfall.

"What are you doing?" Rotrind asked with interest, bending down to examine an identical pebble. "If you're trying to skip stones, I would advise you not to get to close to the cliff edge."

"I know, I know!" Walter sighed. "Once, in my second year as a page, my uncle, Lord Elbert of Ainsworth, took us all adventuring here at Darren's Point. One squi—no, sorry, page, accidentally tripped on a loose rock and fell into the Darfin. He wasn't ever found, and so we never came to Darren's Point again. Except for now, of course," he added hastily.

"Isn't your uncle—Lord Elbert—diseased with leprosy?" Rotrind inquired.

"Yes—how'd you know?" Walter asked, turning to Rotrind. "He really tries to keep it a secret from his countrymen."

"My father told me," Rotrind said proudly, tossing a rock into the unclear depths of Darfin.

"He—my uncle, that is—just singed his eyebrows yesterday," Walter said flatly. "Mother—Lady Juliet—went to the apothecary for the fifth time this morning. All they could recommend was a visit to the barber shop for the necessary surgery."

"Rotrind! Walter!" A loud holler rang out from the camp.

"That'll be Wesley," Walter said grimly, grabbing Rotrind's hand. "He thinks it's his duty as a senior squire to swat the 'minor' squires with Griselda's kitchen ladle as they enter buildings or whatever." Rotrind stifled a giggle.

"It's not funny!" Walter said, irritated. Rotrind bit her lip and said nothing as she followed Walter down back to the camp.

Rotrind felt that dinner was the greasiest meal ever served. Her scrambled eggs were drenched in olive oil, as were her fried chicken and green beans.

"This food is disgusting," she commented to Walter, who was sitting next to her. "Ugh—I rather wish I could throw these eggs under the table."

"Don't," Walter said earnestly. "We usually don't get much food to eat while we're traveling." Rotrind rolled her eyes and took another tiny nibble out of her green bean.

"I could eat the rest of your stuff for you, if you like," Walter offered, pushing his empty bowl aside. "That is, of course, if you're not hungry."

"Thank you," Rotrind sighed, dumping the contents of her bowl onto Walter's plate. "I'm overstuffed." Walter laughed at her feeble joke and quickly **devoured** the food. Rotrind stayed at the table and watched him with interest. Every bite he took seemed to spark a tingling in her veins. Richard had glanced across the table and was watching his daughter nervously, as if expecting something to happen.

"Father," Rotrind said quietly, leaning forward. "I need to talk with you…privately." Walter quickly slipped Rotrind a note and went back to eating. Richard nodded, wiped his mouth with his napkin, and followed Rotrind outside.

"I think I've found someone I want to marry," she whispered as soon as they were out of earshot. "Walter."

"What!" Richard exclaimed. Although he had expected something like this, he had not expected it so soon.

"I love him, Father!" Rotrind cried. "Whether he be of high birth or low birth I do not care!"

"You may love him, Rotrind," Richard said gently. "But you may not marry him."

"Why ever not?" Rotrind demanded.

"He is a low-ranking squire," Richard sighed. "If it were not so, he would be a worthy husband."

"His uncle is Lord Elbert of Ainsworth!" Rotrind exclaimed. "Surely you could not turn away the nephew of Lord Elbert?"

"Walter is the youngest son of the youngest son of Lord Alburn the First," Richard sighed wearily. "He has no lands, money, or inheritance."

"But, Father, surely you cannot turn me against my own true love!"

"Would I ever think to do so?" Richard asked, kissing Rotrind lightly on the cheek. "You may still have long, beautiful romantic dreams. But Ferdinand Castello is to be your husband." Rotrind wept and retired to her tent.

As she lay down to read a page or two from *Romeo and Juliet*, Rotrind suddenly remembered the note Walter had given her. What did it say? It might have a comforting word or two. She unfolded the crackled paper and scanned its contents. The note read "Meet me at

Darfin at the stroke of midnight. Love Walter." Rotrind could barely contain herself. Walter had written "Love"! She quickly dressed in a crimson kirtle and hurried to Darren's Point. Darfin's waters shone with the reflection of the moonlight, the most romantic thing Rotrind had ever seen.

"Rotrind," a voice whispered. Rotrind immediately knew it to be Walter's.

"I got your note," she said, feeling somewhat frightened for no particular reason.

"Good," Walter said, coming out from the bushes. "Come closer." Rotrind did as she was told. Walter kissed her gently on the lips.

"I love you," Rotrind breathed.

"As do I," said Walter. Leaving a brief note for Sir Richard, Walter and Rotrind stole away to a remote forest by the swift waters of the Darfin. So they lived there for the rest of their lives, bearing a long race of seemingly noble, healthy children and living in peace and pleasure.

People Are Not Mute, They Talk

Developing Dialogue in Your Story

Dialogue: Conversation between two or more characters. Dialogue should be included for a reason: it should serve to tell us something about the characters, plot, theme, or setting.

Observing children's early writing, you will notice that either dialogue is absent from the story, or the dialogue is presented in the rudimentary format of "He said" and "She said". It is important to develop the sophisticated dialogue that is multipurpose, perhaps establishing the situation even as it shows action, expresses ideas, develops character, or illuminates themes.

Although Adora understands the need for it now, dialogue is not as prevalent and sophisticated in her earlier writing. When she finally began adding snatches of conversation, it didn't really serve much purpose, though some of her early dialogue was pretty amusing to read.

In the beginning we let her be as silly and whimsical as she wanted. We were all excited to see how much fun she was having adding a new component to her writing. Only a few months ago we began to ask her to think about why or why not to include a segment of dialogue. Adora still has a lot of fun writing dialogue, but because (like most children) she has the desire to improve her strengths, she now welcomes a certain amount of coaching. We try to minimize any kind of direct influence on her style. Instead, we ask questions that lead her to think on a deeper level herself. "How would you feel if someone said that to you?" "What would you say back?" "Do you think your character would react differently?"

Children have two very different types of sources of inspiration for dialogue: real life or books, movies, and television. Using real life as an inspiration is in some ways preferable: entertainment aimed at children is notorious for hackneyed dialogue. Unfortunately, real life conversations are often clouded with meaningless asides and tedious details that do not translate well to the written page. The simple exercise below is a great way to demonstrate how to translate real conversation into the written word.

Try this:

Exploring alternatives to "He said, she said" offers a natural way to include details about character or setting. "Simpered", "roared", "muttered" and "mumbled" all give us a break in the monotony of using the word 'said' twenty times as well as giving us a more vivid mental image of the character.

So, ask your child, "In what tone of voice did your character say this? Did he yell it? Did he roar it?"

Most kids will have a lot of fun with this and it is an easy way to make a story funnier or more energetic. Also encourage your student to use adverbs when describing a conversation. 'He said' can become 'He said snidely' or 'She said shrilly'. Because these phrases provoke a much more vivid mental image, they are a great way to spark a kid's imagination.

For example earlier this year Adora might have written:

"Er, why don't you sit down?" Myles asked.

"You may not remember me," he said "I am your companion of old, Sherwin. The news I bring is urgent."

"Sherwin!" Myles said

"Yes, it is I," Sherwin said.

"And how did you come to earn that magnificent watch?" Myles asked.

Now she writes:

"Er, why don't you sit down?" Myles asked awkwardly.

"You may not remember me," the man sighed, rubbing his thinning hair absentmindedly. "I am your companion of old, Sherwin. The news I bring is urgent."

"Sherwin!" Myles cried, jumping up and knocking his earthenware mug from the table.

"Yes, it is I," Sherwin said, smiling halfheartedly.

"And how did you come to earn that magnificent watch?" Myles asked, eyeing the pocket watch suspiciously.

It's amazing to see how these small tricks and details can add immediate richness to a child's writing. Although dialogue is one of the most difficult skills to master, it's also one of the most fun to learn or teach. Working on dialogue is a perfect opportunity to make a lesson more interactive.

Interview and Tips from Adora

Joyce: When you write your dialogue, do you talk to the characters in your head?

Adora: First I have this picture in my head and the people are talking but I can't really hear what they're saying, but then the dialogue comes to me.

Joyce: How do you make your dialogue so real, so interesting and so funny?

Adora: It just comes to me. Try imaging it in your head.

Joyce: I've noticed that instead of saying 'he said' or 'she said', you'll use something more complex. For instance, in Kathryn you write *"It'll come along," Hum, the victor of their match, assured her.'* Or here you write *"Ew, Kathryn!" Hum exclaimed, disgusted.'*

Adora: If you just say, 'he said this' 'she said this,' you can't really imagine how she's saying it, whether she's yelling it or screaming it or whispering it. It's a good chance to tell the reader something about the character. For example, if you add 'she said snidely,' that tells the reader something about the character, that the character is snobby.

Joyce: When's a good time to put in dialogue?

Adora: Sometimes it's needed, you know? It makes the story more exciting, or sometimes it makes a nice break. Dialogue makes a story interesting because it helps show a character's personality traits.

Joyce: What are the functions of your dialogues?

Adora: I want it to be just realistic enough. Also dialogue is a way to move the story along, and tell the reader what the characters are planning on doing next.

Joyce: So why do you include so much dialogue in your stories?

Adora: People do talk to each other quite a lot in the real world. It's not like we're mutes.

 Tips for Parents and Educators

Have your child play 'spy' and transcribe overheard conversations into a notebook or laptop. Read through the conversations together. It will soon become evident that real conversations sound very different from dialogue in movies, books, and television. Real conversations meander and dead end. They are frequently slogged down by meaningless filler.

Next, ask your child to survey the conversation they have written down, and X out any parts that seem boring, don't tell us anything new about the people in question, or don't seem to be going anywhere. What he/she is left with will retain the flavor of a real conversation, but have more of the snap one craves from fiction. Writing dialogue is about capturing the essence of conversation.

Questions to Ask Students

1. You said before your character was kind: do you think this is really the sort of thing they'd say?

2. This scene is about ———— . How does this dialogue relate to that?

3. What could you have the character say instead that would get us thinking about the main story again?

4. How would you react if someone said that to you?

5. If you were angry in this situation, would you let everyone know, or would you try to hide it?

Tips for More Advanced Students

1. Once you have established who is involved in a dialogue, it is not always necessary to keep adding 'he said' or 'she shouted' each time a character speaks. For example, when writing a scene in which only two characters are conversing, it's okay to skip over this convention until you come to a point in the dialogue you think has the potential to confuse the reader.

2. Sometimes a line like 'Myles stood in the doorway' can replace the more traditional 'Myles said.' The advantage here is that this gives you the opportunity to give the reader a clear mental image of the scene.

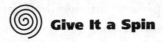 **Give It a Spin**

1. Help your child and another student or friend come up with a scene-by-scene plot outline for a simple play. Have both kids create profiles for the character they want to play, asking them to get as in-depth as possible. Have the kids improvise the scenes while you transcribe the dialogue they create. If things seem stilted or overly dramatic or unrealistic, stop the kids and ask them questions (see above). This exercise gives kids a visceral association with the thought process behind creating a dynamic dialogue.

2. Role reversal play: Ask your child to switch roles with you. You will speak and act like your child and your child will speak and act like you. You imitate your child, the way he/she talks, and he/she does the same. It's great fun and gives your child a chance to observe and express your characteristics, and at the same time have his or her personality mirrored back. After the game, you can have your child write a dialogue based on this activity.

The Realm of Possibilities
Prologue
The Mirror of Zeda

The Duke Raxere of Skere stared at the Mirror of Zeda. His black slit-eyes glowed.

"It is done," he said to his awaiting servant. "Now you must go." Guliset nodded quickly.

"My master, I obey," the old man said.

"And one thing, Guliset. There is a young girl in this mirror. It seems that she will be a threat to you and me. But no mind," Raxere brushed the girl from his mind. Guliset left the room.

Gwen quickly pulled her green gown over her head. It wouldn't do for Lord Esper to catch her in her undergarments! She tied the golden ribbon around her slender waist and tossed back her long mane of brown hair. Her sandals could wait until she went outside to the gardens. It felt good to walk around on the cool marble floors barefoot.

"Gwen, daughter! Are you finished dressing yet?" Lord Esper waited outside the door impatiently.

"I'm coming!" Gwen cried, smoothing her hair one last time.

Esper took his daughter's hand.

"I've an important affair with some ambassadors from Bronsel, so you just stay in the nursery or play outside until then. I don't want you wandering near the rest of the village; there's been a

VOCABULARY LIST

oubliette - a dungeon one can only enter or exit through a trap door in the ceiling

acquire - to obtain, to come by, to get hold of

hastening - hurrying

encounter - to meet or come across something or someone either unexpectedly or with aggression

dilemma - problem, situation in which someone is forced to choose between two unsatisfactory choices

louts - thugs, hoodlums

eerily - creepy, unnerving manner

intentions - aims, objectives

trellis - A wooden structure used to train a plant to grow a certain way

emerged - came out

mock - fake, pretend. To mock someone is to mimic someone or to make them appear silly or ridiculous.

impassively - without any display of emotion

barbaric - uncivilized, cruel

drab - dull in color

flounder - to move with serious difficulty, almost sinking

sinister - threatening, evil seeming

dignity - poise, self-respect

wroth - wrathful (an archaic or literary version of the word, not in general usage) brawl over on the outskirts. I don't want to be bothered until twelve o' clock," Esper said.

"Yes, Father," Gwen said meekly. Although she would have protested in another case, this time it was different. Big men, drunken too, made Gwen nervous.

"And I'm free for the rest of the day, unless an unexpected appointment comes up," Esper said, checking his gold pocket watch. Breakfast was the usual—porridge and meatballs. Gwen picked at her food. Porridge was never her favorite, and the meatballs were hard and tough.

"Are ye done, ma'm?" It was Stella's voice.

"Mmmhmm," Gwen mumbled. Stella took Gwen's plate and added it to her enormous pile. After breakfast, Esper went to meet with the ambassadors from Bronsel, and Gwen went outside to the royal gardens. The gardens were nice, and smelled very good, but they were dull, and no place for a child. Next she went into the nursery. Gwen felt she had outgrown it long ago, but it was fun to play with all of the toys and laugh over her four and five year old drawings. Plus, the thick glass floor allowed her to spy on everyone around the castle. Lord Esper was with the ambassadors in his meeting room. She moved down to the other end of the nursery. In the kitchens, the servants were exchanging gossip as usual.

"Me Amalia's gonna get married off to some garden boy," Gwen could just make out. What garden boy? Ion? Duru? Fells? Oh well. She would see soon enough. Outside, the soldiers were having their daily drills. "Boring", Gwen thought, rolling her eyes and moving away to look at the prisoners in the castle **oubliette**. There were only three men. They were unkempt and filthy, their hands dark and covered with dirt. Although she pitied them, Gwen knew that they were law-breakers and had to be punished.

There was nothing else to see. Nothing else to do, in other words. Gwen lay her head back onto the babyish bed she had slept in when she was younger. She was roused by the sound of wagon wheels. She scrambled downstairs. Outside, a tall man was displaying objects to an interested crowd.

"Stand aside. Make room for me, Gwen, daughter of Lord Esper," Gwen said. The crowd parted to let Gwen pass.

"Merchant," Gwen said, "by whose license do you wander the lands of my father Lord Esper?"

"Forgive me if I was trespassing," the merchant said, "but know this, young maiden, I am Guliset, and I have traveled from faraway, and I have seen many sights, and I have **acquired** many things. It would please me greatly if you could take a look."

"Bring your items," Gwen commanded. Guliset bowed and waved another man over.

"Show her the objects, and be quick with it," Guliset said to the man.

"Yes, sir," the man said, **hastening** away. Gwen, thinking she should follow the man, walked after him. A long tablecloth was laid across on the grass, with many items waiting on it.

"I have knives, which you most certainly would have no interest in, brooms for elderly spinsters, embroidered and perfumed handkerchiefs. Perhaps you would like one?" Guliset said.

"What other things can be purchased?" Gwen asked, pursing her lips.

"Ah, I see you already want to see more of my fine wares! There are crystal vases, fine china, all kinds of cheeses, fancy gowns, ribbons, everything," Guliset said.

"Show me the gowns," Gwen said. Guliset took a number of packages from the wagon. He carefully unwrapped the packages.

"My colors are green, blue, yellow, brown, and white," Guliset said. All of the gowns were so stunning Gwen could not decide which color to choose.

"I think I will have all of them," Gwen said finally.

"And that will be thirty silver coins," Guliset said.

Gwen dug in her pouch to find the coins. Finally she scraped the coins up and handed them to Guliset. After carefully wrapping the gowns again, Guliset handed them to Gwen.

"Thank you for having a look," he said.

"Oh and one more thing," Gwen said.

"What?"

"I want a knife."

"But you are a girl!" the surprise on Guliset's face was obvious.

"And so? I want a knife with a long and sharp blade," Gwen said. Before Guliset could say anything, Gwen took the best knife, pressed some coins into Guliest's hands, and ran off to the castle.

That night, at supper with Lord Esper, Gwen told her father about the **encounter** with Guliset.

"Hmm, I wish to see this merchant. He has a variety of things, you say, daughter?" Esper asked.

"Yes, Father. He has everything!" Gwen cried.

"Very well. On the morrow, then, we shall go out together, and you must show me the things," Esper said, delicately tasting a bit of the perfectly-cooked salmon.

After dinner that night, as usual, Gwen retired to her room, brushed her teeth, undressed for bed, and continued to read *Hannibal: A History*. When she had finished reading, she turned the lights out.

Early the next morning, Gwen awoke, quickly dressed, and ate a hasty breakfast of scrambled eggs and toast. At the Grand Archway Esper was waiting to escort her.

"Take me to this merchant Guliset," Esper commanded. Guliset was found at the same place he had been when meeting Gwen. This time, however, he seemed to have a **dilemma** on his hands.

"Stupid! Stupid! Blasted idiots! Oh, I'll take the livers out of you morons!" Guliset was running, shouting, and spitting at the men who stayed behind. Some saliva missed Gwen's dress by an inch.

"Stop, in the name of Lord Esper of Lien! I command you!" Esper was enraged. The entire area fell silent.

"I beg your pardon, yer lordship," Guliset said gruffly, "but these stupid **louts** just knocked o'er a barrel of me best whiskey." Some of the other men twitched nervously.

"Are you aware of the rule which clearly states that any harmful alcohol is forbidden?" Esper's stare bored into Guliset's face.

"Er, no, yer lordship," Guliset said.

Esper raised his bushy eyebrows.

"Er, yes," Guliset said, fidgeting and twisting his hands nervously.

"Gwen, bring some parchment, an inkstand, and my quill," Esper commanded.

"Yes, Father," Gwen said, running off to do as she was bidden. Within moments, she returned with the parchment and the quill.

"What's it for, Father?" Gwen asked breathlessly.

"Never mind that," Esper said sharply. Turning to Guliset, he said, "What is your full name?"

"Guliset Zeby," Guliset said.

"Occupation?" Esper began writing.

"He's a merchant," Gwen interrupted before Guliset could say anything.

"Gwen, it is not for you to say. Guliset, follow me," Esper said. Guliset remained standing.

"Follow my father," Gwen said. Guliset simply stood.

"Follow me!" Esper sputtered.

"No," Guliset simply said.

"Guards, take this unlawful man!" Esper shouted.

Guliset held his ground and did not even step back. When the guards had hold of his shoulders, he said, "I see no reason why whiskey should be forbidden."

"It is unhealthy and stunts your growth," Esper said.

"Does it?" the look on Guliset's face was bored, uninterested.

"If you were a literary man, you would most certainly know that," Esper smirked, "but I suppose that you have little education."

"I will not hear you insult the noble name of the Zeby!" Guliset lunged at Esper.

"Zeby, eh? Hmm, perhaps because of your grand name, I should give you the grand position of feeding the pigs," Esper said, laughing.

"I - WILL - HAVE - REVENGE!" Guliset roared each word slowly and clearly.

"Guards, take him to the oubliette to clear his head a bit," Esper said.

"No!" Guliset cried.

As he was dragged away to the oubliette, Gwen and Esper went back to the castle.

"Well, er, you know, the ambassadors from Bronsel would like to meet you," Esper said to Gwen.

"Do I have to?" Gwen asked.

"Yes, you have to," Esper said firmly.

The ambassadors from Bronsel were short, fat men with fuzzy beards that looked like caterpillars. They were all almost bald, but they had enormous amounts of hair growing out of their ears. Privately, when talking to her maid, Gwen would later refer to them as "thick lips."

One of the ambassadors, by the name of Count Cedilion, seemed to be interested in marrying Gwen off to his master, Sir Kenkye of Bronsel. Esper dismissed that idea with a wave of his hand.

"My daughter is too young; your master too old. And Kenkye lives far, far away in lands where I would not be able to wander," Esper said.

"Your niece, er, Lady Lindsay, er, perhaps could wed Sir Kenkye," an ambassador named Baron Brockhimer suggested.

"My niece is an orphan, and, as strange as it may seem to you, it is up to her maternal grandfather to decide whom she marries," Esper said impatiently.

"I must warn you, Sir Kenkye is not used to having his requests refused," Cedilion said.

"And I must tell you, Count, that I am not used to people like you questioning what I have clearly stated!" Esper shouted impatiently.

"Yes, well, beg your pardon, friend, no more of that matter," Cedilion said.

"What about what you were saying about that trade of men…" Soon the ambassadors and Esper were lost in a boring conversation, so Gwen took her chance and quietly slipped away.

Raxere looked in the Mirror of Zeda. He saw himself, white hair flowing down past his shoulders. The image faded, and Raxere saw a girl. This time she was holding a knife, and she was killing—who was it?—Guliset! The girl faded away, and Raxere again took the place of the girl. This time he was at the head of a large army.

"So I shall be victorious," Raxere whispered to himself, his thin fingers wrapping **eerily** around each other.

After she had escaped from the room, Gwen breathed a sigh of relief and looked around. Where was she to go? The nursery was at the moment being cleaned by the maids, and it was raining heavily outside. Gwen was too old to beg cookies from Cook as she used to, and the rest of the castle was out-of-bounds to her.

"Why is it out of bounds?" she thought to herself suddenly. It wouldn't hurt to have a peek! There was a series of spiral steps that led up to a small wooden door. Gwen entered. Once inside, she sniffed around. The air smelled damp and musty. It was cold, too. Shivering, she took a peek behind a plain gray curtain that hung from one of the rafters. She was extremely surprised to see Guliset and some other people.

"And now, the main thing is to keep that Esper from discovering our **intentions**," Guliset said. Gwen stuck her head in further, interested.

"Hey! Whaddya be doing here?" One man lunged at Gwen. She ran past the door all the way downstairs, where Lord Esper was waiting.

"Gwen." His voice was harsh. "You were in the out-of-bounds area."

"Yes, Father," Gwen said, bowing her head.

"I told you not to go there," Esper said.

"Father! I heard Guliset, and he was saying things like 'and now the main thing is to keep that Esper from discovering our intentions!'" Gwen blurted.

"Gwen, you speak foolish nonsense. You will be locked in your room for two weeks for going where I told you not to," Esper said. Before Gwen could say anything, he had shouted, "Martha Lucille! Take Gwen to her room." Martha Lucille, a middle-aged, sour-faced maid, took Gwen's hand, and led her upstairs to her room.

"Misbehavin' again, eh?" Martha Lucille asked, raising her eyebrows.

Gwen turned around and did not answer. She shut the door in Martha Lucille's face and collapsed into her chair.

"It's been a very long day," Gwen thought to herself. Luckily, Gwen had her own private library, which was a great source of entertainment. She dragged a stool over to one of the shelves to see if she could find a book she hadn't read in a while. Most of the books were ones that Gwen had already read, like *The Death of a Hag Lord* or *Foreign Princess*. However, as she neared the top of the shelf, Gwen noticed a rather crooked and worn old book with some pages sticking out.

"It's quite a tattered old thing," Gwen said to herself, pulling the book down from the shelf. Opening the book, Gwen spied a yellowed parchment that was folded carefully and stuck between the pages. When she unfolded it, she gasped. The village of Lien was in a far Eastern corner, a mere dot on the gigantic map. Squanee, which was fifteen miles away and the closest trading village, was shown next to Lien. Yugz, yet another trading village, was shown slightly farther away and above Lien. Bronsel lay far to the west, and Skere was far north from Bronsel. Suddenly, the map extended in Gwen's hands.

"Whoa!" she gasped again. Now the map went into more detail, like Stenfot Forest, the Trail of the Realm, the Elea Mountains, the Liness Palace, the River of the Realm, the Rilite River, Tosna Fort, The Meadows of Paradise, and Zeda. "The Realm of Possibility" was printed on the bottom of the map. A gush of air blew through the open window. Gwen looked out. She had spent so much time looking at the map, she didn't even realize the sun was already setting! Just then, she noticed the **trellis** that lined the walls below her windows.

"Why don't I just go for a little walk outside and around the village?" she asked herself. Taking a deep breath, she stuck her foot out onto the trellis. This isn't so hard, she thought. The next trellis was rather wobbly, but it held Gwen. Five more to go, Gwen thought. When she was safely down, Gwen crossed the soldier's field and climbed over the gates. The villagers paid no attention to Gwen, as they were used to seeing her wander around. When it started to darken, Gwen tried to head back, but found herself hopelessly lost and turning around in circles. The streets were dark, and everybody was inside of their hovels, warm and snug. Lights were shining through the windows.

"I can find my way back by myself, anyways, if I try," Gwen told herself. Thinking that the thicket of trees a few feet away was the one that separated the village from the castle, Gwen wandered even further. Unfortunately, a few minutes later, she realized she had wandered too far.

"Stenfot Forest!" Gwen whispered with horror. She didn't even dare look around. All she wanted was to be back home safely, tucked in her own bed, without having to worry about the vicious beasts that roamed Stenfot Forest.

"It's useless to try to find my way in the dark," Gwen said out loud, "so I might as well just climb up a tree for the night." Gwen soon found that climbing trees in the dark and with a long gown on was very difficult, but she made it to a spot halfway up that had many spreading branches, without any injuries except for a small scrape on her arm.

"And now here's where I'll sleep for the night," Gwen said, yawning and reclining on the thickest branch.

Early the next morning, Gwen carefully climbed out of the tree and found herself face to face with the largest species of wolf she had ever seen. Gwen felt like screaming, but quickly calmed herself. *The wolf might attack if I scare it*, Gwen thought. She felt around her gown for her knife and, relieved, touched the blade. The wolf's yellow eyes glinted at her, even though it was broad daylight.

"What do you want? Begone!" Gwen shouted. The wolf continued staring at her.

"Wait a second…" Gwen suddenly had an idea. Her life would probably depend on whether it worked or not, but Gwen was ready for the adventure.

"C'mere, c'mere," Gwen said, gesturing with her hands. The wolf neared closer to her. Taking a deep breath, she jumped onto the wolf's back. Springing forward, the wolf began to run at an extreme speed, covering the fifteen miles through Stenfot Forest, all the way to Squanee.

The villagers turned to stare as Gwen, on the wolf's back, passed through.

"Wolf-girl," one fat little man said, stepping forward, "I congratulate you. Are you aware that wolf has been the terror of our village for many days? Our village braves, full-grown men, attempted to tame the animal. Alas, it was an attempt, and they were unsuccessful. Now you, merely a girl, have tamed the wolf, and your name will be a legend on the Sq'uanak's tongues after your own time."

A great cheer arose. Gwen was about to pet the wolf when she realized it wasn't there anymore. She remembered what her grandmother had told her about forest-demons who took the form of other animals, but she quickly dismissed that idea. If it had been a forest-demon, why, then, she wouldn't even be alive! Perhaps it was a good spirit, sent to protect her. Yes, Gwen thought, that's more like it.

"Anyways, we don't even know your name yet," a man said.

"Oh," Gwen said, blushing. "I'm Gwen."

"Well, anyways, come here," the fat little man who had talked with Gwen earlier stepped forward and took her hand, "and I'm Quincy."

"Great suns! By the moon, you'll be tripping all over on that gown!" a tall, thin woman wearing a man's tunic stepped out of the place Quincy was leading Gwen to. Gwen looked at her in astonishment.

"We women and girls all wear men's and boys' tunics," the woman explained. "Oh, and, I'm Ivy."

"Here, we have a spare," Quincy said, taking another wool tunic out, complete with a thick leather belt and black wooden shoes that were only slightly too big for Gwen.

"Ah, I see you've got a knife! It's very important to have weapons around here. You never know when you may need to defend yourself!" Quincy exclaimed, noticing Gwen's knife. Gwen changed into her new boy's tunic in a different room. She liked the freedom of her new clothes, but the tunic was hot and itchy. Gwen strapped the belt around her waist, buckling her knife on also. When she **emerged** from the room in the tunic, Quincy clapped.

"Ah, bravo, bravo!" he said, laughing so much tears ran down his cheeks.

Ivy looked her up and down with approval.

"You'll do," she said. Quincy invited Gwen to stay for a day before returning back to Lien, and Gwen readily accepted. After having lunch, playing, and talking with Quincy and Ivy, she had dinner and flopped onto the large, soft bed.

The next morning, Gwen arose, washed her hair and her face in the basin of water Ivy brought her. Quincy took Gwen's hand and led her to the breakfast nook.

"We've scrambled eggs, toast, and bacon," Quincy said, "I hope you find it suitable."

The eggs were very well-cooked, with not one bit of runny yolk and the bacon was crisp and crunchy.

"This is delicious!" Gwen exclaimed between mouthfuls of eggs.

"Thank you," Quincy said, beaming, "Ivy cooks just so, so excellent, doesn't she?"

"Mmmhmm," Gwen nodded.

"I've told you, Quincy, my mother taught me a few cooking things," Ivy said, rolling her eyes with **mock** annoyance.

"Not a few, quite a lot!" Quincy cried, chuckling.

"I smell somethin' good, if it ain't by the moon Ivy's good ole bacon!" A tall man walked in.

"You shan't get one piece, Rollan Yord!" Ivy cried, laughing.

"I reckon that there's gonna be some payment I'll have to scrape up?" the man called Rollan asked, raising his eyebrows with mock surprise.

"Aye that's it, if you'll be wanting your meal!" Ivy cried.

"How's grooming the horses?" Rollan asked. Ivy wrinkled her nose.

"Those tender babes, why, they were cowing in their stalls for eight suns after ye did your torture on 'em!"

Rollan chuckled. "Not to worry, me girl, I'll just milk your moon-cursed cow," he said.

"Moon cursed indeed! As if you doubt the noble Sun laid his blessing on our Rana! Oh well, here's the milking bowl!" Ivy tossed a small wooden bowl to Rollan, who promptly caught it.

"I'll be back sooner than you expect!" Rollan promised.

After Rollan had gone, Gwen asked, "Who's Rollan?"

"Oh, he just does odd chores 'round here. I can always trust him to milk the cow," Ivy said, scraping the last of the eggs onto a plate, along with a fresh piece of toast and some bacon.

"He's a good'un, we took him in when he was but a lad, and a clumsy orphan too, and now he's repaying the favor," Quincy explained.

"He's rather like a giant," Gwen said doubtfully. Quincy shrugged.

"He's got big bones, ye know, it comes in the noblest breeds," Quincy said.

"He's a great one for milking," Ivy said as Rollan returned.

"Here's your bowl o' milk," Rollan said, "now where's me breakfast?"

"Right here," Ivy said, pushing the plate over.

"Thanky," Rollan said, wolfing the food down.

"Er, I should be going now," Gwen said, biting her fingernails.

"You know, Ivy's a fortune teller. Perhaps you'd want to get your fortune before you leave?" Quincy whispered into Gwen's ear.

"Sure," Gwen said.

"Ivy, why don't you tell Gwen's fortune before she leaves?" Quincy asked, rising from the table.

"Of course. It would be an honor," Ivy said. She went upstairs and returned with a bright crystal ball.

"Put your hand on the crystal ball and stare at the ball," Ivy commanded. Gwen did as she was told. Ivy put her hand on the ball and stared in also.

"Your full name is Gwendolyn," Ivy said, and continued, "your life will be full of many adventures. Gwen means Goddess of the Moon. The Moon Goddess will protect you on your wanderings, but the Sun God will put you through a number of trials in which you must prove yourself. You must be able to defend yourself, or there will be dire consequences. And...I see one more thing. You will have many enemies, but the main one among them is Duke Raxere of Skere."

After her fortune had been told, Gwen left with haste. She had been planning to go back to Lien, but she decided that she would instead go to Skere by cutting through the Trail of the Realm and passing through the troublesome Elea Mountains.

And so Gwen began her journey to Skere. It was not easy, for the Trail of the Realm was very long and the Elea Mountains would probably be even harder. At least that was what Gwen thought.

It was on one uncertain, foggy day that Gwen was walking past the Trail of the Realm when a tall man stepped up.

"Argh! Why's a wee lassie walkin' 'long?" the man grinned.

"I would not like to be bothered, thank you," Gwen said coldly, staring ahead.

"Not want to be bothered, aye? Hey me buckos, did ye hear the lassie? She not want to be bothered!" A team of about thirty men stepped out from the dust.

"Ha ha ha!" they laughed along with the other man.

"Now, little lassie, ye see how unwise it would be to gimme one o' yer rude answers, aye? I gotta whole force o' men at me back, all awaiting my orders," the man said.

"Tell me your name and I'll tell you why I'm wandering," Gwen said defiantly.

"Ohhoho, does she! Oh well, I'm the Knight Marshal of Zeda, and I am looking for a very important object that is called the Mirror of Zeda, which was stolen from the Zeda Convent by a man called Duke Raxere of Skere," the Knight Marshal said.

"Duke Raxere of Skere!" Gwen exclaimed.

"Yep, he's one to watch out for," the Knight Marshal said.

"And we're wantin' to go to Skere, little missie. Now does that satisfy ye?" another man stepped up.

"I'm going to Skere, too," Gwen said.

"It's too dangerous for you, lass. I'll drop ye off at Zeda and the Prioress'll take care of you," the Knight Marshal said gently.

"No! I am going to Skere and that is final!" Gwen shouted.

"Lass, ye really have to understand, me job isn't to leave young girls like ye on the path of danger!" the Knight Marshal cried, throwing up his hands in exasperation.

"I'm not on the path of danger! I can take care of myself!" Gwen stormed, turning on her heel away from the Knight Marshal.

The next morning, Gwen cut through a small opening in the Trail of the Realm, headed for the Elea Mountains.

"Whoa!" After walking tirelessly for many miles across the bare, dusty plains, Gwen gasped at the sight of the grand Elea Mountains. The grand mountains towered above Gwen, casting a huge shadow on the ground miles around. Winding paths led up the mountains, probably ending up at Zeda.

"I can't believe I'm going up that," Gwen said to herself.

"Not many do, lass," the Knight Marshal strode up in front of her.

"I was hoping I'd seen the last of you," Gwen said, rolling her eyes.

"C'mon, lass, I mean it when I say that you're on the path of danger," the Knight Marshal said.

"I don't care. I want adventure!" Gwen cried.

"Take heed of my words, lass, and you'll thank me," the Knight Marshal said.

"I don't care what you say!" Gwen shouted.

"Beware, lass, beware," the Knight Marshal said. Gwen took a deep breath and stepped onto the mountain path. She knew she had many, many miles to go.

"Lass, look, the least I can do for you is give you my horse. Please accept!" The Knight Marshal had a pleading look in his eyes.

"Fine," Gwen said, mainly to be rid of him. The Knight Marshal's nag was old and worn, and his bones jutted out from his tight, stretched brown skin. The saddle was patched in many places, and the reins were no more than pieces of rope knotted and tied together.

"His name's Fireflake," the Knight Marshal said.

"Fireflake. That's a nice name," Gwen managed to say, trying to climb onto the saddle.

"Here, I'll give you a hand," the Knight Marshal said, chuckling.

"Thanks," Gwen said. The Knight Marshal lifted Gwen onto the saddle with a grunt.

"Well, good-bye, then," the Knight Marshal said awkwardly. Gwen tugged on the reins, and Fireflake slowly plodded forward.

By sunset, Gwen had covered ten miles and was resting, making a small fire out of some sticks and dry grass. Fireflake slowly chewed the grass, looking around **impassively**. Gwen sorely regretted that she hadn't thought to bring some food. *Oh well*, she thought, *there's no use moping about it*. Looking up, Gwen noticed an old, bent woman wearing a black habit walking towards her.

"My daughter," the woman croaked, "I am Mother Giovanna. I do not believe it safe for you to wander these wild lands alone. Permit me to accompany you to the Convent of Zeda, where you will be given food and rest?" Gwen readily agreed. Food and rest sounded perfect!

At the Convent of Zeda, Gwen was immediately given into the care of Sister Irene, who bustled about, exclaiming things like "poor wee little lassie" and "what a tiring journey ye must o' had." Gwen washed herself, redressed, and went downstairs to eat with the rest of the nuns.

"O traveler, we think it right and proper to say this to the Noble Sun God:

"O Sun God, so great and noble, lay your blessing on this bread we eat;

"O Sun God, so just and merciful, lay your blessing on the wine we drink;

"O Sun God, so magnificent and majestic, protect us Sisters of the Convent of Zeda, and we shall take the oath of poverty and promise to give aid to women, orphans, and old people," Mother Giovanna said. The Sisters, along with Gwen, recited the prayer, and then everyone was given a slice of the hard, stale bread and the cheese. The wine was poured into the crudely made wooden glasses and handed out to everyone.

After dinner, Gwen was shown to a comfortable and yet small room on the West Wing of the Convent, where she undressed and flopped down onto the plain bed. All of the candles were blown out at exactly eleven o'clock, so Gwen slept in the candlelight for some time.

The next morning, after dressing and eating breakfast with the nuns, Gwen climbed back into the saddle.

"May the noble Sun protect you, young wanderer!" Mother Giovanna called as Gwen rode away.

Gwen had reached the meadows that lay between Bronsel and the Elea Mountains by sunset. She tied Fireflake to a tree, patted his back, and left him to chew the grass. A few farmers greeted her and went back to cutting wheat with their long, sharp scythes. One farmer stopped working, put down his scythe, and said to Gwen, "And what is your name?"

"I am Gwen."

"Be welcome to my humble abode," the farmer said, and, taking off his hat, he said, "I am Torgish."

"Where do you live?" Gwen asked, glancing around. There seemed to be no houses.

"In Bronsel, of course," Torgish said, looking surprised.

"But is that not far away from here?" Gwen asked.

"If you call a mile far," Torgish said, waving lazily at the west, "although yes, most people would consider Bronsel not to be within walking distance."

"Oh," Gwen said. She had always been taught that Bronsel was a faraway place, a place "her ladyship will never see," and that there were **barbaric** ways of execution. In truth, once Gwen had seen the Meadows of Paradise, which separated Bronsel from the Elea Mountains, all of this floated from her head. Torgish waved his scythe carelessly towards Bronsel.

"Oh?" he said, "oh? You say "oh" when I speak of my great home? Sir Kenkye is a proud man, and he most certainly does not like commoners saying "oh" when his subjects tell them of Bronsel!"

"Beg your pardon, sir, er, I've never been to Bronsel," Gwen said.

"Well, then," Torgish said.

"Hey Torg, whaddya doin' now? Wanderin' off again, jus' like I though ye would!" A big man who seemed to be in charge of them all stepped forward.

"Look, Galis, I can't cut all of those big outlandish stacks the rest of the men are cutting!" Torgish shouted.

"Fine, fine," Galis said, swaggering away.

"Galis is our chief. He's the third cousin of Sir Kenkye," Torgish explained.

"Doesn't Sir Kenkye rule over you?" Gwen asked, confused. In Lien there was no under-chief. Esper took care of everything, no matter how trivial.

Torgish shrugged.

"If you could call it ruling. Drinking, more like. He's also known for his many affairs with the women of the court and even peasant women," he said.

"Are you poisoning people's minds against my dear cousin Kenkye?" Galis swaggered back, waving his scythe menacingly.

"Of course not, Galis!" Torgish exclaimed, trying to resist a laugh.

"Well, then, stop yammering and get working!" Galis shouted moodily, walking away to lecture some other farmers.

"Just go ride to Bronsel, all right? It's easy enough, if you know the way," Torgish whispered to Gwen.

"Okay," Gwen said, mounting Fireflake.

"And good luck!" Torgish shouted.

After an hour's ride, Bronsel came to view. Gwen was amazed by its grand mansions and the summer villas where the people of Sir Kenkye's court spent their leisure time. Everywhere, shopkeepers in clean-pressed shirts and puffed black breeches strolled around on the cobblestone street, commenting on the beautiful weather. Booksellers sat near the small fountains, burying their long, wrinkly noses in big, leather bound books. Young girls in frilly dresses playfully chased each other, exchanging gossip. Sometimes a peasant or two would emerge from some **drab** building, dragging cages full of squawking geese. Shepherd-boys and shepherdesses proudly led their fluffy white sheep. Amidst it all, Gwen was merely a girl—she was no Gwendolyn of Lien there. A queer girl perhaps, but a girl nevertheless.

Torgish met her a few hours later at a hitching post.

"Come in here," he said, leading her into a small, dim shop. He pulled back the plain, moth-bitten black curtains, letting light filter through.

"Let's see…hmm…bit o' milk, some bread and cheese," Torgish hummed to himself as he pulled down a jug of milk, a loaf of bread, and a block of cheese down from a cupboard. After rummaging in a drawer a bit, he also pulled out a somewhat rusty knife.

"Bread and cheese is all I can offer you," Torgish said, cutting a slice of cheese and placing it onto a piece of bread.

"It's all right," Gwen said, taking a bite of the bread and cheese.

A clip-clop sound came through the open window.

"It's Sir Kenkye, come to get the taxes," Torgish said.

"Does he tax you daily?" Gwen asked. Esper taxed his subjects monthly, but she had heard that Sir Kenkye was greedy and needed money to support his ever-growing court.

"Sometimes. It's weekly usually, he has other obligations to attend," Torgish said, pulling haversacks of flour down from a shelf.

"Torgish! Torgish! Open the door and make yourself presentable in the face of your lord, Sir Kenkye!" a voice came.

"Yes, Galis, that I shall!" Torgish shouted back, smoothing his brown vest and opening the door.

"And who is this girl you harbor?" Sir Kenkye asked, raising his thin eyebrows. He was a tall, thin man with long, narrow eyes. Brown hair tumbled down his shoulders. A dagger with a jeweled hilt was buckled on his belt.

"Her name is Gwen," Torgish said.

"Not Gwendolyn of Lien?" Sir Kenkye asked, raising his eyebrows again.

"Er, I do not know what you mean," Torgish said nervously.

"I cannot lie when I am asked a direct question. Yes, I am Gwendolyn of Lien," Gwen said coldly.

"Ha! What does your father think of you running off! Orion, bind her tightly," Sir Kenkye said. The man called Orion grabbed Gwen with his rough, hairy hands. Gwen screamed and broke free of Orion's grasp.

"Get the girl! Get the girl! I'll kill the lot of you!" Sir Kenkye shouted in his fury.

Gwen ran and ran, until she no longer heard any sounds of pursuit. She stopped by a rock to catch her breath. She was well out of Bronsel and grateful she was wearing her tunic instead of her long gown. It was much easier to run in.

"There's the girl! Catch her!" Voices approached nearer and nearer. Gwen started running as fast as she could. She suddenly recalled that Fireflake was hitched nearby. She carefully snuck to the hitching post and leapt onto Fireflake's back. Within moments, they were far away.

By sunset, Gwen had reached the Rilite River. A fisherman was in his boat, with his nets half-full of fish.

"Hello, good fisherman," Gwen said, "is it possible for you to take me across?"

"Gimme ten coins," the fisherman grunted. Gwen rummaged around in the little velvet pouch she kept that was always full of coins. She pulled ten coins out.

"Here," she said, pressing the coins into the fisherman's hands. The fisherman grinned wickedly and rowed away without Gwen.

"You! You!" Gwen shouted, pointing her finger at the fisherman.

"Hey, canna ye swim?" The fisherman dived out of his boat into the water and stuck his head up.

"No," Gwen said, biting her lip.

"Never tried?" the fisherman asked, raising his eyebrows.

"No," Gwen said, tasting blood.

"Fine, fine, I don't want to be put in prison again for leaving helpless girls on the other bank," the fisherman said, rowing back. "But your horse will have to fend for himself. There ain't any space for him on this old boat."

Gwen gently pushed Fireflake into the water.

"Swim, Fireflake," she said.

After Fireflake had **floundered** to the other side, Gwen carefully stepped into the boat. The fisherman moved the nets to make room for her. Then he took the oars and started rowing.

"You know that you're wanderin' into Skere, righto?" the fisherman asked when Gwen stepped out of the boat.

"Yes," Gwen said.

"The Duke Raxere doesn't take kindly to newcomers," the fisherman warned.

"I'll risk it," Gwen said.

"Ah," the fisherman said. Gwen mounted Fireflake again and rode through. Skere, unlike Bronsel, had a dirt road. The girls who did wander around were silent and dressed in drab black dresses. The few houses and shops that lined the streets were far apart from each other, making Skere solemn and **sinister**. The entire place seemed to be draped in darkness.

When Gwen had ridden a good deal and was near the outskirts of Skere, a horse, making a clip-clop noise trotted by, startled her.

"And who be ye?" it was a man's voice, rough and unpleasant.

"Er, Gwen," Gwen said.

"Hmm, newcomer, eh?" the man asked in an uninterested tone.

"Yes, but I have an aunt here," Gwen had the words out before she could even think about her lie.

"An aunt, eh? Who?" the man's tone was suspicious.

"Er, Elaea Wighigh," Gwen had just noticed a sign which said 'Elaea Wighigh, Books.'

"Elaea Wighigh! Oh, then. Good day, young Nlaeia. You must have a touch of sunburn, to be saying crazy things like 'I am Gwen,'" the man said.

"Er, yes, er, I was rather mixed up," Gwen said, relieved that the man had believed at least some of her story.

"Your aunt's waiting for you in her shop," the man said, bowing courteously. When the man had gone, Gwen continued riding north. Soon she caught sight of a large castle with an old creaky drawbridge.

"Who be there? Answer to Sir Tismyon of Partrarrie!" Gwen shuddered as a man dressed in black armor stepped out.

"I'm— " Gwen began. Sir Tismyon smiled wickedly.

"You're a new kitchen maid, girl," he said.

"No, I'm not!" Gwen cried.

"For saying no to me, you will be taken before Duke Raxere of Skere," Sir Tismyon said, stiffening. Gwen grabbed her knife and waved it around.

"Aaah! Put that thing down! I'll let you go, whatever!" Sir Tismyon fled to the safety of the castle.

"Hmm…what have we got here?" Raxere strode up to Gwen.

"Nothing," Gwen said hastily.

"You call challenging one of my most valiant knights…nothing?" Raxere said.

"Valiant? He had a sword, I a knife. I waved it around and he ran back into the castle like a coward," Gwen said.

"You do not notice that knife has a jeweled hilt? Perhaps Sir Tismyon thought you were other royalty and thought he would be put to death if he killed you," Raxere said coolly, quickly regaining his **dignity**.

"That is the worst explanation for it, fool," Gwen said. Raxere was not one to be insulted. He turned red with anger.

"Sir Tismyon, I command you! Bring this girl to the dungeon!" he cried.

"Yes, milord," Sir Tismyon bowed and grabbed Gwen's hand.

The dungeons were not as bad as Gwen thought they would be, despite the fact that they were extremely damp and covered with moss. A small grate blocked the tiny opening through which Gwen could see the Opidit Ocean's waves rolling in. At least the dungeon was big and had space in which she could move around. Through the grate, she could see Fireflake bucking at Sir Tismyon and some groomsmen. She laughed silently to herself. Sir Tismyon couldn't even calm a horse!

"Hey, Raxere's got a new prisoner?" a man's voice startled Gwen.

"Yep, that girl, she challenged me! I took the challenge of course, and I had the sword at her throat, but then she begged for mercy, and that's when Duke Raxere came out, and he wanted to know the story, and there she is!" Sir Tismyon boasted loudly.

"Liar! I challenged you with a knife and you ran away!" Gwen shouted.

"Don't listen to her, men, she's got a touch of sunburn," Sir Tismyon said hurriedly.

"Coward! Coward!" Gwen shouted.

"Ye said ye challenged Tismyon?" one of the groomsmen leaned closer to Gwen.

"Yes, I waved my knife, and he ran away!" Gwen exclaimed.

"So don't listen to her! She's really gotten sunburned!" Sir Tismyon shouted hastily, waving his hands and trying to block Gwen.

"No I haven't!" Gwen shouted.

"Tismyon is a coward, coward, coward!" the groomsmen shouted, circling Sir Tismyon.

"Oh, the punishments I will impose on you!" Sir Tismyon sputtered.

"Punishments? We will no longer be in the company of cowards, but in the company of brave men. Let us move from this place," one of the groomsmen said, and began walking away. The rest of the groomsmen followed suit, after a few glances at Sir Tismyon, who was frozen with shock.

"Girl! You've ruined my reputation! Everything I've got! Now everyone will think I'm the most cowardly knight in the Realm of Possibility!"

"Well, you are, so what?" Gwen asked.

"Oh, you do not understand! My father, he was a knight, by the name of Sir Cedbede! I was the youngest of my five brethren. Now it was the custom that if a knight was challenged for his property by another knight, then their youngest sons would have to joust with each other. I lost my father's property to that other knight, and now, if he is told of my reply to a girl's challenge, he will be so madly **wroth**!" Sir Tismyon gasped.

"How did you come into Duke Raxere's service then, if you are a coward?" Gwen asked, raising her eyebrows.

"I had another, with my shield and coat-of-arms to perform great feats, all under my name," Sir Tismyon said, "and Duke Raxere heard word, and invited me to be in his service."

"If you are brave enough to let me out from this dungeon, I will bring you along on the rest of my journey," Gwen said.

"First, know this. Raxere is plotting against Lord Esper of Lien. He plans to kidnap his daughter Gwendolyn, and hold her for ransom. When word of that reaches Lord Esper, Raxere will offer Gwendolyn back if Lord Esper gives him Lien to rule," Sir Tismyon said quietly.

"He already has Lord Esper's daughter," Gwen said grimly. "She is sitting right in front of you." Sir Tismyon's eyes widened.

"It cannot be true! Therefore, I will most certainly free you. Also, just in case your father does not believe you, here is my message." Sir Tismyon took a piece of parchment from his pocket and quickly scribbled:

Duke Raxere of Skere is plotting against you. Gather an army and stand fast against him. Make sure your daughter is hidden away securely.

Gwen took the piece of parchment, rolled it up, and tucked it into her bosom.

"Thank you. Now I must free you," Sir Tismyon opened the grate, allowing Gwen to exit.

"Good-bye!" Sir Tismyon shouted as Gwen mounted Fireflake and rode away.

Gwen rode with haste. She only stopped at Zeda for a few minutes, to rest, to eat, and to feed Fireflake. At the end of the night, she had reached Lien. The villagers were extremely glad to see her, and Lord Esper was immediately informed of her arrival.

"My daughter," he said when Gwen raced into the throne room, "I am so glad to see you. But what drove you to run away?" And so Gwen told Lord Esper the entire story. But she did show Lord Esper Sir Tismyon's message.

"And, my daughter," Lord Esper said, "I was wrong about not believing that false merchant Guliset was not up to something. We discovered that he worked for Duke Raxere as a spy. By then of course, he had fled Lien."

"But you must gather your army," Gwen said.

"Ah, that is right," Lord Esper said.

After the soldiers had been drilled, they were stationed by the gates, the village, and everywhere around the castle. Gwen was hidden in the hut of the village healer, an elderly man from Yugz. Duke

Raxere was not late in coming after he was informed by some of his men of the conversation between Sir Tismyon and Gwen. But the men had left so hastily to inform Duke Raxere that they did not overhear Sir Tismyon warning Gwen about Duke Raxere coming to take over Lien. So Duke Raxere stormed in with only twenty men, expecting to find everyone unprepared. He was beaten back, although his twenty men fought bravely and well.

The next day, Duke Raxere sent the remaining survivors of his men to gather up the rest of his army and bring them to Lien. Lord Esper had a merry feast to celebrate, where everyone drank rather too much wine. That night, everyone was sleeping soundly, and the guards were asleep at their posts. Duke Raxere had planned carefully, and he crept in early in the morning. One of his men accidentally stepped on one of the guards, so soon the entire castle was alerted with the guard's cries.

"Prepare! Ranks one and two, archers! Rows three and four, swordsmen! Charge!" Lord Esper shouted. Despite Lord Esper's best efforts, his army was forced to retreat back into the safety of the castle.

"See, they are fools," Raxere scoffed, "they celebrate while we plan." Lord Esper, like Raxere, did not like to be insulted.

"I will have revenge!" Esper shouted onto the battlements below.

"As if," Raxere said, rolling his eyes. That night, Lord Esper planned with extreme caution. He had his men dig great underground tunnels. Then he sent his army to stay in the tunnels.

"When you hear the sound of hoof beats and Duke Raxere's men, stay quiet. When they are near enough, creep out of the tunnel with your swords and arrows at the ready. We will have the element of surprise this time. Take prisoners, but do not kill. However, if you encounter Duke Raxere of Skere, kill him immediately," Lord Esper told his army.

The next morning all was quiet in Duke Raxere's camp. Lord Esper took five of his most trusted knights and went to inspect the camp and to retrieve his daughter in the village. As they neared the abandoned camp they became aware of a putrid stench that seemed to arise from the tents. Finding no valuables, they went to the village to retrieve Gwen.

When Gwen heard that the camp was empty and particularly

smelly, she forced herself to stifle a laugh. Her father inquired about what was amusing her and Gwen related what had happened the previous day.

I was tired of all those tedious battles and I wanted to defeat Duke Raxere and his blasted army without a bloody battle. So I dressed in a few rags and stuck pins with laxative medicine on their tips into a few ripe melons. I took great care to cover my face and set about selling the melons to Duke Raxere's army.

I found another chance to sell my useless medicines when Duke Raxere appeared at the healer's door, sword in hand.

"'Give me a medicine or I'll crack your skull,' he threatened. I, dressed in peddlers' rags, gave him a jug full of sleeping potion, telling him it was medicine for diarrhea. He lugged it back to his camp, and he should be asleep."

Suddenly the two were disturbed by an excited messenger who burst into the room. "Greetings, Lord! I bring happy tidings! That vulgar duke Raxere has been found dead in his tent!" the messenger cried, waving his sword merrily. "Well, he wasn't quite dead. But his breathing was ragged, and we heard him muttering about some girl in a mirror. Funny name it had too—Mirror of Zeda or something like that. And then his breathing just stopped!"

"Gwen! I could let you have the entire village of Lien without marrying!" Lord Esper cried, dancing a merry jig.

"Wait for a moment," Gwen said, her brow furrowed. She dashed out of the castle to Raxere's camp. There, in Raxere's tent, was the Mirror of Zeda.

"Tell me who my true love is," she murmured to the mirror. And she saw nobody but herself.

Where and When Did It Happen?
Setting of Your Story

Setting: *Where and when the story takes place. Generally crucial to plot, the setting can also be used to call attention to the characters' strengths and weaknesses.*

Settings pose particular challenges for children when they have limited travel and life experiences, especially coupled with ever-decreasing reading time. Ask them to envision a setting and they will invariably gravitate towards home or school. This is all very well, but it limits their ability to explore various genres, and will often rein in the imagination and make their writing seem more prosaic.

Though Adora's experience is similar to most children's, she compensates for her lack of travel and life experience by reading a wide variety of books. History books and historical fiction, especially, have given her the information she needs to create settings replete with details about food, clothing, and political climate that expand in time and place.

She understands that setting can be crucial to the tone of a story, drawing a reader's attention to key concepts or character traits. For example, stranding her character in a harsh environment gives her a chance to show her character's strengths and weaknesses. She thinks: Does my character have to change in order to adapt to a harsh environment? Descriptions of setting are fine for their own sake, but readers will find them more interesting if they simultaneously tell us something about the character or plot.

Interview and Tips from Adora

Adora's settings range from labyrinthine cave passages to bustling medieval cities. Readers are always curious as to how she dreams up such complete worlds.

Joyce: How do you get ideas for your settings?

Adora: Most from my travel, or mostly from my imagination, a lot of it comes from my reading. Sometimes I'll mismatch, taking one thing I noticed in New York or something and matching it with something I read about. For example there's a subway station in New York, but my story is set further in the past. So I'll make it a carriage station, but include some of the details I noticed at the subway.

Joyce: Does setting a story in a specific historical time period make writing easier for you?

Adora: It's easier for me to write about a time in history that I know about. I can do better on the setting if I know more or less what a village in a given time period will be like.

Joyce: When it comes to fantasy, where do you look to for inspiration?

Adora: I just sort of get the pictures in my head…like the antagonist plotting…But there are some things you just can't describe. Because even if you describe something really well, you're still never really sure if the reader is going to imagine the same thing. Sometimes it's kind of frustrating. Sometimes my words feel empty and I just want to make up new ones.

 Tips for Parents and Educators

1. Finding your child engaging non-fiction reading material can open up a whole world of new ideas. As soon as she began reading about ancient Egypt, Adora found that she had tons of new ideas for everything from costuming to plots.

2. Traveling to new places, going to different restaurants, and staying at different places, especially ones with rich historical backgrounds, will definitely enrich your child's experience in life, and therefore help their imagination to grow.

 Give It a Spin

Ask your child to draw a map of an imaginary country or place they want to live in. Ask the following questions to get them thinking.

1. What is the weather like in this country? Do they have exciting weather like hurricanes, typhoon, tornados, and hail? What does the air smell like?

2. How does the particular weather affect the landscape? Is the ground flat or are there hills? Are the hillsides rocky? What kind of rocks are

they? Is the landscape/house/castle making the protagonist feel happy? Or dreary? Or tired?

3. Do they grow any exotic crops or just normal crops that you are familiar with?

4. What do people eat? How do they eat them?

5. What kind of festivals do they have?

6. What kind of trees grow in the forests? Is the forest dark and sinister or full of light?

7. What do people build their houses out of?

8. Do people have to face crime and danger?

9. What are the main source and form of entertainment?

10. Do they have any new technology and invention that we have not experienced?

Journal of a Pre-teen

Jan. 13 04

Stupid journal! Stupid Mom! Stupid Dad! Stupid everybody! I'm stuck with this horrid thing—it's raining, WHAT ELSE COULD BE WORSE!!!!

Jan. 14

WHY??? Why am I stuck with this journal AS AN ASSIGNMENT!!! Why?? I'm stuck with it! And Mom expects me to WRITE IN IT! HECK!!!

Jan. 15

More rain. And more. There is nothing else to do but write in this THING (I absolutely refuse to call it anything that will make it seem like a THING that comes of any use to the human body!!!)

Jan. 16

There is absolutely nothing to write about in this THING that will be of any interest!!!! Except my name, age, school, and blah blah blah. Name: Lorna. Age: nine and three quarters. School: Home schooled. Which really, really, really sucks!!!!

Jan. 17

Mom *READ* my journal!!!! How dare she!!! And now she says that I have to call this awful thing a journal. HECK!!! Raindrops.

Jan. 18

Still more rain. I'm grounded for hitting Joan.

Jan. 19

Church. I have told Mom over and over again that I do not believe in any sort of religion, but I was baptized nevertheless with some kind of special water and I have to go to church. At least the Communion bread tastes pretty good. Joan's calling.

Jan. 20

WORKBOOK!!! I hate it. I have to do a *FIVE PAGE ESSAY* about some STUPID excavations at ancient Egypt even though I have told Mom recently that I am NO good at writing. And we didn't even get to have any science today!!!!

Jan. 21

I can hear Dad talking with Mom about a vacation to Yellowstone National Park. That would be fun. My friend Violet lives in Wyoming.

Jan. 22

HECK!!!!! We're not going to Yellowstone. Instead we have to go visit our great-aunt Garcia, who is crazy and has to stay shut up in a nursing home for the entire day. Darn, darn, darn!!!! I could fill these beep beep beep pages with nasty words for a week!!! (beep beep beep is my way of describing something that is so horrible it is past describing)

Jan. 23

We all went to the beach today. Joan and I jumped over the waves until Dad called us back. Our jeans were SOAKED!!!!

Jan. 24

We went shopping at Target today. Joan needs a dress for her middle school dance, along with black dress shoes (she already has those) and black pantyhose. I got three new pairs of jeans, one pair of tennis shoes, a small pack of erasers, four mechanical pencils with lead, and an entire thing of lined paper. You know how sometimes jeans can be really loose, and then sometimes jeans can be really tight, and there are some in the middle? I like the kind of jeans that aren't too loose and aren't too tight. I like to have them worn in a lot, also.

Jan. 25

Ow!!! My ferret Tiny bit me on the finger, which is partly the reason I am writing with my right hand instead of my usual left. Not that I write any different with the two hands—but still, I like writing with my left hand better. Joan set Tiny on me after I spit on her because she said that my essay was the worst she had ever seen. It's not my fault!!!!!

Jan. 26

OH MY GOD. I CANNOT BELIEVE THIS HAS JUST HAPPENED. Okay, look. We were going to visit Aunt Garcia in the stupid nursing home. So far, so good. And we entered the nursing home. The beak-nosed woman at the desk told us to wait "a sec". Hour, more like. And then Aunt Garcia comes tottering down, tripping over stairs as usual, muttering in her **fatalistic** way that she's going to die. Her dress is yellow with red polka dots, and her frizzy gray hair sticks out everywhere. **Putrid** liverwurst sticks out from her mouth. Aunt Garcia punched the wall and kicked the chairs and told everyone that they were demons. And then she came to us. TO US! How dare she?! And Aunt Garcia just looked at us—and then—I hardly dare to write this—SHE SPIT ON MOM!!!!

Jan. 27

After she spit on Mom, she just went back up the stairs with everybody giving her the Look. Of course Mom blames the entire affair on Aunt Garcia's craziness, but I mean, well, like to SPIT ON YOUR OWN NIECE!!!

Jan. 28

The cousins—Randy, Arthur, and Elizabeth—are here. And so is disaster. Arthur is about my age, while Randy is Joan's age. Elizabeth is only three and will be kept with Auntie Millie, thank goodness. But I can already see the **mischievous** look on Randy and Arthur's faces. Oh, darn, they're at the door. Gotta go.

Jan. 28

HOW DARE THEY!!!! THE BLASTED COUSINS!!!! Oh, I am **seething**!!! And now I have a worm - a chewed up, slimy, mushy DEAD worm in my stomach!!! To think of that emerging from my gluteus maximus when I am on the toilet!!! And Mom is letting them STAY FOR ANOTHER NIGHT!!!! How dare she!!! When her own daughter is suffering from digestion problems, she lets the CULPRITS stay and BE WELCOME at our house!!! The beep beep beep cousins!!!!

Jan. 29

At least Auntie made them apologize nicely enough. I saw Randy cross his fingers (which makes it unofficial) behind his back, though. There were pancakes with maple syrup for breakfast to brush away the entire affair, though. Yum!!!

Jan. 30

If I ever get this journal published, I think I will take out the first parts. Because I sort of like this journal now. Anyways, nothing that fun really happened today. Tomorrow's Joan's dance.

Jan. 31

Oh, I am *stuffed*. And I mean *stuffed*. You would not be able to guess how many refreshments there were at the dance. And there were SOOOO many cakes and cupcakes and muffins and doughnuts and big dishes of ice cream. Plus Mrs. Chen (whose daughter is Joan's best friend) made her spicy Chinese noodles, which tasted really good. I had THREE BOWLS!!! THREE BOWLS OF NOODLES!!! And furthermore—Ms. Untermeyer from Joan's homeroom made the most delicious chocolate chip cookies!!! The principal, Mr. Osborne, made lemonade and fruit punch!!

~~Jan.~~ Feb. 1

YESS!!! FEBRUARY!!! And it is SUNNY FOR ONCE!!! SUNNY!! DO YOU UNDERSTAND THAT?? Sunny! YESS! We get to have a picnic today at the park, what could be better????

Feb. 2

Joan is complaining AGAIN about Monday. She says that she's forgotten everything, that she has no idea HOW in the world to do pre-Algebra in Mrs. Howard's class, and that her book bag has a hole in it. Which is true. But she is disturbing my reading, for heaven's sake!!

Feb. 3

I keep on forgetting it is February!! But I am very, very, very glad that it is!! I thought January would last forever, and a good thing it didn't last that long!! Because I am tired of FOUR WEEKS OF ONE MONTH!!!

~~Jan.~~ Feb. 4 (Why do I keep on doing that???)

It's Arthur's tenth birthday. I hate when he's older than me!!! (Well, he always was, but STILL!) Whenever he's older than me, he always bosses me around and seems to think that he's in charge!!! Aunt Millie and Uncle Herman did buy an excellent cake, though—chocolate, my favorite!!! We all joined together in a "Happy Birthday" song, although I was crossing my fingers behind my back and very quietly muttering under my breath "ugly toad" instead of Cha Cha Cha like everybody else was doing. Arthur gave me an evil eye-he was standing right next to me, and probably heard me.

Feb. 8

We have just gone on the BEST vacation to Oregon. I forgot to bring the journal—I remembered it just as we were backing up—but the door was locked anyways and it would be too much trouble so we just left. It was pretty fun, despite the fact the journal wasn't with us!!

Feb. 9

Back to regular writing. And also back to lessons. The cousins went back to their house in Rolla, Missouri. They had a rental house here for a while. Unfortunately, there is nothing to write about except

Joan's recent complaints. Which is very, very, very, very, very, very boring!

Feb. 10

I guess there is something to write about. My trip to Oregon. The hotel we were staying in on the border of Washington and Oregon (The Bonneville Hotel or something like that) had a really good swimming pool, and I floated a lot on my back. Dad did laps, Joan sat in the hot pool, and Mom just stayed up in our hotel room, reading or whatever. After two days or so in that excellent hotel, we moved on to Eugene. Eugene has this really delicious ice cream place called Prince Puckler's, and it is just *heaven on earth*. The heater in Prince Puckler's was all nice and warm—a relief after walking around in the cold weather. It was so nice and toasty that I even took off my sweater. (I had to put it back on when we went back outside, though.) After Prince Puckler's, we went to this game shop (I forget what it was called) with a ton of cool stuff. Dad got this game called Cranium. He seemed to have heard about it before, and so had Joan. It looked all right, though. Dad said it was the special Turbo edition. I looked, and it did say that. So that's what we did on our vacation.

Feb. 11

Writing in this journal is getting more and more and more and more tiresome!! Since Dad reads to us from *The Return of the King* from the Lord of the Rings, I don't really have much time to brush my teeth, do you-know-what on the toilet, rush across the hall, change into my PJ's, sort out my covers, and whatever. I'm sneaking this entry in-Mom thinks that I'm writing about parrots and their life cycle. I finished early, though!! Ooops. She spotted me.

Feb. 12

Urrgh!!! I had to sit in the chair until my bottom got all sore, listening to Mom droning on and on and on about this and that. As if that weren't enough, Joan made tons of **snide** remarks. I HATE THAT *DESPICABLE* SNOB!!!!!!

Feb. 13

Joan's friends are here. I am writing this very entry as Joan is leading them in. Unfortunately, Joan and I share a room. Joan tends to turn her stereo very loud with rap songs (which I hate) and pretends not to hear me when I shout over to her to stop. Joan's friends are slightly better. One of them, Dianna Chen, the daughter of Mrs.

Chen, I even like. She is always very nice to me and brings me little Chinese sweets (which I love.) But I absolutely despise Tracey Norris, who has green highlighters in her weird short crooked hair and has these big brass circle earrings which are SO drab. She has SUCH a false voice. Secondly, I hate Emily Wilkins, who has long hair and wears it in a ponytail. She dyed all of her hair this really ugly bright red, and I have to squint every time I look at her because of her bright red hair. She sings really off-key and loudly. Thirdly, I don't like Joan. Mom said that it's just the common sibling rivalry and that it'll wear off. But I think that Joan and I will be major archenemies for the rest of our lives.

Feb. 14

Raining again. Tracey, Emily, and Dianna are staying over for a three-day sleepover. For once I was glad that my bed was the smallest in the entire household and that my feet stuck over the mattress. Had my bed been large enough to fit those horrors, I would have had to give up my bed to Tracey or Emily or Dianna. Not that I would mind giving it to Dianna. But Tracey and Emily both use this weird shampoo that smells horrible, and I would not at all like that smell in my bed. That happened once when I was five years old. Elizabeth was only one year old, and the cousins were visiting. I had to give up my bed to Elizabeth. And guess what she did. SHE WET THE BED!!!!!! Of course Tracey and Emily are too old to do *that*, but, as the **dregs** of society, they might do something just as freaky.

Feb. 15

LETTER FROM GRANDMA!!!! HOORAY!!! As usual, I got the mail. Joan was sitting in the shade of the awning in our big loveseat, reading *THE AVERAGE TEEN*. I didn't really notice that the package I was holding was from Grandma. But I was entering the house from the back, anyways, and then Joan noticed that it was from Grandma. She shrieked and ran at me, grabbing the package from my hands and tearing it open. I grabbed it back from Joan, spit in her face (I find saliva very effective with older sisters) and ran to the safety of the ancient shed wall which Joan believes is infested with worms and snails and slugs.

"Brat!!!" Joan shouted. "Give it!" I heard her stomping and screaming. She finally gave up and went back to the loveseat. I snuck around the front, untied my shoes, and went to the living room to open up the package. First, there was a card from Grandma. I threw it aside onto the couch and dug deeper into the package. I felt something furry. I pulled it out, and much to my disgust, it was a *stuffed animal*. Even though it was very cute, both Joan and I are far too old for teddy bears, and I believe that Grandma should know it. Just then, Tracey came barreling in, her big fleshy tummy bouncing and wobbling as she walked.

"Hey, kiddo," Tracey said, taking a coke from the refrigerator and slurping it loudly.

"Where's Joan?" I asked flatly, even though I already knew the answer. Or at least I thought I did.

"She's up in her room telling us about how you jerk stole that junk from her," Tracey said. *Her* room?!! What was Joan saying?? *Our* room. I guess it was really Joan's, first, because the attic was my room for a while, but then Dad bought all this new furniture and for a while before our auction to sell all of the old furniture we had to store the furniture in the attic. But then Aunt Millie married Uncle Herman, and we gave our old furniture to them as a wedding gift. My bed and all of my stuff had already been moved to Joan's room, and it would be too hard to move it back, so we just made the move permanent. HECK!!

Feb. 16

YESSSSSSS!!!!! THIS IS GREAT!!! YESSSSSS!!! I asked Mom if I could have the attic room back, and she said I could!!! Dad is moving my bed as I write this very entry!!! I have already taken down all of the posters I tacked to the wall, put all of my clothes into boxes Mom gave me, and dragged them up to the attic. Dad is grumbling about this, getting mad at both me and Joan "for getting in the way." Mom says that she thinks that it might cool down some of the "dislike Lorna has of Joan." It probably won't, but at least I won't have to see Joan as much!!!

Feb. 17

YES! I am officially moved into the attic! I have already tacked up my posters, folded my clothes and put them in the drawers, and put all my books into the attic cupboards. I stacked my library books in a pile on the floor, where I can find them easily. I put Dad's old laptop (which is now mine) under the bed where I won't step on it, **resolving** to put it somewhere later. For now, I just need a good night's sleep.

Feb. 18

Uh-oh. There is a problem. Dad cannot read to us from the *Fellowship of the Ring* if Joan and I are in separate rooms. Joan and I were both quarreling about who Dad should read to, but Dad stopped us by threatening to not read to us at all. Finally he said that we both could gather in the living room (at least if we brought our covers and wore our warm PG's) to listen to him read. He knew that it would cause too much bickering to ask for us to gather in Joan's or my room. So with that taken care of, we went back to our rooms to do our stuff. By that I mean write in this journal, do pinball on the laptop, etc, etc.

Feb. 19

OH MY GOD. I CANNOT BELIEVE THIS IS HAPPENING. Mom and Dad have just finished the adoption papers making this Chinese girl named Yin Lotus Flower my sister and their daughter WITHOUT MY CONSENT. Another girl in the family. If I had a say in this thing, I would ask for a boy. But I don't even want another kid in the household!!!!! I don't want to go to China and stay on the plane for, what, like a damn sixteen hours!!! Since there's nothing else to do, I'll make a list of Joan's bad and goods.

Pros and Cons for Joan Goldstein

Pros

Makes good s'mores
Doesn't wear "sexy" dresses
Doesn't bother me if I don't start a conversation
Never ducks me underwater while we're swimming
Rarely has hurt me physically

Cons

Gets into big arguments with me
Blabbermouth
Tattletale
Has tried to steal my posters before
Very nosy
Always treats me like I'm a baby
Always very gossipy
Always invites Tracey and Emily over
Drinks all the Coke and Gatorade
Hogs the backseat in the car

Feb. 20

We're packing our stuff today. Mom turned the entire thing into a vacation (thank goodness), and she says that we'll have to pack a lot of stuff. We're going to China tomorrow.

March 1

If you're wondering why I haven't written for such a long time, it's because of this stupid jetlag. We're still in China. Lotus Flower is nice and all, but she doesn't speak English. Which is a serious rip-off.

March 4

Back in U.S.A. There was a lot of turbulence on the plane, delaying my good night beauty sleep. Well it wasn't a beauty sleep anyways. Lotus Flower kept on leaning over onto my legs, looking at me with big brown eyes. Mom taught her some basic English, like "hello", and Lotus Flower was toddling all over the place saying that to people until Mom got her back to our seats.

March 5

Urgh!!!! Having a new kid in the family is HARD!!! I hate Mom!!! She is just basically picking on me like a bully, saying "you haven't done this" and "you haven't done that". HECK!!!! I am seriously thinking about running away!!!! Joan's calling. Gotta go.

March 6

I think that I'm going to turn this journal into a scrapbook. There isn't really anything to write about. I'll switch back and forth. Anyways, here's some of my drawings:

I did that just yesterday. I had to cut it out, though, to paste it on here. My hands are all sticky with glue, ugh!!!

This princess is a doodle I just did. Well, anyways, dinnertime.

March 7

Scrapbooks are so cool! Joan said that they're babyish, but I detected jealousy in her pimply face. Joan has quite a number of pimples on her forehead, nose, and cheeks. Oh yeah. And her chin. She has this huge zit on her chin. It's all red and popping out. Mom's tried to pull it before, but Joan was crying and screaming. I know that it's probably wicked to write this about Joan, but I can't help myself. I really wish that I didn't have to grow up and get all of those pimples like Joan!!!! Being a teenager would be even worse. All of the jeans they sell for teenagers are these really tight jeans that make your bottom look really big and have all of these stupid black glittery belts. Whenever Joan walks, her hips sway back and forth. That's another thing I don't want to have!!!!!

March 8

More doodles:

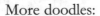

Anyways, back to what I don't want to have when I'm a teenager!!! I do not want to have any pimples, tight jeans, glittery black belts, hip swaying, weird voice (like Joan's), be considered annoying, nor anything like that. Mom says that all of that is just a part of growing up, but who says that *black glittery belts* are part of growing up?????? Here are my illustrations of belts:

No, never mind. Let me just tell you, whatever I drew would NOT be glittery. And a good thing, too. But I just do not want a stupid black glittery belt and have stupid cartoons drawn of me that show me having a date with some kind of stupid Tom Cruise guy. Joan never lets me borrow her glitter after the "glitter incident."

This is what they will draw of me once I am a teenager!!! I don't want this slipped onto my desk, and then some kind of beak-nosed professor expels me just for passing notes, etc.

March 9

DISASTER!!! ALERT!!!! DISASTER!!! The cousins will be here, and they will tear the wallpaper to shreds! Plus—if they find my journal they will laugh over it and rip out the pages! What embarrassment! I must find a place to hide you, dear journal!!!! Under my pillow??? No, way, way too common, you would be smashed!!! Uh oh, I HEAR THEM APPROACHING, in the cupboard??? No, would be opened!!!! Under my bed with all of my clothes on top of it??? Zipped up in my beanie bag purse? The bed will have to do!!!! They're coming!!!!

Later tonight

Sore pounding relief. (I don't think you can really describe it that way, but my heart is pounding with relief.) They didn't come into the attic at all. Randy and Arthur and Elizabeth were too interested in Lotus Flower. Hurrah!!!

March 10

Anyways, Auntie Millie brought chocolate chip cookies over for dessert. They were really good, nice and crisp and golden-brown. Randy had three cookies until Auntie told him to stop "eating the cookies." He passed gas right next to me (ugh, that putrid stench!) Mom fed Lotus Flower just a tiny nibble of cookie, and dumped the rest on my poor dad.

March 11

Oy. I am so sick. My throat is sore, I've got a headache, and I'm dizzy. I can barely write this. Gosh, searing headache.

March 14

Finally. I'm slightly better from this ibuprofen stuff. Joan the Fusspot is avoiding me, in case she gets some "bacteria" in her so very divine (as if) body. Mom and Dad are being unusually nice to me (advantage!!!) Lotus Flower is steadily improving with her English, and even the abominable cousins made me a get-well card in the short time they were not roughhousing around.

"With each of our personal DNA, of course," Randy had said grandly, while I lay shocked with horror in my bed. By personal DNA, he had meant a hair and a whole bunch of spit from each cousin.

Elizabeth had written her name in her shaky little letters, Randy had written his in his dirty scrawl, and Arthur had written his in those big blocky bubble letters that he always uses. I wish I could paste the card in here, but I can't, since there isn't enough room.

March 15

Yum!!!! WAFFLES for lunch!!!! WAFFLES WAFFLES WAFFLES, YEA! I am writing this in the morning (by the light of the window— whatever I say, Dad still won't give me a candle) and Joan is taking an extra long snooze. She calls it a short siesta, but I know better. She can sleep for hours on end. Part of the reason I always hated rooming with Joan was because she makes this really loud noise kicking her covers off and moving and everything. I used to sleep with Joan when I was five or so and one time she kicked me over to the very edge of the bed so that I almost fell off. Now I don't have to sleep with Joan, luckily. Mom says that Joan needs her "own bed space to grow", "get rid of typical hormones" and blah blah blah. I am still thinking about those delicious mouthwatering divine waffles. Mmm…Mom's special golden brown, crisp but not in the least bit burnt…with tons and tons and tons and tons and gazillions of whipped cream on top…

Later this afternoon

I am floating away on a vessel of whipped cream. Lunch was simply indescribably heavenly. It was…simply waffle paradise. I had four waffles, all with my special whipped cream seal or emblem or symbol or whatever you want to call it (well, I just only invented it). It was a very wavy L with a circle around it. Get it?? Lorna? Circle — for O?? And L. Which stands for the first two letters of my name. So anyways, we also had organic strawberries on top of that. That tasted even better. I tried to smear my whipped cream everywhere on my waffle with my fork (another excuse for eating whipped cream by itself) and a lot of the whipped cream ended up on my fork. Mom and Dad didn't even glance at me once.

March 16

Leftover waffles for breakfast. They don't taste as good as ones fresh from the waffle thingy (I think you call it a griddle). But they do taste pretty good. Dad doesn't let us have any whipped cream for breakfast, because he says it has too much sugar. HECK!!! It has only one or two grams of sugar, for heaven's sake!!! Oh well.

March 17

Shame. There's no more waffles left, and I have to eat the regular cornflakes for breakfast. Plus an unfortunate discovery made yesterday— I was ranting on about whipped cream having less sugar than milk. But then Dad was like "It's one gram of sugar every serving. But there are seventy servings in the entire can. So, tell me, how many grams of sugar are there?" I sat stupefied for a moment. But of course I couldn't stay mum for that long. Finally I admitted that it would come to a grand total of seventy grams of sugar. Joan looked triumphant, how dare she gloat!!! And the regular bagels with cheese for lunch. And the regular vegetables and toasted bread for dinner. Joan is now criticizing Mom's food. Dad says that if she shuts up then we can go to MacDicken's or Coldway's sometime soon. Well, he didn't actually say "shut up." He never says anything like that. But he did say that if she didn't do that anymore, we would get to go to MacDicken's sometime soon. So Joan did shut up. And that was a good thing—she was getting on my nerves!!!!

March 18

Shopping. Regular stuff—shampoo, body soap, scented lotion for Mom, shaving cream and deodorant for Dad, new backpack for Joan, binder for Joan, pencil pack for me, eraser pack for both of us (DRAT! Joan will steal again), a few office pens for Dad, and a frozen pizza. After dropping that stuff at home we went off to MacDicken's. I just got something randomly off the list—Fish 'n chips. Joan, who is too old to get the kid's menu, ordered salmon with clam chowder as a side dish.

March 19

Man. Back to regular lessons. Horrible stuff. Mom brightened us up a bit saying that if we read books for the summer, we will get a prize from the library. Some reading program thing. It's called Reading Deeds. We get this little booklet thingy in which we record all of our time in which we read. But first before that we have to set a goal. By goal I mean something like, say, uh, one hundred books. There's really a choice of goals. The First Level Goal is one hundred books. The Second Level Goal is two hundred books. And The Grand Level Goal is three hundred books. You can choose between the First Level Goal, the Second Level Goal, and the Grand Level Goal. I chose the Grand Level Goal. Joan scolded me saying that it was only because I thought that the Grand Level Goal would get me a bigger prize, but hey, aren't bigger sisters supposed to encourage their little sisters!!!!??? But I suppose that it is true. About the prize, I mean.

March 20

SWIMMING!!!! We just went swimming today!!! My hair is dripping as I write this very entry. Mom let me take some time off from my nap to write this, but she didn't really take any time to dry my hair. Just a few swipes with the hair dryer. Write more later.

Later

Ugh! I have the terriblest (yes, I know that's not a word, but still) headache. Mom thinks that it might be due to the fact that my hair was dried inappropriately, and on top of that I slept on all of my wet strands of hair. Can't write anymore - it hurts.

March 21

This is Mom writing, if you're wondering about the change in the handwriting. I told her to make her writing as big as she could, since normally she writes very small. Anyways—to the most frustrating part. I have a raging fever which makes me unable to write with my own handwriting. Mom measured my temperature, and it came to 101. 3. Unbelievably horrid. Joan, who is normally very **squeamish** about sick people, bought some orange cough drops from the drugstore and even came up to my room, which she usually doesn't due to the large amount of dust there is on the floor, wall and cupboards.

March 22

Lorna wishes for me, her father to record her day due to the fact that my wife now does not feel well and lies in bed. From here, I will continue on from what Lorna dictates.

Dad typed this up on his laptop and printed it out and pasted it in. He doesn't want to use his own handwriting! He says it's illegible, but I think that it's perfectly alright. Joan has a fever, too, along with Mom. Dad also has headaches occasionally, along with a running nose, so we're basically all sick! There is going to be the annual Summer Festival soon, and it's going to be in two days, so I really hope we don't miss it. Mom seems to be the sickest of us all. She has to take naps constantly, as well as ibuprofen to reduce the fever. I have doses of it too, although it's the children's kind, fruit punch flavor.

March 23

Finally!!!! I HAVE RECOVERED!! Joan is worse and I know that I should feel sorry for her, but I can't help feeling happy that I am, duh, BETTER!!!!!!!!!!!! Dad and Mom do not have to write this for me, I do not have to unwrap any more of those troublesome cough drop packages, and I am free from the confinement of my extremely filthy bed!!! I jump with joy!! I chirp with merriness!!! I drink with relish!!! Mom is somewhat better, too, but she's still sneezing and has an occasional cough. She doesn't need to take anymore stupid ibuprofen. A good thing, too—I was getting tired of washing that medicine spoon!

March 24

A new boy named Dylan and his parents just moved in. They have a pet dog and a hamster, too. Mom baked some brownies and gave them to me to deliver to our new neighbors. Dylan lives in what used to be Ms. Wellsgood's house. He is about my age, has regular boy's hair, and is a bookworm. Or at least so I was told by Mrs. Herman, who is Dylan's mother. When I knocked on the door, the door was answered by Mrs. Herman, followed by Dylan, who had his long pointed nose in a book. I could just barely see the title—*Daring Expeditions of Christopher Columbus*. Mrs. Herman was unlike any of the other women who lived on Westgate High with us. Instead of wearing regular jeans and a shirt, possibly with a sweater, she wore a short, almost knee-length dress that was bright yellow with red strawberries dotted all over it. It was actually quite a few inches above her knees, so that I could see most of her bare legs and her bare feet. I said hello and the other necessary greetings. Blah blah blah. I came inside, but Dylan still didn't put down his book. Instead he plopped down onto a black leather sofa. Mr. Herman was in the study, printing something (directions I think) out. He was a very tall man, with long wrinkles on the side of his chin and around on his cheeks. His hair was thinning, and it was bald at the very top. He wore a white shirt with the sleeves rolled up and a very dark blue tie with stripes across it, as well as dark blue pants which matched the tie (excluding the stripes.) Dylan looked like both parents. His eyes were brown, his nose was pointed (as I have said before) and his face was the same shape as his parents'. I didn't want to say anything, and Dylan's eyes were glued to the pages of his book, so it was sort of boring for a few minutes. Then he *finally* looked up and was like, "D'ya want to see our backyard?"

"Uhhh…sure," I said, following him out the back door onto their gigantic patio. Their deck made a big shadow on the patio so it was really cool under there. And I mean cool both ways. There was a small whitewashed table with gaps in between the white planks and matching chairs. It wasn't there when Mrs. Wellsgood lived there, so I assumed Dylan's family purchased it. There were stairs which led up to the really, really, really sunny deck. But the ABSOLUTE BEST part was the swing. It was nothing like those normal plastic swings with plastic seats and chains holding them up in the park. It was old-fashioned, with a rope tied to their enormous maple tree holding the swing plank up. It was a real wooden plank as a swing, with real rope holding it up. Dylan had a dog named Capricorn and a tom cat named Dipper. They didn't even have collars!!!! Capricorn was a bloodhound and Dip was a tom cat. Didn't I say that before?? Oh yeah. So anyways, Dylan just hoisted himself onto the swing and started swinging. Unlike me, he could start the swing by himself. I stared at him.

"Can I come over to your house?" he asked. Without my reply, he unlatched his yard gate and ran out.

"Wait! Shouldn't you tell your parents?" I asked, breathless as I caught up with him. Dylan shrugged.

"Doesn't matter much," he said. "Do your parents care? They must be fusspots like my aunt Louisa."

"Don't call them fusspots!" Hot rage over took me. Where in the world did I learn to write so dramatically? Never mind. Mom always said that I had the blood of Shakespeare in me.

"Well, if you have to tell them every single time you leave the yard, they are fully qualified as fusspots," he said, shrugging again. I gritted my teeth. I was not going to get anywhere with this obstinate boy.

"Fine!" I ran after him, my temples pounding. WHERE AM I GETTING THESE WORDS?????!!!!!! I was in hot pursuit of him, despite my sweat and my torn jeans. Just one more step—and I'd have him. Except—well, Dylan was nowhere in sight.

Should I Sprinkle Some Sparkles?

Descriptive Writing: Using Five Senses to Arouse Readers' Imagination and Immediacy.

When children write they often deliberately don't use adjectives to describe the things or people and adverbs to describe the actions—instead, they skip straight to the action. Interestingly, most kids know a lot more about their subject than they put on paper. When a story lacks descriptions, it doesn't mean that the writer lacks imagination. Sometimes a young writer needs to be reminded that readers are literally left in the dark without descriptions. When Adora first began writing, she often forgot to include descriptions of a character's appearance, facial expressions, intonation, or locale. However when asked what something looked like, or what someone felt, she would immediately have a detailed answer.

"What does the fortress look like?"

"Masked beneath the darkness of night, it looks like a dim black shadow."

"What did the royal lady wear?"

"A long gown of green, which shone brightly as she walked and had the light of one thousand stars reflected on its skirts."

One simple question, and suddenly she had a paragraph of new material. We have found that most kids respond well to this strategy, especially if you encourage them to use all their senses, including sight, smell, touch, hearing, and taste to describe and present what they imagine so their readers can enjoy what they are describing that much more. Remind the children that they have complete power over the realm they are creating, and are free to be as dramatic or silly as they like.

Adora also enjoys making drawings of her characters and the scenes in her stories. She often has the mental image of her stories before she sets out to write. For many children drawing is a pleasurable activity, so encourage your child to draw pictures to help them learn to bring alive their descriptions of characters and actions.

Interview and Tips from Adora

Joyce: When you're writing descriptions, are you conscious of deciding what things look like, or do you just know?
Adora: Sometimes I know what it looks like and sometimes I don't, but when I do know I like to have a mixture of my imagination and what it really looks like. I know whatever I'm writing about looks like in my head, or else I just randomly choose a description.

Joyce: If you don't know what something looks like, how do you make it up?
Adora: I imagine it, what do you think!!!

Joyce: When you describe your characters, do you have a picture in your head of how they should look like?
Adora: Usually I do for protagonists. When I imagine minor characters sometimes I just see half of them or see them in my mind blurred. But I can see them well enough to describe them.

Joyce: How do you link the description of your character to the type of character you are writing about?
Adora: It really just comes along with my imagination.

Joyce: How do you match the descriptions of your characters to the personality traits?
Adora: It seems to just fit in when I imagine them. I prefer having ugly antagonists, but sometimes I make them handsome and sinister instead.

Joyce: When do you decide that certain phrases and sentences need more descriptive writing?
Adora: I look over my stories a lot, and usually I notice those things, so usually I like adding in a few extra descriptions.

Joyce: Why is descriptive writing important to you?
Adora: It gives the reader and me a clear mental image of my character or setting. It's also fun to describe people and things.

Tips for Parents and Educators

Because most kids spend their lives getting 'bossed around' by parents, siblings, coaches and teachers, having free rein to make decisions about an imaginary universe can be an exhilarating experience. Emphasize that they have complete control over the world they are creating. Children who are used to more regimented academic assignments will frequently ask "Can I put this in my story?" And you can assure them of their freedom to create with the answer, "Of course, when you're writing you can do anything you want. It's your decision. Create hurricanes, give pigs wings."

You can use the inquisitive approach to loosen up your child's imagination and thinking by asking questions like these: Does the window have curtains? What color are they? Are they soft? Is it cold in the room? Is the character barefoot? How hard is it raining? What is the view like? What does the character see? What is another word for this? How does it make the character feel? What does this character think about it? What does this character look like? Where does he/she live?

 **Give It a Spin**

1. To get the creative ball rolling, ask your child to elaborate. It's amazing how a little prompting of the imagination can turn a basic sentence into something vivid. For example, perhaps your child writes: "Ben went to the window and looked outside. It was raining." Then ask your child to imagine the scene with eyes closed. Most kids imagine more than they initially put on paper. Encourage your child to rewrite the sentence incorporating some of these new details. Before you know it, you might end up with something like this: "Ben pushed back the dusty red drapes and looked outside. The rain came down in sheets, obscuring the dark hills. He shivered a little, though it was warm and cozy inside the house." Next, have your child pick five people they know well and use five or more adjectives to describe each of them and then five or more adverbs to describe one's actions.

2. Ask your child to write a description of a painting or photograph. The internet (Google image search, MSN and Yahoo) is a good source for images.

The Rebel's Reward

Kathryn Karlsman looked up from where she had been digging in the damp dirt with her **grubby** fingers. The Mistress of the Gardens, Lady Anna, looked at her disapprovingly.

"Brush up," Lady Anna said, frowning. "You look like a **street urchin**."

"But Lady—" Kathryn's pleading made no difference.

"Brush up," Lady Anna repeated, this time her lips in a tight line. "Elsie will help you. And change your dress!" Anna stared at Kathryn's smock. It was one of Kathryn's favorites, because it allowed her to move and breathe freely. Of course Anna was asking her to change!

> ## VOCABULARY LIST
> **grubby** - dirty
> **street urchin** - scamp, brat
> **curtly** - a rudely brief manner of speaking
> **disdainfully** - in a scornful way
> **despicable** - loathsome, deserving of contempt
> **reprimand** - scold
> **sly** - crafty, mischievous, cunning
> **distinctly** - clearly
> **reluctant** - hesitant, somewhat unwilling
> **hastily** - hurriedly
> **bickering** - arguing
> **dilapidated** - ramshackle, falling to pieces
> **scurrilous** - foul mouthed or vulgar

"And don't put on those square boots," Anna reminded Kathryn just as she was about to leave. "They are so manly. I do not know what your father was thinking when he brought those from Kenswell."

"But they are so comfortable!" Kathryn exclaimed.

"You must make a good impression upon the public," Anna said **curtly**. "Now leave and do wash your hands!"

Kathryn ran into her class five minutes late. Dame Giovanna, the teacher of the class, glanced **disdainfully** at Kathryn's soiled gloves, her hurriedly plaited sandy braids, and her wrinkled burgundy gown. The rest of the girls sniggered in their horrible high-pitched tones.

"Sit," Giovanna ordered Kathryn, pointing at an empty chair next to the most **despicable** bully in the Academy, Reana Broadsmat.

"So, you've been rolling with the goats, heh?" Reana whispered, leaning towards Kathryn.

"Reana!" Giovanna said sharply, looking up.

"I just needed to get a closer look at my book, Dame, you know how bad my eyes are," Reana said in the high-pitch fakey-fakey voice she always used to trick the teachers. Kathryn rolled her own eyes. Bad eyesight indeed! But she knew better than to protest, and settled on ignoring Reana.

"Yes, Reana," Giovanna said, turning to **reprimand** Reana Brodsmat for putting her elbows onto the desk.

"Fire, fire, never tire," Reana muttered under her breath, aiming her stare at Kathryn's desk. Within moments, Kathryn's desk was in flames.

"Kathryn!" Giovanna shouted, hurrying over and almost tripping on her black dress. "What are you doing!?"

"I didn't start it!" Kathryn shouted.

"I'm sure you did," Giovanna said. "You have been practicing your magic ever since you arrived, even though, outside of magic arts class, magic is strictly forbidden here at the Academy. You will receive detentions this week. I will be expecting you in my office."

Hot tears ran down Kathryn's face at the unfairness of it. She had been practicing magic when it was forbidden, yes, but everyone always accused *her* of wrongdoing without even thinking twice! Kathryn jumped from her chair, slid her things into her magic pouch, and ran to the upper chamber, where her brother, Hum, was practicing various spells.

"Hello, Hum," Kathryn said, throwing her pouch into the closet.

"What's up?" Hum asked, removing a charm he had just put on Asweet, his toy elephant, and turning to Kathryn.

"Reana set fire to my desk," Kathryn said. "I got the blame. Now I've got two detentions this week, Dad will be so disappointed in me after all I've tried to do." Suddenly, stomping her foot, Kathryn spun around to face Hum and cried, "I don't even want to be a lady! I never will be, anyways! Dad promised to take me beyond The Twin Gates into the Unknown Land, and far away to the Valleys, where Mum was born, and even farther to the Realm of Iosis!"

"You don't know that, do you?" Hum asked **slyly**.

"Oh, shut!" Kathryn exclaimed irritably, turning back to the closet and taking her smock down from the crude wooden hanger. "I'm going to change now, so go." Hum, who had no desire to see Kathryn in her undergarments, quickly ran off. When Kathryn was sure she was quite alone, she took off her hot dress, flung it into the back of the closet, and redressed in her smock.

"You look better in *that*," Hum said, eyeing the smock respectfully as he came back into the room.

"Lady Anna would swoon if she saw me like this," Kathryn lifted up her dress to reveal her square boots. "They're so manly," Kathryn mimicked in a high-pitched voice.

Hum laughed so hard he fell over onto his knees. He hastily rose, and said, "You're not like those other girls."

"Yes, well, what do you expect?" Kathryn asked. "Dad didn't marry one of those awful noblewomen who 'train' their daughters. Pamper, more like, seeing how these girls are terribly spoiled. Heck, I'd like to do some Dark magic on Reana."

"Well you can't. You know that," Hum said regretfully, muttering a few choice words under his breath.

"It's not fair you boys get to do magic at the Academy without it being within the time limit of Magic Arts," Kathryn said crossly.

"Look," Hum said, "Boys get to do magic because they'll need magic —defying demons, slaying wrongdoers, and defending the old and the weak. Girls of noble birth like you only need magic in time of emergencies, um, like…like when the tea is too hot or cold, you can change that with a few words."

"But it's not fair!" Kathryn shouted. "I *want* to slay wrongdoers, I want to defy demons, and I want to be a Magi Knight!"

"And you won't be able to," Hum said shortly. "You're a *girl*."

"Kathryn?" It was Lady Anna. "You're to go with me to Lady Edith's office."

"I didn't start the fire, I told you!" Kathryn exclaimed crossly. "It was Reana!"

"Er, well, about that," Anna said, blushing. "We did a Truth Spell on the rest of the class about what kind of detention you should get, and, er, Reana, under the power of the Truth Spell, was forced to admit that she had started it."

"So you were wrong," Kathryn said.

"Er, well, yes," Anna said. "But Lady Edith wants to see you anyways."

"Fine," Kathryn said, running past Anna and into the adjoining room, on which there was a plaque inscribed *Headmistress: Lady Edith*. A hurriedly tacked schedule hung on the low arch of the wooden door. Anna knocked twice with the large brass lion knocker.

"Enter," came Lady Edith's sinister voice. Anna opened the door, pushing Kathryn ahead of her.

"Kathryn?" Edith barely looked up from the handkerchief she was embroidering.

"Headmistress," Kathryn said, trying to curtsy but instead falling on the floor.

"You are a hopeless one to teach, as I can see," Edith said, looking at Kathryn with her sharp eagle-eyes.

"Er," Kathryn said, not sure what to say. Other headmistresses in other Lady Schools had always been saying things like "good job, sweety plums," or "you're certainly charming." Only Edith said what she really thought—and what was true. Kathryn *was* a hopeless case—in her own mind at least.

Kathryn pushed herself up and brushed off her smock.

"And you dress most inappropriately," Edith said calmly, pulling her drawer out and putting her handkerchief and her needles into the drawer. "You know, that smock is from The Valleys. If you read runes, which, I believe, is a most unladylike and manly task, then you would understand that. Unfortunately my own mother, Lady Emma, did not understand that runes were not a lady's best interest and enrolled me in a class based solely on runes." Kathryn was growing impatient. Dad could read runes, and, after all, he was one of the wealthiest men in all of Darrin! Even the scholars of Kenswell were not as prosperous as he.

"Excuse me," Kathryn said to Edith when the conversation had reached a stop. "But what did you really want me for?"

"Oh yes," Edith said, her black eyes glowing. "This." She pulled out a few papers from her drawer. She handed them to Kathryn, who flipped through the pages.

"Nothing but coggleshpwat, I bet you'll say," Edith said, smiling secretively. "It's your and Hum's report. I will present this to your father."

"Can I see it again?" Kathryn asked, biting her lip.

"Yes," Edith said, handing back the report. Kathryn scanned the paper. It looked like this:

The Academy for Young Girls and Boys of Noble Birth

Kathryn Karlsman, etc. Daughter by the rights of Sir Roland Karlsman.

Progress:
　　Magic and the like: 10) on a scale of one to ten
　　Lady Lessons: 3) on a scale of one to ten
　　Embroidery: 1) on a scale of one to ten

The Academy for Young Girls and Boys of Noble Birth

Hum Karlsman, etc. Adoptive Son and Heir by the rights of Sir Roland Karlsman.

Progress:
　　The following progress is based on the scale of one to ten
Magic and the like:10　Fencing Sessions:8　Defense of the Shield:3
Archery Sessions:6　Squire Training:4 To Address One's Overlord:9
To Bow to One's Overlord:8 To Address a Damsel:2　Close Battle:2

Kathryn handed the report back to Edith.

"Impressive, is it not?" Edith asked. "Take this back to your chambers, and be sure to show it to Hum. He is such a good learner." Kathryn bit her lip. Everybody said that — but the only reason they said that was because Hum was the heir to all of Dad's estates, which were vast. People who managed to get on Hum's good side now would be very powerful one day. Or so they thought.

"Well, I'll be off," Kathryn said quickly, running back to the chambers.

"You just missed this great stampede I made with the animals," Hum said excitedly. "I put a Limit Charm on the room so that only I would hear it, though. Shame."

"Yeah, here, have a look at this," Kathryn handed the report over to Hum.

"Kathryn! How many times do I have to tell you to say 'yes' instead of 'yeah'?" Anna peeked through the door, wincing when she said "yeah".

"Ditto," Kathryn said.

"And do not say that *slang* either, understood!" Anna shouted.

"Yes, Lady," Kathryn said, mostly to get rid of Anna. When Anna slunk off, Kathryn plopped down onto her bed. Hum sat down next to her.

"It's not fair you get to have fencing and all of that stuff," Kathryn said, sighing.

Hum wrinkled his nose.

"I feel sorry for you, Kath. I mean, you have to do stuff like *embroidery*," Hum said.

"And you even get to have classes on how to address an overlord!" Kathryn exclaimed.

"I hate that," Hum said.

"But you got such high marks in it!" Kathryn exclaimed.

"I hate it, still," Hum said. Suddenly, Kathryn leapt up.

"I know!" she shouted. "You can teach me fencing and all of that stuff!"

"How would we get the fencing swords?" Hum asked.

"You could sneak them from the room," Kathryn said.

"The Vault!!??" Hum shouted. "That big thing is locked, double-bolt! Plus," and at that Hum grimaced, "it's got wand magic protecting it."

"Oh, heck!" Kathryn shouted. The only wand in the entire Academy was in Edith's office, and it was locked in a gold cupboard that was locked with different keys each time. Wands were only for the most powerful and learned wizards and witches, and there were only three witches and four wizards who had wands and could legally use the wand's stored power. Hand magic was more popular, especially among the trainee wizards and witches.

"So I can't teach you fencing," Hum said. "I can't defy wand magic with hand magic. They're different things. After all, even if I tried to, it would sap my strength."

"We could do fencing with sticks," Kathryn said.

"Sticks?" Hum said doubtfully, scratching his chin. "That wouldn't work as well."

"Still, it's something," Kathryn said. "Remember, Dad used to shave our sticks and we would pretend that we were great knights battling each other with lances?"

"Have you a knife to shave *with?*" Hum asked.

"Well…" Kathryn's voice trailed off. It was true—she had left her small hatchet back at her cozy room in Dad's large manor house. Even if she was able to use magic to summon it, Kathryn remembered **distinctly** that she had put a variety of spells (with Hum's help) on the hatchet, so that nobody could steal it.

"Along with Amaa, Sharp Eyes, and two perfectly antique bronze kings, Edith took my *magic* knife away from me," Hum said sullenly. Amaa was Hum's *minclops*, a tiny winged horse who had the magical ability to unlock anything, even things protected with the strongest wand magic. Sharp Eyes was Hum's *semieagle*. He had the wings, the sharp beak, and the eyes of an eagle, but he could change into a different animal at any time desired.

"Wait—Hum—that's it!" Kathryn breathed. "Amaa will be able to unlock the room with all of the fencing swords, and, there we are!"

"Excuse me?" Hum raised an eyebrow. "Did you forget that Amaa is locked also?"

"No!" Kathryn exclaimed, rolling her eyes. "But I've seen where Edith hides the keys. You create a distraction; I'll sneak the keys and get Amaa."

"Why do I have to create the distraction?!" Hum shouted.

"Well, do you want to get Amaa instead?" Kathryn raised her eyebrows.

"No," Hum said hurriedly.

"Good," Kathryn said. "Now no arguments."

Hum grumbled a lot for the rest of the day, but Kathryn felt happy and lighthearted. She was going to learn *fencing*—a boys' art!

Master Taylor was **reluctant** to let Kathryn and Hum inside the fencing area, as he did not like anyone "ruining the things." But when Kathryn said that Hum had lost something, he hurriedly said a few words, and the door swung open into the area. Kathryn let out a gasp, only to receive an elbow in the ribs from Hum.

"Stop it," Hum said, gritting his teeth. "You're supposed to look like I've really lost something." Hum stooped down, pretending to pick something up.

"I've got it, Master Taylor!" Hum shouted, pretending to pocket his "lost thing."

"All right then, I need to be off to a conference," Master Taylor called back.

"YES!" Hum accidentally shouted. Master Taylor quickly doubled back.

"What was that, young man?" Master Taylor said, his eyebrows lifted.

"Oh, Hum was just thinking about his birthday," Kathryn said, much to the displeasure of Hum, who considered birthdays to be of no importance.

"All right," Master Taylor said, going back upstairs.

"Got him away," Hum said. "Now, you get Amaa. Be sure to lock me in, all right?"

"Okay," Kathryn said, quickly sliding the latch closed and running out to Edith's office, weaving in and out of the magnificent corridors.

As soon as Kathryn was gone, Hum began shouting, "Help! Help! I'm locked in here!" Within minutes, the entire Academy had rushed to help —all except for Kathryn. Edith's door had been left slightly ajar in the uproar. Kathryn tiptoed in, took the keys from Edith's drawer, and unlocked the cupboard. Amaa squealed, delighted to see her.

"Ssssh, Amaa," Kathryn said. "You need to be quiet, okay?" Amaa nodded her shiny little head.

"Good," Kathryn said, taking Amaa down from the cupboard. Sharp Eyes stared at her from the corner.

"I guess I'll take you, too," she said, lifting Sharp Eyes from the cupboard.

"Hum, you will be receiving a detention. What you were doing in the fencing area I don't know," Edith's voice drifted over. Kathryn quickly stuffed Amaa into her pocket and ducked under a tapestry with The Academy's coat of arms on it, just in the nick of time. Edith walked in, stopping short when she saw that the cupboard was ajar, and Amaa was gone.

"Hum!" Edith screeched. "Did you have a part in this?!"

"No, how could I, headmistress?" Hum asked innocently. "I was locked in the fencing area!" Kathryn giggled from behind the tapestry.

"What was that!?" Edith looked around sharply.

"Oh, I think it's just one of the girls back there," Hum said **hastily**.

"Hmm," Edith said.

"Anyways, Kathryn should be waiting in the chambers," Hum said, "I'll be off." And so before Edith could protest, Hum was speeding out of the room. Much to Kathryn's surprise, Edith muttered a few swearwords under her breath.

When Edith had gone off to eat supper, Kathryn ran (with Amaa squealing noisily in her pocket) back to the chambers, where Hum was waiting.

"I've got Amaa," Kathryn said, taking the little miniclops from her pocket.

"Poor little thing," Hum said gently, stroking Amaa's short little mane of fiery red hair, which was not unlike his own.

"Enough happy endings," Kathryn said quickly. "You've already said hi to Amaa, now we need to get on with the important stuff."

"Fine, fine," Hum said reluctantly. The fencing area was deserted, just as Kathryn had hoped.

"Coast clear," Kathryn whispered to Hum, who nodded and turned a pale greenish color.

"Are you sure this is going to work?" he asked timidly.

"Yes!" Kathryn shouted impatiently, and, lowering her voice, she said, "Well, if we get expelled, there's none the worse of it."

"Oh, fie!" Hum exclaimed. He stepped forward, holding Amaa up to the lock. Amaa studied the lock for a little bit, and then bit around the edge. The door swung open with a click.

"Oh, Venus!" Kathryn gasped. The fencing swords were hung all around the room, all shiny and bright with their jeweled hilts.

"Here," Hum said, handing her a sword and some tough leather armor from a nearby hook. "We can practice in here."

"Okay," Kathryn said.

Kathryn soon found that fencing was not as easy as it looked. By nighttime she was covered head to toe in sores and bruises.

"It'll come along," Hum, the victor of their match, assured her. "You just need practice." Since the fencing swords were spares and would not be missed, Hum and Kathryn hid the swords in the sturdy oak chests under their beds.

The next day, in her excitement, Kathryn could hardly pay any attention to the lady lessons. Even Reana could not bother her or sink her high spirits.

Kathryn met with Hum in the cellars, where piles of cheese and meat, and casks of cider and wine were stacked against the walls and packed in tightly with straw.

"Except for Peb and Bee, hardly anybody comes in here," Hum said. Pebble, the old, gnarled, and grumpy cellar-keeper, was away in Berrbury, anyways. His twin (although they were always **bickering** over who was the elder), Bee, who was also extremely ancient but very friendly, had gone off to Kenswell.

"To black me boots," he'd muttered as he departed.

"It is quite deserted," Kathryn said. "Ew!" A rat scurried across the creaking planks of wood. Another rat hung by its tail from the rotting wooden rafters.

"Phew!" Hum had been sniffing at some of the casks of wine, and he shot back. "This junk smells musty."

"Well, yeah, it's been preserved in here for about a year," Kathryn said. "You drink that stuff every day."

"Ew, Kathryn!" Hum exclaimed, disgusted. "By Jupiter, you can't possibly know what you're saying!"

"Well, anyways, we should get on with our practice," Kathryn said, holding out her fencing sword. Hum picked his up from where he had left it on the ground.

"And begin!" Hum shouted. The two swords clashed. Kathryn circled Hum, always defending herself against his attacks. By mid-afternoon, both were exhausted and called it a tie.

"Let's go back upstairs," Hum said wearily, setting down his fencing sword.

"Oh, fie!" Kathryn exclaimed, but on the overall she was rather glad that Hum had suggested it; she was getting tired as well.

"Anyways, don't you have your lady lessons, that horrid torture stuff?" Hum asked. Kathryn's mouth dropped open with horror. She had completely forgotten about that!

"Um," Kathryn said, checking her gold-and-ruby watch. "Yes. They'll be doing—I don't want to talk about it."

"What a lady should and should not do, such as *the thing* without asking her guardians?" Hum asked, raising his eyebrows. He was entirely used to Kathryn's schedule by now.

"Well…yes," Kathryn said. "But I have to go." She lingered a bit longer, uneager to begin the dreaded lady lessons.

"Go then," Hum said. "I won't keep you." Kathryn nodded regretfully and raced upstairs.

Dame Shirley was not at all happy to see her. At least Reana wasn't there to make fun of her.

"You are late," Dame Shirley said shortly.

"Yes," Kathryn said, fidgeting uncomfortably. Dame Shirley stared right into Kathryn's green eyes, which most teachers found difficult, as Kathryn stared right back in a way that usually made adults uncomfortable.

"Your hair is a mess," Dame Shirley said, her lips pursed. Kathryn turned red. "And I think that your clothing could do with some washing and ironing." Kathryn turned even redder. *Hellgates!* Kathryn thought. She looked down. Wrinkled and much stained, the dress hung loosely on her scrawny body.

"But no mind," Shirley said. Turning to the rest of the class, she said, "My ladies, a most distinguished visitor honors us with his presence. Sir Hemlin of Kenswell and the Lord Protector of the Twin Gates."

A young man stepped into the class.

"Sir Hemlin, you are most welcome," Shirley said graciously. "Would it please you to have food and drink?"

"Well, of course! We've been driving along a dusty road, and we're famished," Hemlin said, laughing. One of his attendants tweaked his nose. Shirley looked surprised for a moment, but quickly regained her senses.

"Yes, of—of course," she said. Normally when she asked a visitor if they wanted refreshments they would politely (and solemnly) refuse. But Hemlin was a different case. When he received fresh hot bread, he broke it into small pieces, threw them up, and caught the pieces in his mouth. Kathryn couldn't help laughing, although she received a sharp slap from Shirley when Hemlin wasn't looking.

"Now, I hear you're wanting a wife who could continue with you on your voyage to the South Realms and The Valleys?" Shirley asked, sitting down in her rocking chair. Kathryn perked up.

"Well, yes," Hemlin said. "Although most girls practice silly things like embroidery and don't spend a millisecond of their time doing useful things like real magic and reading and writing, all of which are the qualities I wish to find in a future wife."

"One candidate I would propose to you would be Reana Brodsmat. Unfortunately, she is not here with us," Shirley said.

"Can she read and write?" Hemlin asked.

"Well, er, no." Even Shirley could not lie when asked a direct question.

"Then who can read?" Hemlin asked.

"Kathryn Karlsman," Shirley said. Kathryn felt a surge of hope. She had been taught to read and write when she was only three years old, and she was quite a bookworm.

"Where is she?" Hemlin asked.

"Kathryn, stand up please," Shirley said. Kathryn stood up. Hemlin surveyed her, a smile on his face.

"Now," Hemlin said. "Would you please write for me the word **'dilapidated'**?"

"Yes, my lordship," Kathryn said. She quickly wrote out the word.

"What about **scurrilous**?" Kathryn scribbled the word. Then:

"True or false—Sir Gareth Mayflower's shield was decorated with daisies."

"Yes, I believe Sir Mayflower's shield was decorated with daisies…"

"Good, good!" Hemlin exclaimed, clapping his hands. "Who is your father?"

"Sir Roland Karlsman," Kathryn said.

"Sir Roland! Yes, I have heard many a thing about your father," Hemlin said.

"Good or bad?" Kathryn asked.

"Ah, I see! Both, of course," Hemlin said. "On the whole, I believe that he must be quite the gentleman."

"Well, yes, if you put it that way," Kathryn said, blushing.

"Sir Hemlin?" Shirley asked. "You…er…were searching for a wife?"

"Quite true," Hemlin said. "I think I've already found her." Just then, Reana entered.

"Dame," Reana said in her fake-sweet voice, "is Sir Hemlin here?" Just then, Reana turned and noticed the knight sitting in the chair.

"Oh!" Reana squealed. "Sir Hemlin!" Kathryn rolled her eyes. She knew Reana's routine. It was all false.

"Er, well, I'm glad to know that…um…someone supports me," Hemlin said awkwardly, shifting in his chair. Kathryn wished more than ever that she could kick Reana.

"This is Reana Brodsmat," Shirley said, putting on a false smile. "I've told you about her before."

"Yes," Hemlin said, scratching his stubbly beard. "You're the one who can't read and write?" Reana turned pink. Kathryn had to put her hand over her mouth so that nobody would hear or see her laughing.

"Would you like to meet the rest of the girls?" Shirley asked hastily. Kathryn pretended to cough, although she was really laughing.

"If they know how to read and write, yes," Hemlin said doubtfully.

"I like Kathryn here the best." Kathryn was satisfied to see Reana's face turn white.

"Would you like to take her on a private walk through the grounds to…get to know her better?" Dame Shirley asked, her fingers twitching nervously.

"Well, I'm not sure. I really came past here to see my father, who is ailed with a terrible malady," Hemlin said, leaning against the blackboard. "My mother wished for me to find a bride along the way, so I am merely cooperating with her wishes. If I had Sir Roland's permission, I would take Kathryn along with me to Verlliones." Kathryn could barely contain herself from jumping up and down. *Take me to Verlliones!* she thought. *That would be a **real** adventure!*

"I am sure that I could contact Sir Roland, if it be your wish, Sir Hemlin," Dame Shirley said, batting her eyelashes.

"I can do so myself," Sir Hemlin said, leaping up from his chair. Kathryn watched with awe as he closed his eyes in concentration and murmured a few words under his breath. Finally, he opened his eyes.

"I have Sir Roland's permission. But most importantly, Kathryn— I need yours," Hemlin said impatiently. Kathryn was so pleasantly surprised that she stood gaping at Hemlin. Finally she said "yes."

"Good!" Hemlin cried, evidently pleased. "Then we shall make our leave, shan't we?"

As they left the sinister iron gates of the Academy, Kathryn looked into the distance and smiled. Far, far away, the great castles of Verlliones could be seen.

What Happens Next?
Key Concepts for Plot Development

Plot: *the sequence of events that serves as the backbone for a story.*

Although many kids know that a story has a beginning, middle and an end in theory, some students still feel that it's tough to get the first sentence out, difficult to make the transition from one action to the next and hard to end the story with the right note. In fact, it takes practice... It takes practice to gain the intuitive understanding of how a plot should be structured throughout a story.

Since Adora has learned many tricks of the writing trade intuitively through her extensive reading, she can't articulate the concept and theory of plot without guidance. Although she understood the basic concept easily enough and could soon explain the key components of plot, she has had to struggle more than usual to apply this understanding to her writing. The stories she is writing today are structurally much stronger and more complex than the stories she was writing a few months ago. Repeating the same plot related exercises and activities on a daily basis has been an important part of Adora's learning process.

Our motto has always been: master an art or skill through doing/practicing it before you begin to elaborate on it or offer variations. Giving a child the basic precepts of plot while they are doing/practicing it will give them a framework to fall back on when they feel stuck.

Key concepts for plot

Inciting Incident: the event at the beginning of a story that gets the ball rolling. Generally an inciting incident should contain the seeds of other events or themes that will be crucial to the plot.

Goals: Traditionally, most plots are based around the main character's quest to attain their dream or goal.

Obstacles: A story is generally not going to be very interesting if everything moves along without a hitch. Therefore it is necessary to dream up obstacles that block the protagonist's path to their goal. These obstacles can be other people (generally referred to as antagonists), physical barriers (mountains, roadblocks), or physical or internal weaknesses (fear of public speaking, lack of confidence) that the protagonist must learn to overcome.

Crisis: Situated before the climax, the crisis is the point in the story that ups the ante, or to put it another way, throws the protagonist or another key character out of the frying pan and into the fire. The crisis is a moment or incident that really tests the protagonist's resolve.

Climax: The most exciting point in a story, usually situated close to the end. The climax of a story should generally incorporate both the protagonist and antagonist, and should relate somehow to the protagonist's original goals.

Resolution: The end of the story, in which other plot points are resolved.

 Interview and Tips from Adora

Joyce: What kind of obstacles have you used in your stories to block your protagonist's path to his/her goals?
Adora: I like to use particularly pesky people and oftentimes creatures of my own imagination.

Joyce: Why do you think obstacles are important to a story line?
Adora: If the character does not have any obstacles, she/he could zip right through the story, which would make it boring and uninteresting.

Joyce: What do you think is important to include in the climax of a story?
Adora: I like including big decisions. I think they hold the reader in suspense.

Joyce: What do you do when you get stuck?
Adora: Usually I run off to terrorize my sister. If I don't feel like facing a mimicking monster, I have my Mommy Time or draw.

Joyce: Do you ever experience difficulties in ending your stories?
Adora: Definitely, I review my story and brainstorm possible endings. When I go back to finish stories for the book I usually don't finish it exactly along the lines of my plans because I have a different idea for it. If you look at some of my old stories you can find some unfinished

tales that drifted off into the fog of a writer's block. When I start another story and abandon my old one, I lose interest with my old one because I have improved my writing on my new story significantly.

Joyce: How do you usually come up with minor characters in your stories?

Adora: They just follow the story. I can't have a story without a large quantity of people, no matter how minor. I have to put them in somewhere. A story would be boring if you're just reading on and on and on about one single person.

 Tips for Parents and Educators

Encourage your childen to share their idea for a new story with you. Most children love to hear their parents' appreciation when they have something interesting to say. Adora used to come up with a new story idea every day and she had a hard time finishing the stories she was working on. In order not to discourage her, I encourage her to write down her ideas so she can work on them later. Have your child discuss a story idea with you before he/she sits down to write. Telling you the plot for a new story creates a chance to organize and analyze ideas. Support ideas and encourage your child to write them down. To keep on track, sometimes it's helpful to have your child map out a plot in advance. Encourage your child to imagine a character by asking him/her the following questions: What does this character want in life? Who or what might get in the way of this goal? How might the character overcome this obstacle? Although it's important to avoid cookie cutter plots, it is useful to create a simple graph to illustrate the story arc. Have your child fill in the blanks, identifying inciting incident, key plot points, etc. The following worksheet is a great learning tool.

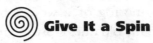 **Give It a Spin**

Fiction Writing Blueprint

Protagonist:

_____

Antagonist:

_____

Minor Antagonists:

_____

Protagonist's Main Goals:

_____

_____

External Obstacles:

_____

_____

Internal Obstacles:

_____

_____

How does the protagonist change during the course of the story?

_____

_____

Why does the antagonist want to stop the protagonist?

_____

_____

What are the protagonist's greatest strengths?

_____

_____

What are the protagonist's greatest weaknesses?

_____

_____

How do these strengths and weaknesses tie into the plot?

_____

_____

What makes the protagonist happy?

_____

_____

What makes the protagonist sad?

_____

_____

What makes the protagonist angry?

_____

_____

Does the protagonist try to hide any of these feelings?

_____

_____

Inciting Incident: (the event towards the beginning of the story that jump starts the action)

_____

_____

Theme:

_____

_____

Setting:
How does the setting tie into the story? Can you use the setting to emphasize the characters' strengths and weaknesses?

_____

_____

Climax:
Questions to ask oneself about the climax:
How does my climax emphasize the way my protagonist has changed during the course of the story?

_____

_____

How does my climax force my protagonist to make an important decision?

_____

_____

A good climax should force the protagonist to do or say something that is difficult for them.

_____

_____

A good climax should emphasize the story's underlying theme. (Examples: love is more important than money, the journey may be more important than the destination, etc.)

_____

_____

Think about an event or scene that would dramatically illustrate underlying theme, while simultaneously tying together plot points.
Plot Outline:

_____

_____

Subplot:

_____

_____

Questions to ask yourself about every new scene in your story:
How does this scene tell the reader anything new about any of the main characters?

_____

_____

How does this scene propel the plot forward?

_____

_____

Danger Ship

"**A**mber!" The gruff cry of an old sailor startled the girl, who spun around and nearly tripped on a coil of rope which was directly behind her.

"Steady, steady," the sailor said as he made his way up the wharf. "Ye wouldn't want yer Uncle Ian to see yer dress mussed. Oh, here he comes." The sailor said this with a twinkle in his misty gray eyes as Ian drew nearer to them, increasing his speed when he noticed Amber's sandy hair.

"Amber! Hurry—and get your sisters. Edmond's in my cabin, but we have to leave soon," Ian said impatiently, shivering and burying his hands in his pockets.

"I'm coming…just wait," Amber said crossly, taking one last deep breath of the London air and stepping onto the rocking ship.

The White Minnow was not quick in leaving. A few of the sailors had to be dragged out of a pub by a disgusted Uncle Ian. Amber privately thought he looked out of place wearing his fine suit in the muddy streets of one of London's nastiest slums.

Finally, with all of the sailors grunting with effort, the battered ship gave a great lurch and pulled away from the dock.

Once Amber was aboard the ship, she joined Edmond, her sickly brother, in Ian's cabin. Edmond was very white in the face and laid propped up in a narrow bunk.

"Why did we ever have to go on this horrid old soaking hulk?" Edmond moaned, pulling the thin covers over his face.

VOCABULARY LIST

forecastle - raised section of deck at the front of the ship
accustomed - familiar, used to
collided - crashed into
hoisted - lifted up
lurched - moved violently and unsteadily
seething - a pent-up quality, usually applied to anger or resentment
traversing - moving up, down, over, or across
scurrilous - insulting
commotion - hubbub, ruckus, noisy disturbance
cringe - flinch or shy away in embarrassment or fear
sufficient - enough, adequate
relish - savor, enjoy
menacingly - threateningly
gnash - to grind one's teeth in anger
kirtle - a long dress or skirt popular from the Middle Ages through the 17th C.
mutiny - sailors' rebellion
flamboyant - showy, flashy or colorful
scalawags - troublemakers

"You know quite as well as I do that Uncle Ian is the closest relation we have," said Amber, lying back on the bunk, "and unless you want to go to live in an old shack, you shall have to stop your complaining this instant." Just then Ian opened the door, looking as though he could have done with some serious rest.

"Oh, Amber. It's you," he said, collapsing into a rickety chair and gulping down a mouthful of a steaming hot liquid. "I just had to pull your sister, er, Joanna, away from the **forecastle**." Amber had no idea what a forecastle was, but she did not want to show her ignorance by asking. From the bunk, Edmond gave a moan. Ian looked over at the boy, putting down his mug.

"I hope you're doing well, Edmond," Ian said weakly, attempting to smile. Amber rose from the bunk, brushed herself off, and made a move towards the door.

"Where are the ladies' facilities?" Amber asked curtly, not bothering to look at Ian.

VOCABULARY LIST
brig - ship's prison
malady - illness
sufficient - enough, as much as is needed
furrowed - forehead wrinkle, groove, plow trench
galley - a boat's kitchen
scandalous - disgraceful or shameful
indignant - angry at unfairness
cherub - a chubby faced child angel
trump - in a card game the suit that has a higher value than others, slang for an outstanding person
rigging - the ropes that attach to masts and sails on a boat
vigor - strength, vitality
cartilage - the substance that our noses and ears are made of
hysterically - uncontrollably
grog - a mix of rum, hot water, sugar, and lemon juice
dehydration - loss of bodily fluids

"What?" Ian asked blankly. "Oh, er, well about that…perhaps I should do some construction on the ship later. But for now, could you please just do it in here?" Ian held out a soaked wooden bucket, held together with an assorted number of rags. She jumped back with a shriek, gasping.

"Amber!" Ian shouted.

"I refuse to use that filthy bucket!" Amber shouted, shuddering as a slug wormed its way across the rim. "Now please show me my room!"

A sailor took Amber to a small room a few feet away from Ian's cabin. It had an unusually low ceiling, so Amber was forced to stoop down as she entered. A small lantern hung from a large beam, swaying each time the ship rocked. It was very dim, and also very hard to get **accustomed** to the musty smell.

"What!" Amber shrieked, enraged. She kicked the bunk. "These are unacceptable lodgings!"

"Good enough for the rest of the crew," the sailor said darkly. "We share this, sleeping in hammocks. In the pitch dark to boot."

"Why would you think that I care?" Amber exclaimed. "I must see my uncle about this immediately."

"He has his orders. None are to see him but his nephew," the sailor said, making a move to block the door. *His nephew!* The words rang in Amber's head. How she wished she could have stopped the carriage accident. The duel. Just everything. Everything that had led to this horrible ship.

"Well, then bring me some food," Amber said haughtily, placing her hands on her hips.

"Find it yourself. I have my own duties," the sailor said, walking out and closing the door, leaving Amber in darkness.

Amber awoke the next morning with aches in her arms and legs. She had spent the night being tossed around in the bunk, and had **collided** with what she was sure was some kind of rat. Everybody was busy, muttering and swearing. To make matters worse, Ian put Amber in charge of her little twin sisters, Joanna and Mary.

"Just get off me!" Amber cried with disgust as Mary clambered onto her arm. Ian merely sighed and turned away. It was to be a busy day, with everyone knocking each other about and general confusion. Amber was going to have a hard time. She had her heart set on exploring the ship, and the only way to calm Joanna and Mary and keep them from jumping and hiding from everything they saw was to give them a piggyback ride. There really was no other way. Amber sighed as she **hoisted** first Joanna up to her shoulder and then Mary. Carrying them was going to be no easy task.

It was not really Amber's choice to go below decks, but everybody seemed to want the girls out of the way, including Ian, who was obsessed with Edmond's worsening fever. Amber groaned as she staggered down the creaking stairs. Her lantern bounced against her side, making Mary shrink back with fright. It was wet and damp, not at all Amber's dream liner. She grasped the wooden railing to steady herself. The ship **lurched** again, making Amber trip and the lantern fall. As Amber shrieked, the passage was plunged into darkness.

When Amber woke up, she was lying in the bunk with Ian hovering anxiously over her.

"What happened?" Amber asked, somewhat annoyed at the previous event.

"That was quite a fall you had back there," Ian said, whistling. "Can't you learn to keep your balance?"

"Not when the thing I'm on has to be this old ship," Amber said fiercely, her pride stung by the scathing remark.

"Well, I suppose you've made up your mind about it. The next port should be about, say, about a day. There we can stop and pick up fresh supplies. And you can get some proper care," Ian said, taking a step back. Amber threw back her covers and slid out cautiously.

"I need my baggage," Amber said impatiently. "It has my things in it."

"Your trunk will be below decks," Ian said, making no move to the door.

"Where is a sailor who can bring my baggage up?" Amber asked, unintentionally betraying her impatience.

"What?" Ian asked blankly. "Oh, er, I suppose you'll have to do it yourself."

And so it was that Amber left the cabin **seething** and angry. She had not had a pleasant experience when **traversing** the stairs last time, and although an undersized sailor accompanied her this time, Amber was not reassured by the tiny sailor's scurrilous words.

The hold where Amber's baggage was kept was dark and dank. Amber pulled her trunk out from the corner and shoved it into the sailor's hands.

"Here. Carry it up," she said coldly.

"No," the sailor said calmly, sliding the trunk back to Amber's feet.

"No!? You dare refuse a lady's wishes!" Amber cried, enraged. "I am the daughter of the Earl of Cambridge!"

"You ain't no lady," the sailor said, chuckling. "Look at ye." Amber looked down and to her surprise realized that it was true. She was not at all the image of a fine lady. Her dress was spattered with mud and saltwater, and her hair was tangled and loose around her shoulders. Nobody would have mistaken her for an elegant, refined lady of high society. She was somewhat disheartened at this. After all, she had been sent to the best finishing school in all of London. Why hadn't she come out right?

"If ye don't move yer legs, I'll leave ye." The sailor's voice disturbed Amber. She gritted her teeth and dragged her trunk back up the stairs.

Once she had pulled one of her favorite dresses out of her trunk, Amber dabbed perfume behind her ears and then dressed herself. She combed her hair and braided it into two long plaits, washed her face with a damp towel, and joined the rest of the company. Dinner that night was nothing more than some biscuits and sea beans. Ian was extremely worried about a storm that was gathering, and could be seen pacing the deck with a sharp eye focused on the foggy skies.

"There's a storm out there," he said grimly as he came back in the kitchen, shutting the door. "We'll have rain tonight, as well as some lightning and thunder." There were groans from crew members.

"It can't be stopped," Ian said wearily, sweeping the dishes up from the table and dumping them into one large bucket. "Maybe we'll have better weather as it nears midsummer."

The days passed. Soon Amber had lost track of time aboard *The White Minnow*. Edmond's anguished cries could often be heard faintly from the cabin, and although many medicines were prescribed, none really did anything. Storms came and went. New cargoes of black slaves were loaded, unloaded, and reloaded.

One particularly warm day as Amber stood on the deck of the ship, staring out at the yards of endless water, she was startled by the cabin boy in the middle of a grand daydream.

*What'd he have to come now for? I was just having that pleasant daydream about me dressed in a long beautiful **kirtle** with my hair braided into long plaits, while everyone was serving me and…*

"Ma'm," the boy said, trembling. "Ye are wanted to tend to one of the n-negroes below d-decks."

"The slaves!" Amber exclaimed. Regaining her prim, elegant posture, she said quietly, "By whose orders do you summon me?"

"Y-your uncle's, ma'm," the cabin boy said, looking positively terrified.

"Fine, then," Amber said, pulling away from the deck railing. She followed the cabin boy to the steps that led down into the hold. She had scarcely put her foot on the first step when she was hit on the back of her head and blindfolded.

When Amber opened her eyes, it was dark and dim. She groped around and tried to get up, only to find that she was tied with strong lengths of rope. A large sailor came barreling towards her.

"Right, you've finally woken," he said roughly, starting to untie the cords that bound her. A few other sailors came up from behind him and stared at her.

"Right, boys, now that we've got her, we need the boy," the sailor said. The rest grunted. One made a move towards the stairs. The sailor who had been untying Amber grabbed the other sailor by the arm and pulled him back.

"What do you think you're doing?" the sailor who had been untying Amber hissed. "You could've just signed your death warrant, fool! Did you know that if you went up there, that blunderer Ian would have asked how everything was going and then come down here to check! He would've shot us all with that darned pistol of his!"

"You should really control your temper, Tom," the other sailor said calmly. Amber screamed, her own shrill voice piercing her eardrums. She had heard enough, seen enough. It did not take more than a few long statements to assure her that there was **mutiny** in the crew. Ian would have to be notified at once. And there was no other way to notify him with the sailors guarding the steps.

"What do ye think yer doin', girl?!" Tom exclaimed angrily.

"Quick! Hide her!" The other sailors immediately dragged Amber to a dark, shadowy corner as Ian's thin figure came into view.

"Who screamed?" Ian asked mildly, straightening his **flamboyant** jacket.

"Nobody," Tom said hurriedly, and, at Ian's raised eyebrows, he said, "Well, I think it might have been the cabin boy. Uh…he might've tripped on a shard of glass."

"Help!" Amber bit her captor's wrist (she was happy to note she drew blood), and struggled wildly to break free.

"Amber! What in God's name are you doing here?" Ian asked, his hand immediately touching his pistol.

"The sailors kidnapped me," Amber said rapidly. "A mutiny's been started against you."

"To arms, men! Fight for yer lives! Every man for himself!!!" Tom barked, firing a crude pistol he had pulled from under his shirt. The smoke and confusion which followed next was so unpleasant that Amber wanted to just forget it. Whether it was luck or a mysterious force, Ian continually avoided the shots until one sailor had been killed and two more wounded. Finally the **commotion** died down. Tom was cursing as he sunk down onto the ground, shot in the thigh. Amber pushed herself up and ran to where Ian was crouching.

"That was a close call," Ian whistled, tucking his pistol back into his belt.

"Now can we go back to your cabin?" Amber asked.

"Yes, but first I need to take these—" here Ian grimaced and kicked one of the sailors, "**scalawags** to the **brig**."

"I'll be in the cabin," Amber said quickly, sprinting up the steps.

More days passed until finally it was Amber's fifteenth birthday. Ian apologized for not being able to make a cake, but the cook scraped up a pie out of a few special ingredients. They all sat down at the table, munching on the delicious treat.

"This is wonderful. What is it made out of?" Amber asked, swallowing a mouthful.

"I'd rather not tell you," Ian said, **cringing**. "You might...er...find it rather dissatisfactory after you were made aware of the ingredients." Edmond groaned from his seat.

"Oh," Amber said, disappointed. She glanced at Edmond, who looked as if he was going to be sick.

"Edmond! What's wrong?" Amber exclaimed.

"My stomach," Edmond groaned.

"Are you feeling all right? Why don't you just go back to the cabin?" Ian asked.

"Alright," Edmond groaned.

There was a large amount of commotion on Saturday as the black slaves were unloaded from the ship and given to the hands of white slave traders on the warm shores of Louisiana. Ian had some extra dealings with a plantation owner, so he had rented a room in a nearby inn.

"It'll be fast," he promised Amber. It was really the wrong thing to say. Amber wanted nothing more than to stay in the town for as long as possible.

"Can we please stay for just another week?" she begged Ian. "This is the first civilized town I've seen since we sailed off from England."

"No, I've told you! I have business dealings elsewhere that need to be taken care of, and there's bound to be a storm on the open water once we leave!" Ian exploded, spinning around. Amber shrunk back, hurt.

"I'm sorry," Ian said. "But it's very hard to be patient with all of this happening. A crew mutiny, trading with some of the most impatient plantation owners, it drives a man mad!"

"Fine," Amber sighed, walking away.

Their leave was delayed by the plantation owner, who proposed to throw a farewell party.

"Jus' thought might do good to ya'll," he growled, clutching a bloody rod which he had used to beat a slave just moments before. Amber turned away with disgust at the brutality. Ian protested against the party, but the owner insisted. The party was hosted by the owner's wife, who was a thin, solemn woman named Deborah.

"I wouldn't take her for a wife if I had a choice," Ian whispered to Edmond and Amber as they were seated at the long broad wooden table.

"She is not at all someone I would like to be acquainted with," Amber whispered back, staring at the numerous stains which dotted the threadbare linen tablecloth. Ian ignored Amber, instead turning to Edmond.

"How are you feeling?" he asked the pale boy loudly, patting his stomach.

"Not—very—well," Edmond croaked.

"You, lad! You've got any spots on ya?!" the plantation owner, Alec, barked. *If he yells at his slaves like he's doing to Edmond, they'll attempt running away soon,* Amber thought, staring at Edmond sympathetically.

"No, he hasn't got the spotted pox," Ian said hurriedly, dropping a spoonful of cilantro mashed potatoes onto his plate.

"What's that?" Amber asked, certain it was some terrible **malady**.

"Smallpox. You haven't heard of it?" Ian asked Amber, raising his bushy eyebrows.

"Yes," Amber said, irritated. "Of course I have. I just didn't exactly…grasp what you were talking about."

"Most feared disease in the entire civilized world," Ian said, winking at Edmond. "Most certainly brings death. Of course, there is ways you can avoid it…but it spreads like wildfire."

"Yes, I know," Amber said, even more annoyed. "News of a recent epidemic was on the cover of *The Informed Englishman.*"

"P'raps you need a checkup, too, gal?!" Alec roared across the table.

"No—you have my assurance that Amber is most delightfully healthy. She eats well and has sufficient weight, although I may say myself that outlandish girdle which young girls now wear so tightly does spoil a regular complexion," Ian said, blushing as he finished his statement. Amber glared at him, tenderly stroking the fine leather on the belt which was strung tightly about her waist.

"Yah, I agree," the man growled, somewhat calmer. "Me Deborah don't wear nothin' of the sort."

"And perhaps I should wear one, Alec, just to make you aware that I am not a household tool to be spoken of freely," Deborah said coldly to her husband.

"Whaddya thinkin' of, woman!" Alec roared, bringing his fist down on the table with a splintering crash.

"Let's not get into an argument here," Ian said quickly. Amber nodded superiorly.

"Fine, fine," Alec said grudgingly. And so all was well for the rest of the evening.

When she woke up in the morning, Amber washed in the water-basin that was beside her bed, dressed in a pretty dark green gown, gave her thick hair a quick brush, plaited it, and skipped downstairs. Ian looked grave and serious as he sat in his chair by the inn's fireplace. His stubble of a beard looked more ragged than usual, and his usually neat brown hair was unkempt.

"Is there anything wrong?" Amber whispered to Edmond with some anxiety.

"Another one of Ian's ships—*The Merry Waters*—was taken by pirates," Edmond whispered back, his little round face white with fear.

"Damn. Darn it all," Ian swore from his chair. Amber shuddered.

"And there's more," Edmond whispered. "We'll have to go on a rescue mission to the site where the ship was attacked! *Us!* "

"Amber, I'm sorry to disappoint you, but we'll be going on a different course today, er, to some important—" Ian was cut off by Amber's "I know." She tried to sound cool and calm, but the trembling in her voice betrayed her fear.

"You know about the pirates?" Ian asked, his eyebrows raised.

"Yes. Everything," Amber said grimly. "Now I suppose we'll have to board the wretched ship and forget about all the nice times we've had here."

"Well, actually, about that," Ian said, blushing. "Another one of my ships, *My Fair Lady*, just arrived. It is larger and more luxurious—more fitting to a young lady of your rank. I am switching *The White Minnow* with the captain of *My Fair Lady*, so we will have comfortable sailing for the rest of our journey." Amber was so overjoyed that she was at loss for words. She stood gaping at Ian.

"Yes, I know, it is a delightful change," Ian said, smiling. He grimaced, then, and went on, "But the Indies won't be. Our destination, of course."

"The Indies!" Amber gasped, clutching her hands even tighter. "You cannot be serious! Savage heathens reside there!"

"Savage heathens do live there, but still, I have my duty to my men," Ian said grimly. "I'm afraid my other captains are not feeling up to the job. If you had been with me earlier, I could have made the arrangements to leave you at finishing school. But unfortunately you were dropped on my hands just when it was most inconvenient."

"Indeed!" Amber exclaimed. "When are we to depart?"

"After breakfast. I want to leave as soon as possible. An old sailor's proverb—the sooner you leave, the sooner you return," Ian said, brushing back a few stray locks of hair.

"I do indeed understand that," Amber muttered, although she was very unhappy. She had been hoping to leave in the late afternoon, or even the next day. But she knew that it was impossible.

My Fair Lady was indeed a pleasant change from *The White Minnow*. It had large, bright cheery rooms with clean washed decks and a large dining room. The crew was very kind to Amber, Edmond, and the twins, welcoming them aboard with a hearty "Howdy, children!" Even sickly Edmond looked better—his cheeks were starting to look red, and he walked around chattering amiably with the sailors. Ian was back to his normal self, talking with everyone and making jokes. Amber even enjoyed below deck, where despite the lack of windows there was a **sufficient** amount of air from the bright blue sky above. There were no further signs of a storm, and Ian no longer paced the deck staring at the sky with his brow **furrowed** in worry. Mary and Joanna were cared for by the ship's washerwoman and cook, a jolly woman named Eva, who was the wife of Ian's second mate. Amber was relieved to have the two troublemakers off her hands and into Eva's rough, floury ones.

"I love these little girls, and they're like me own chyldren," Eva had said croakily, and grinning, showed Amber her crooked yellow teeth. Mary and Joanna immediately warmed towards the old woman, and were often seen running to the **galley** accompanied by a relieved and leisurely Amber.

"It's a relief to have some things off of my hands," Ian told Amber and Edmond at the dinner table. Mary and Joanna had already eaten their fill, and were in their room listening to Eva tell a story.

"Yes," Amber said, tossing back her rebellious strands of hair. "Mary and Joanna can't bother me anymore, and I'm free to do as I wish. I do believe that this ship is fit for Queen Victoria."

"No," Ian said, grinning. "The royalty have luxury yachts. Edmond would do quite well on one." He turned back to the boy, who was sitting comfortably in a chair with many cushions. "How are you, Edmond, anyhow?"

"He's fine," Amber cut in. "I make sure that he gets plenty of fresh air on the deck every morning before and after breakfast." In truth she had not really bothered much with this routine, but she was eager for her share of attention and wished to display the fact that she was being a responsible lady.

"Yes, yes," Ian said. "Very good. I might just make this switch permanent—I'm sure that Captain Williams wouldn't mind. After all, my old crew on *The White Minnow* seems to need an older and tougher man who can deal with them."

"Certainly!" Amber exclaimed. "About making the switch permanent, I mean. Although I certainly won't be staying on this ship long."

"That's the thing," Ian said thoughtfully.

"What do you mean?" Amber asked, quite alarmed.

"About your staying on the ship. I would certainly welcome a new crewmate," Ian said. "Not to do any heavy work lifting splintery ropes and all of that. But a cook's companion or somebody of the sort."

"No! Most assuredly not! I am not going to sink to the position of a ship's servant!" Amber shouted, enraged at the very thought.

"Just asking," Ian said slyly, taking another orange and spitting the seeds of the previous one out into the dish.

The next morning, Amber was still angry about Ian's suggestion and pursed her lips as she dressed. She let Mary and Joanna run into Eva's arms without even a single "hello." Ian did not talk to her much, and Amber made no effort to talk back. Edmond had an ugly purple bruise on his knee and was taking a nap.

"So, Amber," Ian finally said as they sat at the table in an uncomfortable silence. "I suppose you did not seem to **relish** the idea of becoming a crewmate."

"I would rather not bring up that **scandalous** idea!" Amber exclaimed shrilly.

"As you wish," Ian said. "But you may decide to change your mind."

"I most certainly will not. I will not serve another!" Amber snapped back.

"Perhaps you shall," Ian said calmly, although his smile was gone.

"I am sure I shan't, for it would displease Mama and Papa!" Amber exclaimed.

"Do as you wish," Ian said. "But I am sure that you will at least consider the idea."

"Consider the idiotic idea, indeed!" Amber fumed.

Amber forgot the heated conversation later in the day, as pleasant breezes swept the warm deck. Eva had brought the washing up to enjoy the sunshine, and Mary and Joanna came with her. Amber was standing in a corner on the deck, breathing in the sweet air.

"Hello, Amber!" Eva cried out to Amber, who turned her head as the old woman said the words. Mary and Joanna were scampering along carrying two large buckets overflowing with putrid yellowish liquid.

"Washing soap—or rather, urine," Eva said unblushingly.

"Ugh! How can you wash with such despicable fluid?" Amber exclaimed, jumping back as a large portion of the urine sloshed out of the bucket.

"It be collected from the crew members," Eva croaked. "We have chamber pots with caps on 'em." She set down a large basket filled with every manner of clothing as she said this. Amber stared at it, and was surprised to see many torn and tattered vests, shirts, and breeches.

She had always imagined Ian's crew to be like a grand navy, dressed in full uniform that was clean and pressed thoroughly.

"Why are all of these articles of clothing so worn?" Amber exclaimed, turning to Eva.

"Ah, the life of a seaman is hard," Eva said dreamily. "Me husband comes back every night from work tired with his clothes all torn. I mend 'em, but I can't repair the fact that if you choose this life, you're in for a hard life." Amber stared at Eva's rough, wrinkled brown hands, which had taken the bucket of urine and poured it on the clothes in the basket.

"Can I help?" Joanna asked Eva.

"No! Joanna, to think that you would even ask such a thing! I forbid it!" Amber cried, indignant that Joanna would want to do such disgusting work.

"Yes, my darling," Eva said as if she had not even heard Amber's words.

"I want to," Mary said, taking a torn shirt and examining it with curious eyes.

"No!" Amber cried again, her temper flaring. "It would be shameful!"

Just then Edmond came walking up to the deck.

"Hello, Amber!" he cried joyfully. "Are Mary and Jo bothering you?"

"Yes, immensely," Amber said, irritated despite Edmond's friendliness. "They are going on about nonsense how they want to do washing."

"The little **cherubs**!" Edmond exclaimed, cuddling Mary's chubby little face in his hands. "Aren't you **trumps**? Volunteering to do the washing…" Amber scowled and stormed off in a huff.

That night at the dinner table Ian was very quiet.

"The worst of the journey is ahead. The Indies are very storm-prone," he said grimly.

"Why?" Amber asked, alarmed.

"The Lord wishes it to be so," Ian said shortly. He had not been talking to Amber much after their heated conversation. Amber left her plate and bowl at the table and stalked off.

Ian was right. A fierce storm came just three days later. The entire crew rushed to the deck. As men scrambled to the **rigging** to tame the billowing sales, the great howling winds tossed some into the raging waters. Some unluckier men fell onto the hard wood of the deck, breaking every bone in their body. Others came down successfully, panting and sneezing. The worst was still yet to come. In the midst of the chaos, a grim watchman informed Ian that a ship flying the Jolly Roger had been seen on the distant horizon.

"Prepare the cannon," Ian ordered. "And do make haste."

"Yes, sir," the watchman said, tipping his cap. In moments a large, rusty cannon was wheeled out onto the deck. Amber thought that it was the ugliest thing that she had ever seen.

"Don't start shooting until the pirate ship comes in sight," Ian commanded the four men whom the watchman had brought with him. "I don't want to waste gunpowder. Our stores are low."

"Yes, sir," the watchman said again, although this time there was more anxiety in his voice. Ian put one hand on his pistol, and the other reassuringly on Amber's shoulder.

"Don't worry, I don't think they'll make any attempts to try and board the ship," Ian said, but the tone of his voice betrayed his doubtfulness. Amber broke away.

"I'm going below decks," she said, sniffing as she turned away. Ian grabbed her waist.

"No!" he exclaimed. "We might need you if one of the cannon men falls." Amber scowled, but she stayed. The pirate ship neared, and could be seen without the help of Ian's long telescope. Sailors pulled out any type of weapon they could find—pots and pans, chopping knives and broken saws, ancient cutlasses and rusty rifles, and broken beams of wood. A large pile of putrid fish was piled up near the deck to prevent the pirates from boarding, and the supplies were safely hidden and locked securely away in the storerooms. Even Eva wielded small stewpot, brandishing it about **menacingly**. Ian forced a cooking pan into Amber's hand, despite her protests.

"You might need it," he growled. Amber scowled again and accepted the tool. Other sailors grabbed hammers and sharpened screwdrivers from a small box that the first mate was passing around. Two men stood beside the pile of fish with buckets of water at the ready to stop the pirates from setting the ship on fire.

Fire. The most feared word a seaman could mutter. He could swear, curse, and stomp his feet, but nothing could be as dangerous as the hot red flames on the open waters. Rags soaked in urine were hung about the sails, and the sails themselves were drenched in water to prevent them from catching fire. The pirate's ship came so near that Ian ordered the first shot to be fired from the cannon.

"Fire!" he shouted. Amber jumped with surprise at the deafening noise of the cannon. The pirate's ship responded with a burning brand of hot shot, which landed harmlessly in the water.

"Swivel up, around the pirate ship. Fire at the back gunpowder magazine!" Ian shouted to the sailors. Sailors ran to the wheel, immediately following Ian's command. Within minutes the air was filled with hot smoke. Red flashes of fire exploded up into the air. Amber's eyes watered.

"Fight for your lives!" Ian cried again as a pirate dived into the water and grabbed hold of a rope that had been forgotten in the turmoil.

"Cut the ropes!" Ian cried. Amber, being the nearest, suddenly grabbed a rusty cutlass from a nearby sailor and hacked at the thick cords. With a cry the pirate fell backwards into the water.

"Yea, Amber!" Ian cried. Amber handed the cutlass back to the sailor, but, grinning widely, he handed it back to her and grabbed the kitchen pan.

"Ye deserved it," the sailor said. But there was more trouble. One of the sailors who had been standing around the pile of fish to prevent the pirates' attempt to board had been shot down as his comrade was wounded, and nobody had really noticed that the two had fallen from their posts. When Ian finally turned to look, he saw four filthy pirates jumping up onto the deck, waving glinting knives.

"Up and at them!" Ian cried, firing his pistol at the pirates. But hearing his command, the pirates ducked, letting the bullet fly harmlessly overhead. A few sailors rushed to Ian's defense. Amber was among them, slashing her cutlass left and right, forward and backward. She pleasantly surprised everyone that night. Her dress was torn, her hair was tangled and hanging over her eyes, and her hands usually so white and delicate were blistered and rough. She killed and wounded pirates like an unstoppable machine.

While slashing madly with her cutlass, Amber kicked and bit, elbowed and threw. Although she tripped once, she immediately rose and attacked with renewed **vigor**. Pirates stopped to gape at her, which only gave her a better chance to cut them down. Ian took this opportunity to fire at the pirate ship's unprotected parts, splintering their helm with another shot from the cannon. Finally the last pirate had been thrown into the water. The smoke and fire started to clear, and Ian swiveled up next to the pirate ship.

Ian spent that night selecting a choice crew and captain to take control of the pirate ship. The galley slaves were freed and recruited as midshipmen on the pirate vessel. They thanked Ian heartily again and again, shaking his hand and muttering thanks to God. Ian's spirits were lifted mightily. He thanked Amber for "her services to the battle," as well as the other sailors for their courage. Still, there was a tiny part of gloominess left on the ship. The waters were bound to be teeming with pirates, bigger and better trained than the ones they had just faced.

"They'll have firearms and gunpowder, as well as numerous cannons," Ian said glumly.

"This is not a war!" Amber cried, wringing her hands with frustration. "They might have more firearms than us, but it's not like they'll have a fully loaded warship! They're not English privateers or...or ancient warlords!"

"Fine, fine, fine, but they'll be prepared for any major battle," Ian said wearily. "Anyways, I'll be up in my cabin deciding the route we're going to take." And with that he strode off, leaving his soup cold and untouched.

Amber awoke to the sounds of crashing and shooting. There was a cry and then silence. Without bothering to dress herself in fitting attire, she leapt out of bed and raced to the scene of commotion. When she reached the deck she found a sailor with his head split open. The deck was already soaked with blood. Ian stood next to him, unable to move. The rest of the sailors jabbered at each other and talked excitedly, while the wounded sailor writhed in agony and shrieked. Amber felt queasy at the sight of so much blood, and yet she knew what to do. She tore off the lace on the low-necked collar of her nightgown and wrapped it around the sailor's head to stop the flow of blood. She helped the poor man up and accompanied him below decks into the hold. Ian joined her as she stood anxiously by his bunk, watching the man snore soundly.

"He will live, won't he? How did he split his head?" she asked Ian anxiously.

"Yes, I'm certain he will live, with the work you did on him. As for the reason he split his head, he fell about ten feet from the mainmast," Ian said, smiling crookedly. Amber looked at her bloody hands, and grinned back.

"Yes, I do suppose it was worthwhile," she said.

From then on Amber helped with small chores around the ship, tending the sick or wounded, and occasionally helping with a few side dishes for dinner. Everybody agreed that she was very helpful now that she actually had volunteered to help, and their words (which were very audibly spoken) made Amber's cheeks glow with pride.

"My girl," Ian said one morning as they neared the shore, "I do believe that you are as good, or better, than a sailor. Your help is enormous. That pie you made yesterday was simply delicious. Now—I again ask my question. Do you want to stay aboard the ship when we land in Great Britain?"

"Ye—no—yes," Amber stuttered, really unable to make up her mind.

"Good!" Ian exclaimed, obviously overjoyed. "Why don't we throw a party in honor of your decision!" And with that he grabbed Amber's arm and danced a merry jig. Amber was forced to do likewise should he step on her toe.

Eva made a marvelous cake with white frosting and little white sugar-doves on the second layer. Candles were placed along the rim of the first layer, letting out a marvelous light.

"Oh—it's simply divine," Amber breathed, hardly daring to talk. Ian stared at it, his eyes like glassy pearls. Edmond stood with his mouth open, gawking at the splendor of the cake. The candles let off a radiance which seemed to reflect on the cake, and the radiance was working its magic on the three spellbound people. Amber was the first to regain her senses, and sat down in a wooden chair with a *plop*. Edmond came next, closing his mouth as he dropped onto his cushioned seat. Ian finally collapsed into his chair at the head of the table, ranting on and on about how it was "simply magnificent and wonderful."

Next Eva unmasked another surprise—bread pudding. Ian immediately dug into the bowl with his spoon, dumping it onto his plate and wolfing it down as soon as it touched the rim. Finally he wiped his mouth with the back of his hand and lay back in his chair.

"Well, it looks like this eater is quite enthusiastic about his food!" Eva exclaimed, laughing.

"And why shouldn't I be?" Ian asked teasingly.

"Oh, do come off it," said Amber impatiently. "Let's just eat."

"Hear, hear!" Edmond cried. Amber at once took the knife and cut the cake into slices, sliding a slice onto everyone's plate. Then Eva spooned out the bread pudding into small little dishes, and everyone took some. Amber retired to her room with a full stomach. Edmond stayed out on the deck to play a game of chess with Ian in the sunset, with the shadows of dusk just beginning to fall.

"We'll be at the island before midnight," Ian said happily as he was coming down the hall, which neighbored Amber's room.

"Without another pirate attack, I certainly ho—" Amber's hopes were shattered as a sailor's cry cut through her sentence.

"Captain! Pirate ship nearing!"

"Oh, dear," Ian buried his face in his hands, but ran along. At once the crew was assembled and handed assorted weapons. Ian offered Amber a pistol, but she politely refused and took a cutlass instead. Four men raced to attend to the cannon, wheeling the heavy weapon onto the deck. The fish were again piled up on the deck to prevent the pirates from boarding. Three men stood ready with buckets of water.

Just as Ian had feared, these pirates were tough and had a larger ship. Pirates who wore nothing but torn blue vests and ripped gray canvas trousers shouted and flexed their bulging muscles. Instead of brandishing knives, most of them wore pistols tied with cords to their sides and a huge variety of glinting daggers. Many wore black eye patches and red headbands tied on their heads, or else rags around their feet. The leader of them all stood in front, shabbily-dressed but still better off than the rest. He wore a ragged blue vest around his bare chest, which had a tuft of hair growing in the middle. One long scar ran down the side of his face, and Amber shuddered to see it. His temples throbbed, and his veins stuck out of his large brown hands.

"Fight for your lives!" Ian ordered. With a deafening blast of the cannon, the ship shook and rolled. The pirate ship replied with grapeshot, which knocked out several sailors in the front line.

"Hurry," Ian whispered. "The pirate ship is at close enough range that we can attempt hot shot. Just hurry!" Sailors rushed to fulfill Ian's command. Amber took their place in the front line. The pirates

gnashed their teeth at her, waving their daggers menacingly. Ian shot a burning brand aimed at the pirate ship's mainmast, which instead set the deck of the pirate ship on fire. Roaring angrily, the pirates attempted to stomp the fire out. Amber could just barely make out their captain shouting,

"You lily-livered landlubbers! You scurvy sea dogs! Get water to put it out!" Although the hot shot had not met its exact mark, it was doing quite a lot of damage to the pirate ship. The flames had spread, nearing what Ian guessed and hoped was the gunpowder magazine.

"They're preparing to ram us in or board the ship! Our only chance is to run for it!" Ian gasped as the pirate ship neared. He immediately ran to the steering wheel and swiveled away from the pirate ship. The sailors shot the cannon for the last time and retreated to convenient hiding places that would allow them to ambush the pirates when the time was ripe. Amber chose a spot behind the mainmast, where she could easily spring out and slash at the pirates if there was need. Though Amber was aware that he was heavily armed, she still felt worried that Ian's visibility would lead to his downfall.

Edmond was put in a bunk below decks, and Mary and Joanna were sleeping next to him. Two sailors went to guard the gunpowder magazine, wielding long rifles and short broadswords. Slowly the dilapidated pirate ship drifted towards *My Fair Lady*, gaining speed as its decrepit sails caught the wind. Pirates leapt from barrels, some landing in the murky depths of the swirling seas, but most landed on the deck's broad wooden railing.

"Hiyah!" they shouted, waving burning torches and throwing them onto the ground. Amber jumped out from behind her hiding place, with the rest of the sailors. A few sailors poured water on the hot flames, while Amber slashed wildly at the pirates. The ones who had fallen into the water were climbing up the sides of *My Fair Lady*, and their captain (who was still on the pirate ship) was bringing it even closer towards *My Fair Lady*. Amber gasped with horror and amazement. The two ships were almost colliding! Ian gave a turn of the steering wheel, and they went off at a much faster pace.

"They're getting away!" the pirate captain roared, smashing his pistol against the pirate ship. "Get them!"

"Go away to where you belong—the hanging noose!" Amber shouted, thrusting her cutlass down on the shoulder of another pirate.

He collapsed, groaning and cursing with pain, blood running from the wound. With a powerful kick, Amber bashed the pirate against the wooden railing and into the deep water. There he could be seen floating on the surface, a grotesque, bloody figure. As she spun around to face another, Amber saw one large, burly pirate barreling towards her. He had two knives in his hands, and he looked dangerous. He barred his teeth threateningly, his eyes burning with hatred and enmity.

"Go away!" Amber cried, slashing at the pirate's hip. The unsuspecting pirate jumped away with blood trickling down his thigh.

"Damned girl," he muttered, collapsing onto the ground with a groan. Amber quickly finished him off with a flick of the cutlass.

"Good going, Amber!" Ian shouted from the steering wheel. "That was the captain you just got right there!" The few remaining pirates spun around with surprise. Seeing that Amber had sliced their captain's **cartilage** into finely chopped white powder, they shrieked **hysterically** and jumped overboard.

"Well, that takes care of them," Ian said, wringing his hands, "but much of our crew has been killed or wounded. Take them to the forecastle. I'll attach this pirate ship onto the other one so that we'll have a whole fleet."

More were killed than wounded, and those who were wounded had only minor injuries. Amber quickly washed their scabs and cuts, and then put them off to bed with a dose of **grog** to help them sleep. When she was done, she went off to her own room, where she was horrified to find the window panes shattered. Shards of glass lay about in her bed and on the floor. Amber called for Ian, who dashed in at once.

"Oh," Ian said, looking around. "It hasn't happened in my cabin. I'm sorry, Amber, but right now I can't repair it. You'll have to sleep below decks with Edmond and Mary and Joanna."

"Fine," Amber sighed, and staggered wearily off to join Edmond. In a few hours' time, Ian woke them excitedly.

"See, that's the island where my men are stranded!" he exclaimed, pointing to a small blob of land in the distance. "I've doubled the speed, so why don't you just stay up on the deck to watch?" Chairs were brought out, and soon most of the crew was squinting towards the island. Finally, a few palm trees came into view, then some grass, and finally a group of haggard men. Some were naked—others were dressed in dirt-filled rags and loincloths. Their hair and beards were filled with grime and mud. Their hairy arms were covered in grass and scraps of bark. Their lips were chapped from weeks of **dehydration**.

"Hi! Our savior is here!" the men cried, jumping up. Ian waved to them and brought *My Fair Lady* to an angle at the island. A few sailors threw the anchor out, and then they all stepped onto the island. As the light of dawn began to show its colors, Amber noticed specks of water shining in the green grass. The palm trees towered above their heads, giving them shade. Ian was already deep in conversation with the tallest of the men.

"So we were attacked by pirates twice," Ian was explaining, "and we captured both of their ships. Amber was just killing those pirates like a maniac, having no mind of the danger around her." The other men started to grumble at having to wait so long, and Ian immediately brought them onto the ship for refreshment and clothing. When they had been clothed in a more presentable way, he shooed them off to the pirate ships for nightly slumber.

The next morning Ian started them all off with some breakfast, and then steered *My Fair Lady* away from the other two ships. He gave a signal to the captains of the other ships to follow him, and so soon they were cruising speedily along. When Amber and Ian were alone in Ian's cabin, Amber said solemnly,

"Uncle, I need to tell you something."

"What is it?" Ian asked, taking a biscuit and popping it into his mouth.

"I don't want to stay aboard the ship," Amber said hurriedly. "I want to go to finishing school to become a schoolteacher. I…want to be more…independent. Not a grand lady who has to entertain stuffy old guests. I used to want to be a lady, but I think it would be far too…too…boring, after…this experience. Teaching would be like a whole new adventure to me. If I just was a grand lady with some big manor house, it wouldn't be exciting enough."

"I was actually going to tell you that if you didn't want to stay aboard the ship anymore, I wouldn't really need you," Ian said, smiling. "So I suppose it all works out."

Who Are the Players in the Story?
Character Development

Character: *one of the people, animals, or objects portrayed in a book, movie, or television program; the set of qualities that make something or someone distinctive.*

Children intuitively know that characters are the essential part of any story. However, if you ask them to describe and define their characters, they are generally unclear about it. Because they haven't been around as long, the range of people a child writer has been exposed to is naturally less than that of an adult writer. Reading can help develop empathy and broaden perspectives, but purely mimicking other fictional characters can again limit a story's dimension. It is crucial for young writers to begin mixing fictional and real life influences. To help your child make the connection between the people they know and the concept of the protagonist is to tangibly enrich both their life perspective and their writing. *People are not always perfect, or good at everything. Your protagonist doesn't need to be either. This doesn't stop them from being likeable.* Additionally, to help your child create more real and believable characters, you can ask questions that lead them to think about how their characters link to the whole aspects of the story itself.

Adora's approach to creating characters largely depends on the tremendous number of books she reads and the playmates she has interacted with at her school, Seeds of Learning. To create the characters she needs, she picks and chooses, mixing and matching real and fictional influences. Initially, she would focus on one aspect, such as physical appearances, and neglect other aspects such as thought and emotion. She purely enjoyed the process of creating stories and did not make a conscious effort to include the necessary and important elements of characterization. As she creates more characters in her stories, we gently guide her to think about the relationship between characters. We ask her questions as loyal and interested readers: *I love this character, can you tell me more about him? Ah, so he's like that. Has he always been that way?*

Character development can become an ongoing game. What do spies, private detectives, and writers have in common? It's their job to observe, make educated guesses about the people around them, and later use this information in their work. When Adora and I take a walk, we play a game. Look at that house! Based on the clues in their yard and in the house's appearance, who do you think lives there? Are they young or old? Liberal or Conservative? What are they going to eat for dinner tonight? I remind her that many great writers are able to use small details of dress or location to provide readers with amazingly complete character sketches. When we get home we both sit down and write a description of a house and ask each other to guess who lives in it.

The following character profile worksheet is a good way to get kids thinking about what makes each of their characters different and interesting. Explain to your child that it is not necessary to include all the information from the worksheet in their story; but that knowing a character well is an important part of describing how the character reacts to each new situation.

 Interview and Tips from Adora

Joyce: Where do you find your characters? Or do they just enter your mind?

Adora: Oftentimes I am inspired by characters from other books. However, I am creating more and more of my own characters from my imagination now that I am maturing as a writer.

Joyce: What kind of characters do you enjoy writing the most? Why do you enjoy writing them?

Adora: I find it very amusing to describe evil antagonists, due to the fact that I believe I can describe more about evil antagonists than about normal, everyday people.

Joyce: What kind of characteristics do you like to give to your protagonists? How about your antagonists?

Adora: The most typical characteristics I give my protagonists are often along this line: clever, independent, and adventurous. I usually put my antagonists on a strictly wicked road, but there are times when they are only mildly malicious.

Joyce: What are your methods of mixing and matching characters from your imagination and real life?

Adora: Usually my entire character is mainly based on my imagination and I add on a few characteristics from people in real life.

Joyce: Do you put yourself in the character you are writing about?
Adora: Occasionally in the protagonist.

Joyce: What would you tell other kids when they can't think of characters for their stories?
Adora: Think of people in real life. Think of characters you've read about. Sit back and imagine.

Joyce: Why is it fun for you to create so many characters in your stories? Do you have a favorite one? Why?
Adora: It is fun for me to create characters because it gives me a chance to really use my imagination, and simply think and ponder about what they're like, what they do, what they look like. My favorite characters are often the protagonist and the antagonist. Some minor characters have a special place also, but my thoughts are usually set on the protagonist and antagonist due to their importance to the story.

 Tips for Parents and Educators

Ask your child to think of a person or a pet in their own life who interests them. Why is this person/pet interesting? Are they kind? Are they always easy to predict, or are they sometimes surprising? Encourage your child to create a fictional character based on this person/pet. Although it's important for a protagonist to be likeable, perfection is rarely interesting. Remind your child that sometimes it's okay for a main character to have weaknesses. A story will move too smoothly if the characters don't have any personal obstacles to overcome. Nobody is perfect, everybody has fears and weaknesses, and readers will find it easier to root for a character who they can identify with. You can ask your students the following questions to get them thinking: Who are your favorite fictional characters? How would you describe their physical appearance? Are they handsome or ugly? Are they tall, short, heavy or light? Does anything about their face stand out? How do they talk? Clear and loud? Horsy and raspy? Is this character always good? Is this character good at everything? What are some of this character's personality traits? How do you know?

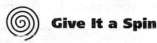 **Give It a Spin**

List making is a great non-threatening way to free up the imagination. It also provides ready-made details to add to a story. Ask your student to make a list of things their character might have in his/his private quarters. It's amazing how one item leads to another, and how an entire list of items can lead to a remarkably clear character sketch.

Propose the following scenario: Imagine a room with three people you know in it. Suddenly a bear lumbers into the room. How do these peoples' reactions differ from one another? Try the game with more everyday events, such as a flat tire or a terrible haircut. Then apply the same scenarios to three fictional characters.

Character Profile Worksheet

Character Name: _____

Age: ____ Physical characteristics (eye color, shapes etc.): _____
_____
_____

How does the way your character looks affect his/her everyday life?
_____
_____

Check box for character traits
Is your character

- ☐ happy
- ☐ outgoing
- ☐ snobby
- ☐ picky
- ☐ jealous

- ☐ optimistic
- ☐ impatient
- ☐ sarcastic
- ☐ lazy
- ☐ gloomy

- ☐ friendly
- ☐ funny
- ☐ grumpy
- ☐ messy
- ☐ adventurous

What does he/she eat for breakfast?
_____
_____

Is your character like anyone you know? If so, who?

_____

_____

How is your character similar to this person?

_____

_____

In what ways is your character different from this person?

_____

_____

Is your character a cat person or a dog person?

_____

Name an event in your character's past that had a big impact on him/her:

_____

_____

How does this affect the way your character acts?

_____

_____

What makes your character happy?

_____

_____

What is your character afraid of?

_____

_____

What are your character's greatest strengths?

_____

_____

What is your character's favorite movie?

_____

Why does your character like this movie?

_____

_____

What are your character's greatest weaknesses?

_____

_____

What does your character want?

_____

_____

Why doesn't your character already have this?

_____

_____

How can your character get around this obstacle?

_____

_____

How can your character overcome his/her weaknesses?

_____

_____

Does your character have to win in order to be happy?

_____

_____

Agymah and the Amulet

"**A**gymah!" It was Lapis's shrill voice again. Why did she waste her time interrupting Agymah's privacy?

Trying to ignore Lapis, Agymah rolled over to one side.

"Agymah!" This time Lapis's voice was pleading. "Father is troubled, and he wishes for you." Agymah immediately jumped up. Although Abubakar was not his real father, Agymah loved him deeply, and of course he knew that Abubakar was dying.

"You will come?" Lapis asked hopefully.

"Yes," said Agymah, running.

Khepri, the eldest of Abubakar's daughters, awaited Agymah at the gate.

"Does Father wish to see *you*?" Khepri asked with a hint of **contempt** in her voice. She took pride in being the eldest and the favorite of Abubakar's four daughters, and she did not look upon the others kindly.

Agymah ignored her, much to Khepri's dissatisfaction.

"Be sure to pay your respects to Father!" she hissed in Agymah's ear.

After the long **mummification** process was over, Abubakar's mummy, in a magnificent coffin decked in precious jewels and amulets to keep away bad spirits, was carried away by four of the pharaoh's strongest men to the tomb which awaited him.

Abubakar's daughters were married off to powerful officers in the pharaoh's court, but Agymah was taken as a slave because he was not really related to Abubakar.

VOCABULARY LIST

contempt – disgust or hatred
mummification – process of drying and treating bodies to avoid decay
gangly – long limbed
solemnly – very seriously
muse – to speak thoughtfully
tarry – waste time
sulkily - resentfully
hastily – hurriedly
hallucination – a vision of something that is not really there, altered perception
flinched – reacted protectively in response to sudden movement or sound
barbarian – uncivilized person
oblivious – completely unaware
asp – a type of poisonous snake
tourniquet – a tight band applied to stop bleeding
prompting – urging into action
vividly – clearly, intensely
sinister – suggesting evil or malevolence
Spartan – simple and plain
bewildered – confused

Autumn passed and winter sct on all of Egypt. Agymah hardly noticed—winter in Egypt was only slightly colder than autumn. His job as a slave was easier, since many of the markets which he was sent to buy food from were closed, giving him more time to spend in leisure, eating his meager slices of bread.

It was just about sunset and Agymah was sitting on his hard reed sleeping mat when one of the messengers came into the slave quarters, and said,

"The pharaoh wishes to go on a hunt, and must have five slaves to attend to him. I was given the task of choosing the honored few." Agymah's heart leapt. A hunt? He had never been on a hunt before— he had only heard about them. But his hopes were shattered quickly. *The messenger won't choose me, obviously,* he thought. He didn't have much muscle. He was tall and **gangly** and bound to be clumsy. The messenger ignored him, and was about to say something to the boy next to Agymah when a vase that had been wobbling on the shelf fell. Agymah easily caught it with his long arms. The messenger gave Agymah a searching look.

"I think I will take you, boy," he said.

The pharaoh seemed pleased with most of the messenger's choices, but when he came to Agymah, he said,

"Where did you get this one? Why did you not get Nizam, or Nassor?"

"I am sorry, O supreme son of the great gods."

The messenger kissed the hem of the pharaoh's linen kilt.

"It can be forgiven," the pharaoh said, mounting his camel. Agymah and the other slaves walked behind the pharaoh, swift and silent. Two archers whom Agymah had never seen before stood beside the pharaoh, also silent.

"We hunt today the crocodile," the pharaoh said **solemnly**, "and my wife, Chione, has already said the blessing so that we will not run into danger. I, of course, also have the amulet which will protect me from all dangers."

The Nile River was full of crocodiles at sunset, giving the pharaoh's men a good opportunity. The men tried to kill the fierce crocodiles with their long sharp spears. The archers shot at them repeatedly, trying to pierce their skin, but their hard, tough scales sent the arrows flying harmlessly into the river. Having nothing better to do, Agymah sat down on the grassy bank

"You!" The pharaoh turned around, and slapped Agymah with the back of his hand. "You! Get up, idle boy!"

Agymah had no idea what to do. The other slaves giggled.

"Boy! You again!" the pharaoh shouted. Just then, the pharaoh slipped on a loose rock, into the fast-flowing river full of crocodiles!

"Help!" the pharaoh shouted, kicking wildly. Obviously, he didn't know how to swim. The other men looked on with horror. Ignoring the crocodiles, Agymah dove into the water, grabbed the pharaoh's hand, and pulled him to safety on the bank.

"I thank you...what is your name?" the pharaoh asked, water dripping from his beard.

"Agymah," Agymah said, kneeling down to dry the pharaoh's feet.

"Agymah? The adoptive son of my loyal officer Abubakar?" the pharaoh asked.

"Yes," Agymah said.

"You must be given a promotion," the pharaoh **mused**. Finally he said, "I will make you the head of all the slaves. You must be given new quarters, of course."

One of the pharaoh's archers frowned and whispered something to his companion.

"Abasi! Adofo!" the pharaoh turned to the archers. Abasi quickly tucked something into his kilt and said,

"Yes, O supreme son of the gods?"

"Try to shoot arrows into the crocodiles' mouths. That should stun them," the pharaoh said.

"Yes, O supreme son of the gods."

When Agymah returned to the palace, he was immediately shown to his new quarters. He was not surprised at the splendor of the suite, mostly because when he lived with Abubakar, he had been accustomed to fine rooms like this. A messenger soon came to Agymah and said,

"The supreme son of the gods, the pharaoh, wishes for your presence. He and his queen are watching the strongmen."

The slave helped him into a clean wrap-around kilt of white linen, similar to that of the pharaoh's, except simpler.

When he was dressed, he went to the richly ornamented courtyard where the pharaoh was watching the strongmen. The pharaoh noticed Agymah and walked over, his wife following.

"Chione," the pharaoh said to his wife, "this is Agymah, the boy who saved me from the hungry crocodiles." Chione smiled, her beautiful red lips shining. Agymah breathed in the sweet smells escaping from her long black hair, which had been soaked in bear fat to look attractive and smell better.

"I thank you," Chione said, her beautiful brown eyes resting on Agymah.

"We must not **tarry**," the pharaoh said, glancing at the strongmen anxiously, "or we shall miss the performance." Just as the pharaoh finished speaking, twin boys ran through the gateway. They grabbed at the pharaoh's legs, whimpering.

"Be quiet, Ata, Atsu!" the pharaoh exclaimed, impatiently shaking the boys off his kilt.

"I am sorry, O supreme son of the gods." Ata and Atsu's nurse came in, her hair disheveled. "But…could I be so brave as to ask you to if I could watch Kesi, perhaps?"

Chione opened her mouth to speak, but the pharaoh raised his hand for silence.

"No, Kesi already has a suitable nurse. I need you to watch Ata and Atsu."

"Yes, O supreme son of the gods," the nurse said **sulkily**.

"But, do find Kesi and tell her to come here. I want them to meet someone," the pharaoh said.

"Yes, O supreme son of the gods," the nurse said, running off.

Kesi was tall and slender. She looked beautiful in her sheath-like wrap-around dress, and Agymah could not help staring at her. Kesi returned the stare with her long and narrow hazel-colored eyes.

"I wish you good, Father," Kesi said in a rather cool tone of voice, touching her head to the floor and kissing the air before the pharaoh.

"Ah, Kesi! My good daughter! Be introduced to Agymah, the head of the slaves in the palace," the pharaoh said. Undoubtedly Kesi was his favorite daughter like Khepri had been Abubakar's. Agymah bowed awkwardly.

"You must kiss the air around the princess," the nurse whispered to Agymah, her forehead creasing in worry. Agymah **hastily** kissed the air in front of Kesi.

"Agymah," Kesi said, staring at Agymah without blinking. Her tone of voice was still quite cool. Agymah found this staring so uncomfortable that he took a step back. Kesi turned to her mother, who took her daughter into her arms.

"Agymah," the pharaoh said, "you must consider this very carefully, although it is not altogether a difficult question. Would you like to be a playmate to my children, and perhaps watch over them somewhat?"

"Of course!" Agymah exclaimed. What could be better?

"Kesi," the pharaoh said, "Agymah will be your new playmate, as well as Ata and Atsu's. He will have the rooms next to yours, eat our meals with us, and have every single extended courtesy."

"Yes, Father," Kesi said, glaring at Agymah when her father turned around.

The next morning, Agymah moved into the room next to Kesi, Ata, and Atsu's. He actually was rather in the middle of Ata and Atsu, with Kesi in the room behind his.

That night, he was awakened by a sharp pain in his head. He opened his eyes and found that he was repeatedly slamming his head against the heavy oak door.

"What is it?" Kesi came running into Agymah's room, anxiously looking around.

"Oh…it's *you*," she said coldly, glaring at Agymah.

"I bumped my head."

He was red with embarrassment and reflected that it was lucky Kesi could not see him in the dimness.

"Funny. I did too, but I thought it was a ghost," Kesi said. From Ata and Atsu's rooms, a great wailing arose.

"I need to see what's up with those brothers of mine!" Kesi exclaimed, running off. It turned out that Ata and Atsu had woken up to find themselves slamming their heads into their doors as well.

"What is wrong with us?! Why are we all bumping our heads?" Kesi moaned, shaking her fist.

"Perhaps someone's put something into our food, some sort of poison that causes **hallucinations**," Agymah said shakily.

"Impossible!" Kesi snapped. "Nobody's dared try that since my great-great-grandfather was pharaoh!"

Agymah **flinched**. He thought his idea was rather a likely one, but Kesi had dashed his hopes.

"The **barbarian** spell-casters who live on the border of Egypt perhaps did it," Kesi mused. Now it was Agymah's turn to scoff.

"Spell-casters? All children's legends," he said, although he really was unsure himself.

"There still are some, you know!" Kesi nearly shrieked.

"As if," Agymah muttered under his breath.

The pharaoh stood in the doorway.

"Kesi," he said solemnly, "did you bump your head? Ata and Atsu tell me you did, but I want your words."

"Yes," Kesi said excitedly, "Agymah too."

"Chione and I have too," the pharaoh said.

"Perhaps it is food poisoning?" Agymah asked.

"Great gods, no! My testers could detect no trace of poison."

"Perhaps they were struck dumb by the poison," Agymah said, although this time he was doubtful of his own idea.

"No, no, no! More likely those spell-casters on the border!" the pharaoh exclaimed. Kesi sent Agymah an I-told-you look, and held her head up high.

"But—" Agymah began. It was too late. The pharaoh had already left the room.

The next day, the pharaoh went on another hunt, taking Chione, Agymah, his children, and a few choice slaves with him. They were to hunt snakes. A servant fanned Chione, who sat under a palm tree. Agymah was given a sharp hunting knife, and Ata and Atsu held mock battles fighting with sticks. Kesi lay down in the sun to watch.

Suddenly, it happened. A snake glided along swiftly, carefully concealing itself in the sand. Two more followed it. Chione rested against the palm tree with her eyes closed, **oblivious** to the danger.

"Oh! Oh! An **asp**!" Chione's servant dropped her fan and raced off. Frozen with fear, Chione was an easy target for the snake. Agymah seized his spear, hurled it, and hit the snake dead on.

It was too late. The snake had already delivered its deadly bite. Blood streamed from the wound on Chione's leg, and Agymah knew that the poison was probably already spreading through her body, poisoning her heart. The pharaoh was beside himself. Only Kesi and Agymah did not panic.

"Ata! Atsu! Find the nearest doctor and bring him here!" Kesi shouted to her brothers. With one fearful glance at Chione, Ata and Atsu tottered off as fast as their short legs could carry them. Kesi ripped up parts of her dress.

"Quickly! Squeeze out all the bad blood, and I will put this **tourniquet** on her!" Kesi shouted. Despite Agymah and Kesi's frenzied efforts, Chione's breathing became more and more labored. Her eyes rolled back in her head, and she shivered in the intense afternoon heat. Within moments she was dead.

The pharaoh was beside himself with grief. He remained confined to his rooms for the next few days, and then composed himself. A gaunt man dressed in black stepped out of his quarters. Agymah hardly recognized him as the pharaoh. His matted hair stuck out in places, his high cheekbones jutted out of his face, and his hands were thin and bony.

Agymah turned fourteen on the fifteenth of October. Nobody really celebrated it, but Kesi shyly presented him a band of gold necklaces and some sandals which she had made herself. Ata and Atsu (with Kesi's prompting, of course) gave Agymah a beautiful platter on which they had painted Agymah's name in very messy handwriting.

The pharaoh soon took a new wife, Akila. Akila was intelligent if not particularly beautiful. The pharaoh was distracted from his mourning when Akila gave birth to a baby girl, whom they named Jamila.

Several months later, Agymah was out playing with Kesi, Ata, Atsu, and Jamila when, suddenly, a giant cloud of sand flew at the small group.

"Run!" Kesi shrieked, dropping Jamila. Agymah picked the little girl up before she was buried in the sand. Ata and Atsu grabbed onto Agymah's kilt in fear, crying. The sand flew even faster, getting into Agymah's eyes and into his nostrils. When the sand stopped flying, Agymah collapsed onto the ground in exhaustion.

"That has not happened since the pharaoh Adeben's time!" Kesi cried.

"What has not happened since Adeben's time?" Agymah asked rather stupidly.

"A sand storm, of course!" Kesi shouted impatiently.

"Oh, right," Agymah said awkwardly. His and Kesi's eyes met. Agymah hastily turned away.

"Perhaps we should…be getting back now," Kesi said, staring at her feet.

"All right," Agymah said. Kesi scooped Jamila up in her arms, much to the discomfort of the squirming and drooling baby.

When they arrived at the palace the pharaoh was awaiting them, leaning on his scepter, his forehead creased with worry.

"Thank goodness you're alive!" he exclaimed. "Egypt has not seen a sand storm for centuries!"

"The sand storm stopped almost as soon as it came," Kesi informed the pharaoh. "We were lucky."

"Hmm," the pharaoh said. "I am getting suspicious of those spell-casters. But no mind. I must inform Akila."

When Akila was informed of the sand storm, she screamed and pounced on Jamila, kissing her everywhere and saying, "My baby, my precious baby!" Agymah shrunk back, feeling he had no place in the room. "Kesi," When Akila turned to Kesi, her voice was hard and cold. "You were foolish. You should have never gone outside. My poor Jamila! As for you, Agymah, you could have done something."

"How could we predict the sand storm?! Why blame Kesi?" Agymah exploded.

Akila looked surprised at his outburst, but she quickly composed herself, and smirked. "Boy," Akila said, "I was not saying that you had the terrible powers to predict the unsure future. You could not be much worse if you did. But," and here Akila stopped, "at least, perhaps, you could have been more cautious."

"Cautious? Again, we could not predict the future, which would tell us that we would need to be cautious!" Agymah exclaimed.

"Boy! You are disrespectful to your elders! Be gone all of you— Kesi, Ata, and Atsu too!" Akila screeched.

Agymah stepped out of Akila's chambers, Ata and Atsu clutching his kilt in fear.

"Kesi, Akila is as much as a witch as I've seen!" he exclaimed.

"Agymah! That's it!" Kesi shouted.

"Ssssh," Agymah said, already guessing what Kesi was going to say.

"All right," Kesi said, hardly able to keep her voice down. "Perhaps it was that Akila was putting the spells on the pharaoh—from afar! And that is why she married the pharaoh—to get a closer aim!"

"When the Lion pounces, the mouse will see—and can escape and the Lion finds himself with nothing," Agymah said.

"What has that to do with this?" Kesi asked, frowning. She looked rather pretty when she frowned, Agymah decided.

"We are the Lion. Akila is the mouse. When we pounce—in this way, accuse her—she will escape. You likely are making hasty judgments, Kesi," Agymah said slowly.

"Hasty judgments?! Who are you to judge me?!" Kesi burst out laughing.

"No, no. Akila very well might be guilty. But she will escape. I am sure of it. You see already how close the pharaoh fondles her, how he feeds the witch her food on a silver spoon, how he looks at you with more and more distrust? Akila is feeding your father tales. Your father already spends more time with Jamila than with you, Kesi, and it is that witch Akila's fault," Agymah said, gritting his teeth.

"No, no, this cannot be true! O Isis, protector of women and girls, help me!" Kesi gasped.

"But," Agymah said, "I also remember **vividly** the two archers who stand by your father's side on hunts—Abasi and Adofo, I believe they are called. One of them—Abasi, if I remember, tucked something into his kilt, as if hiding it. This was on the evening that your father almost drowned. There was also a great deal of whispering between the two."

"The archers? Them? No, I do not think so. Akila is my guess," Kesi said carelessly.

When Akila emerged from her chambers, she found Agymah and Kesi.

"What are you doing here?!" Akila shouted.

"Nothing," Agymah said hurriedly.

"Nothing! As if! I will let you go this time, but rest assured—" Agymah had already dragged Kesi, Ata, and Atsu away by that time.

The next morning, the pharaoh met Agymah and Kesi rather nervously in his leisure room. A servant fanned him while another rubbed soothing lotions and oils on the pharaoh's long legs. Not making eye contact with Agymah and Kesi, the pharaoh began,

"Kesi and Agymah, Akila is rather…uncomfortable with your presence here. You will be sent to a place where many priestesses, priests, and monks have gathered to follow the religious order of Isis and Osiris."

"Sent away!" Kesi exploded. Agymah could only open his mouth, but no sound came out.

"The camels have been made ready," the pharaoh said, "now I dismiss you. Ride safely and well!"

Agymah was enraged. After all he had done for the pharaoh, the pharaoh was sending them away! To a religious order, no less!

"I cannot believe that this is happening to me," Kesi moaned, facing Agymah and not looking at her camel. "I am absolutely sure that Akila is poisoning my father's mind against us! If only we could get Akila out of the way!"

"Mmmm," Agymah said. He was in deep thought, and it was hard to think while being jiggled on the camel's rough back. Kesi's babbling didn't help.

"Agymah?" Kesi asked crossly. "Are you listening?"

"Sorry," Agymah said. They rode in silence for a few minutes. Finally their guide stopped them at a tall, silent building. It had no windows and was dark and **sinister**.

A woman emerged from the building. She wore undecorated sandals of rough wood on her brown feet.

"Isis, from the above, welcomes you," she said, folding her hands and surveying Kesi.

"I give you the message of the pharaoh, supreme son of the gods," the guide said with great importance, taking the pharaoh's message from the saddle-bag. After scanning it for a few seconds, the woman said, "Come in, come in!"

Inside the building was no better than the outside. Kesi and Agymah were made to take off their sandals and shake them free of dust, and then enter the building barefoot. Then Dalila (for that was the priestess's name) took Agymah to meet Anum, a monk who showed him to his room.

Agymah's room was more **Spartan** than the room he had been sleeping in as a slave. When Agymah protested, the monk replied,

"This is the best room. Accept Osiris's gift thankfully."

"Osiris's gift! Osiris's curse, more like!" Agymah muttered under his breath.

"It is not good to scorn those who are in close contact with the gods," the monk said cheerfully, surprising Agymah, who had thought the monk would not be able to hear him.

"Yes, I can hear your words as well as the gods," the monk said, as though he had read Agymah's mind. "The very words which you believe none other to hear." Agymah said no more after that.

Agymah stood waiting. Why is Kesi taking so long? he thought. As if answering his call, Kesi came running, breathless.

"One of the priestesses called for me to stay," she explained. "I pretended I didn't hear her, but we must find someplace to hide. I have something I must tell you without the possibility of anyone listening in." Agymah nodded, and pointed outside. Kesi frowned.

"Hmm," she said.

"It'll do," Agymah hurriedly put in, for fear of the priestess coming.

"I suppose," Kesi said following him outside.

Agymah headed for the shade of a palm tree. Kesi wanted to lie on the burning hot sand, but Agymah hastily opposed that.

"Somebody would be bound to see us—and after all, it's much nicer here," Agymah said. Kesi finally gave in.

"First, I need to tell you something," Kesi chattered excitedly once they were settled down, "my father's amulet has been stolen. It's protected him from dangers before, but now that it's stolen, anything will be able to kill him!" At this Kesi resumed a sober face.

"If only we were back at the palace!" Agymah stormed. "If only!" he stubbed his toe against the tree's trunk in frustration, which only made him all the more frustrated.

"Calm down!" Kesi was obviously scared. Agymah hurriedly sat down, scratching his kilt on the trunk of the palm tree as he did so.

"Now, as I was saying," Kesi said, "since my father's amulet is stolen, he will have nothing to protect him, and Akila will do her spells over him or whatever!"

"Poison maybe," Agymah said.

Ignoring Agymah, Kesi continued, "Perhaps we could get back to the palace somehow."

"In disguise?" Agymah suggested.

"No! As ourselves!" Kesi shouted.

"There'll be no other way but to be in disguise," Agymah said, sighing wearily.

"I will not go in disguise! It is dishonest, and I don't want to fool my own father!" Kesi exclaimed, jumping up.

"If we don't go in disguise, there will be no way we will be able to enter," Agymah said.

"Fine!" Kesi said after thinking about it for a little while.

"The question is what shall we disguise ourselves as?" Agymah asked.

"I know!" Kesi exclaimed, her eyes shining. "We can pretend that we're the gypsies, come from the north of Egypt!"

"I doubt gypsies come at this time of the year," Agymah said, raising his eyebrows doubtfully.

"Oh whatever! Do you really think that they would think about *that*?" Kesi exclaimed impatiently.

"Yes! And people would get suspicious of us—after all, we would only be two gypsies! Gypsies come in groups!" Agymah shouted.

"Don't worry about that!" Kesi shouted. "I've got it all under my sleeve!"

At exactly sunset, Agymah and Kesi excused themselves from dinner and ran to Kesi's room. Kesi already had a rope ready, which was tied securely to the granite bust of Isis.

"I'll go down first," Kesi volunteered bravely. "I'm older, so I'm bound to be heavier."

"You're not older!" Agymah hesitated. He had never thought about it before.

"You're thirteen, right?" Kesi asked.

"No!" Agymah exclaimed. "I'm fourteen!"

"Strange. I am too," Kesi said.

"I'll go first," Agymah said, although his stomach churned as he said it. The sand below, harmless enough, now seemed like poison.

"No, I will," Kesi said, and lowered herself onto the rope before Agymah could say a word. Suddenly, before he could stop himself, Agymah felt tears filling up his eyes.

"I love you, Kesi," he croaked. Kesi looked up at Agymah, still keeping a firm grip on the rope.

"I never thought you would say that," she said, her eyes shining with tears. "I love you too."

By the time both Agymah and Kesi reached the ground safely, a monk had discovered their absence and had the good sense to check outside. He shouted after Agymah and Kesi, but they had already run away.

Kesi and Agymah stole some tattered and outlandish clothing from the nearest gypsy camp and snuck away quickly before the theft was discovered. They changed their clothing on opposite sides of a palm tree. Before he had changed, however, and was still naked, Agymah stooped down to look at a party of ants that were eating a worm. He accidentally bumped into Kesi, who was also naked. After staring at each other for a few seconds, Kesi began laughing.

"We better change now!" Agymah was very angry and embarrassed at being caught naked.

"Yes, yes," Kesi said, walking off.

Agymah and Kesi looked strange in their new gypsy get-up.

"My father will mistake us for just anybody!" Kesi said proudly, tightening her green hair ribbon one last time as they approached the pharaoh's palace.

"Sssh," Agymah said to Kesi. "There're the guards."

"Aren't gypsies late to be coming?" the guard who was standing by the great gates said suspiciously.

"We were injured, and left behind," Kesi said, in the most syrupy voice she could possibly think of. Agymah pretended to walk with a slight limp.

"Go on, go on," the guard said, pushing Kesi and Agymah past.

The pharaoh received Kesi and Agymah with great interest. "I hear you were left behind?" he asked, twiddling a tiny golden likeness of Ra between his fingers.

"Yes, O pharaoh," Agymah said, remembering just in time not to say "O supreme son of the gods."

"For some reason you remind me of some people," the pharaoh said. "But no mind. You will be given lodging, of course."

Kesi and Agymah were invited to have dinner with the pharaoh and Akila. As the meal neared to an end, Agymah noticed that Akila had crept out of the room. All of a sudden there was a loud crash. Agymah ran to the kitchen, followed closely by Kesi and the pharaoh.

Akila was in the middle of it all. Water ran down her face. Chicken bits clung to her dress.

"What has happened?" the pharaoh asked, **bewildered**.

"Some blundering oafs spilled this all over me!" Akila said, not slow in making her excuse.

"Is there any way we can help?" Agymah asked, a plan already forming in his mind.

"Not really *you*," Akila said, "but the girl can help."

"At least let me brush you off a bit," Agymah said. Brushing the chicken bits off of Akila's dress, Agymah caused a little vial to fall out. It was made of glass, with a small sapphire stopper. The vial immediately broke, letting forth an odorless fluid.

Ain, Kesi's unruly little puppy, ran forward and licked at the liquid. He immediately fell down dead. Akila's face scrunched up into an ugly ball of wrinkles.

"What is the meaning of this, Akila?!" the pharaoh shouted. "Why do you have this poison concealed in your dress?"

"This was meant for you, not this stupid dog!" Akila kicked Ain's cold little body scornfully.

"She's plotting against you!" Kesi shouted. "Father, please listen to us!" The pharaoh turned, and saw his own daughter, and Agymah.

"You fooled me!" the pharaoh shouted. Akila broke free of the pharaoh's grasp and ran out of the room.

"Catch her!" the pharaoh shouted, so enraged he forgot any anger towards Kesi and Agymah.

Akila was promptly caught by the palace guards, who dragged her screaming and cursing before the pharaoh.

The execution of Akila and the two bowmen (now found guilty) was to be a grand event, with food and drink and much merrymaking, despite the desperate shouts of Akila. Agymah, who had been made a prince by the pharaoh and granted permission to marry Kesi, rode next to Kesi on a large litter carried by four men. Suddenly a servant ran up to the pharaoh and cried:

"O supreme son of the gods, the archers have escaped with your youngest daughter to the land of the spell casters!"

"Be this news true?" the pharaoh demanded, turning to the other slaves.

"Yes, it is truth, O supreme son of the gods," the minions replied.

"Then with Akila I am much wroth," the pharaoh said, wringing his hands. "But I will not trouble my soldiers by sending them into the barbaric lands of the spell casters. Let the execution continue." So with those words Akila was dropped into the mouths of the hungry crocodiles. And it was said that those crocodiles never ate the flesh of humans again.

What Should I Call My Hero or Villain
How to Come Up With a Clever Name

For story writing, coming up with the characters' names can be the first major challenge for many kids. Without a proper name, your child feels stuck before they even begin. Helping your child establish a character name they feel connected to and proud of is one step further to the success of their story. Adora imparts great importance to her character's names. She often consults me with the question of "What do you think of this name?" During workshops we often find that kids will stall when they can't think of a name. Naming problems occasionally lead to complete writer's block. Conversely, the joy kids get out of a good name can be very inspirational and motivating

With the convenience and the speed of an internet search engine, coming up with a name that that reflects the personality of characters while still staying true to the era or culture in question is as simple as a few keystrokes. When Adora was writing *Agymah and the Amulet*, and she needed a male name that sounded Egyptian, she turned to the search engine and found many sites that featured Egyptian names. Not only did she find what she was looking for, she also landed on sites that explained the origin, meaning and significance of the names. It broadened her knowledge as well as her research skills. For fantasy stories, Adora favors made-up names, and enjoys scrambling the letters of real words.

 Interview and Tips from Adora

Joyce: How do you make up names for your fantasy stories?
Adora: I just sort of go through the alphabet and mix the letters up to make these names and if I don't like them I just switch them around. When I get to B, I'll think of a word that starts with B. Say, 'bran.' So then I'll think Bran, that could be a name. But it sounds too plain. So I'll say maybe Branabal. Or even Branavuel. For C, hmm, maybe Curver.

Joyce: So C, Curve, Curver.
Adora: Yeah, I was thinking that would be a good name for a gang leader. But I don't like it all that much. How about E, for Erise?

Joyce: What kind of character would Erise be?
Adora: Probably a main character.

Joyce: But what type of main character?
Adora: I don't know why, but it seems to me she'd be a really snide main character.

Joyce: What other strategies do you have?
Adora: A lot of times I keep up a bunch of names in my head because I know that they'll come in handy. For instance if I'm reading a book and I see something that I like the sound of like, say, 'Great Wexely,' I'll file that away. But when I come down to using it, I don't want it to sound too much the same, so I'll change it to say, 'East Yurxely' instead.

Joyce: Anything else?
Adora: Sometimes I just like to take an appropriate word and switch around the letters. For example in *The Tools of the Trade* they go to the Great Cathedral of Aroda.

 Tips for Parents and Educators

Unlock the mystery of naming characters. Unleash your children's creativity and give them the freedom to choose what they please. Play naming-your-character games by jumbling the letters of familiar names. Or talk about the names of people you know and ask your child what those people would rather be called instead. Once your child understands that a name is just their creation and there is no right or wrong, they will enjoy the process of picking a name for their characters.

 Give It a Spin

Write down the names of your child's favorite role models or celebrities then have them take the names apart to form new names. Have your child use a search engine to look for appropriate categories, such as "English Male Names" or "Chinese Female Names" and you will find many names you can use for your story.

Ask your child to write down the names of your relatives, neighbors, teachers, friends and the characters from books and movies to use them as names of characters in the story.

The Tools of the Trade

Myles looked up from the book he was reading. Didoni Marcelleni, his master, frowned at him.

"I believe I told you to wash my paintbrushes," Didoni said, putting his large, bony hands on his hips.

"Sorry, master," Myles said, grinning guiltily. "My mind wandered off for the moment."

"Wandered off!" Didoni snorted. "Forgot, more like! But no mind. Tomorrow we are off for Bulrox, where the Duke himself resides. If luck is with us, the Duke himself may ask me to paint his portrait, or perhaps **commission** a portrait of his Duchess!"

"Then, master, won't we be lucky indeed?" Myles asked, his grin even wider.

"Don't be **pert**! Now hurry up with the tasks I give you!" Didoni exclaimed. Myles stowed his book in the gray-brown **haversack** he habitually wore slung over his shoulder and said,

"Yes, master."

Washing the paintbrushes was no easy task, as he had to haul water up from the stream. Simply washing the paintbrushes in the stream would never do, as the current was swift and strong and could easily carry away the delicate paintbrushes, "which cost me a fortune," as Didoni always said. Myles hated the brushes, but he knew they bought the daily bread and kept his mouth shut.

VOCABULARY LIST

commission – an order to produce a piece of work
pert – jesting, bold
haversack – a heavy bag carried on back
cottar – someone who works on a farm in exchange for a place to live
ascertained – found out, determined to be true
odoriferous – having or diffusing a strong odor
trudged – walked wearily
vagabond - homeless wanderer
brandishing – waving something about in a menacing or threatening way
flagon – a large narrow-necked bottle used to store alcohol
treachery – betrayal
minion – a servant or enslaved person
pomp – ceremonial splendor, self-importance
abyss – bottomless
pilgrimage – religious journey
relic – something that has existed for a long time, often the only thing that still remains of something that was once grand
habit – clothing of religious order
sluggards – lazy person
relish – enjoy
skulk – to move furtively
dabble – to participate in something without ever becoming seriously dedicated
dryly – with subtle

Myles had a great interest in painting, but he had never dared to try. Didoni kept all of the paints locked in his sturdy painter's chest, which had quite a number of delightful springs, drawers, and little niches. Even if he had been able to pick the chest's ornate lock, he rarely had time to spare. Didoni always assigned a million little tasks to keep him on his toes. Myles sighed and inhaled a deep breath of fresh air. He remembered the old **cottars'** house with not even a proper roof, where it had always been very smoky and dirty. There were certainly some advantages to his new life as an apprentice.

"Myles!" Didoni shouted impatiently, walking towards the boy.

"You're not much of an apprentice," Didoni said, sighing heavily as Myles jerked to attention. "I need to dry out my painting canvases from yesterday's rain, and the least you can do for me is concentrate."

"Anyways, it's your choice." Didoni said, managing to sound as though the exact opposite was true. After he had **ascertained** that Myles looked appropriately guilty, the old man limped away, wearily shaking his head.

Myles hastily filled the buckets with water to the brim, put the buckets on a long, thick oak branch, and hoisted the branch onto his shoulders. He plowed his way through the long stalks of grass, avoiding any fallen branches or other things that would make him trip. When he finally arrived at the camp, Didoni was waiting for him.

"You're late," Didoni said crossly. "Now you'll have to continue washing our clothes until midnight." He flung a pile of dirty clothes at Myles's feet. "Start the washing early," Didoni said. "You can finish the rest of the chores early at sunrise."

Myles collapsed with exhaustion onto his haversack, which he had emptied and laid across the ground to sleep on. Didoni snored loudly next to him, not even opening an eye. Myles checked the dark sky and guessed that it was ten past midnight. He was quite right.

Early in the morning, after Myles had finished his chores, Didoni and Myles mounted their donkeys, and set out for Bulrox.

The Twin Gates of Bulrox were, as usual, extremely crowded. Two soldiers were posted at each of the magnificent gates. They made crude jokes and belched loudly while patting their jiggling tummies. Their spears lay forgotten in the dirt.

Didoni and Myles passed through without difficulty. The soldiers opened the gates at four o'clock and it was normal for folk to be crowding around Bulrox. Myles stared openmouthed at the lavish tapestries that decorated the stone walls, gasping with amazement at the towering buildings.

"Shut your mouth, youngster," one soldier said rather rudely to Myles, poking him in the side with his grubby finger. After that, Myles learned to hide his awe at the wealth of the grand city.

Didoni stopped right in the town square. A young violinist, probably sixteen, was grinning at the crowd as he played his gleaming violin. Some people were putting coins in the cap he had set out, while the rest merely applauded. Only a few acknowledged Didoni and Myles's arrival. When Didoni gave Myles a tweak on the nose, Myles knew it was time to start shouting.

"Portraits! Paintings! By the most learned artist in the world, Didoni Marcelleni!" he shouted. Gradually people began to drift away from the violinist and stare at Didoni, who was making long and graceful brush strokes on his canvas. A young lady stopped and asked how much a portrait would cost.

"Twenty coins, ma'm, one sitting," Myles said, bowing as Didoni had told him to.

"Hmm," the lady said. Finally she smiled and said, "I think I'll have it. My name's Marie, by the way." Myles at once dragged out a folding chair.

"If it pleases you, sit," Myles said, pointing to the chair and bowing again. With a graceful sweep of her green skirts, Marie seated herself. Didoni was already busy arranging his paints and his charcoal pencils.

"A smile, please," Didoni said, staring at Marie. Marie smiled, light reflecting on her shiny red lips.

"And...good," Didoni said, taking a charcoal pencil. "Myles, write *Marie* right there, will you?" Myles nodded with excitement and took a pencil.

After Marie had received her portrait, an entire crowd gathered around Didoni and Myles, clamoring for paintings. As the summer heat grew hotter and hotter they began to drift away.

"Portraits! Paintings! By the most learned artist in the world, Didoni Marcelleni!" Myles cried again. He was met with the silence of the deserted square. Didoni pocketed the forty coins he had made and rose stiffly from the bench.

"It will be enough for today's bread," he said, taking Myles's hand. "But we'll have to sleep outside again."

"Yes, master," Myles said, picking up the brushes as Didoni scanned the horizon. It was not at all easy to find a shop, as most shopkeepers closed their shops at six o'clock in hopes of a cool escape in their huts.

The only shopkeeper still waiting in his shop was a small, brisk-mannered man called Mug. Mug was not at all happy to see Didoni and Myles. He preferred no customers to any, and frowned when Didoni entered.

"Whaddya want?" Mug said, crossing his arms.

"Just some bread and cheese," Didoni said, not surprised at Mug's unfriendliness.

"Maybe one of those thingamajigs," Myles added hopefully, pointing to a small axe hanging from the wall.

"Do not listen to my apprentice. He has many fancies," Didoni said quickly, cuffing Myles on the ear. "Just some bread and cheese." Mug grunted, taking a moldy loaf from a cupboard and a block of **odoriferous** cheese.

"Thirty-two coins," Mug said. Didoni handed the coins to Mug.

"Now go!" Mug shouted. Myles and Didoni were not slow in leaving. As the day settled into evening, they **trudged** to the outskirts of town. Though the cornfield they slept in wouldn't be at all mistaken for luxury accommodations, it felt like home after an entire day of contending with the hostile city folk.

That night, Myles munched contentedly on a slice of bread with cheese. Didoni had already eaten his fill and was sketching the landscape. Myles lay down on his haversack, which he had spread across the grass. He stared up at the grayish-blue sky, with the mixed sunset colors of reddish-pink and dark violet. He swallowed his last slice of bread and cheese, and then rolled over to one side. Soon he fell asleep.

The next day, Didoni shook him awake.

"Hurry!" Didoni shouted. "The Duke himself is coming out, and we need to attract his attention!" Myles quickly roused himself. Since he had slept in his clothes, he had no need to dress, and followed Didoni to the high road where the Duke was being carried in a litter, sitting on purple cushions with his wife, the Duchess Joanna.

"Long live the Duke! Long live the Duke!" the townsfolk cried, throwing up caps and bonnets.

At Didoni's impatient gesture, Myles cried, "Portraits and paintings of fine quality! By the grandest artist in the world, Didoni Marcelleni!"

The Duke turned his head. "Stop," he said to the men who were carrying his litter. Didoni and Myles stepped forward.

"Didoni Marcelleni?" the Duke asked, his eyebrows raised. "I am the Duke, as you probably already well know, and I govern Bulrox. But you say you can paint?"

"Yes, your Grace," Didoni said, bowing with a flourish. "If it would please your Grace."

"Hmm," the Duke said. Then he turned to Myles.

"You, boy," the Duke said roughly as he dismounted from the litter. "Is this artist good?"

"Very, sir," Myles said, ignoring Didoni as he mouthed 'your Grace'. "He is very skilled with the brush, and has the rare ability to mix paints and produce beautiful colors."

"Joanna!" the Duke turned to the Duchess, who nodded.

"Yes, my lord?" Joanna asked, tilting her head.

"There's a painter who can do your portrait," the Duke said. Turning back to Didoni, he said, "How about seventy coins?"

Myles gasped. It was an enormous amount, much more than the cottars back in his hometown had to pay in taxes to Lord Horace!

"What ye gawkin' at, lad?" An old man with a gray patch over his eye came limping forward, waving a rough wood cane. "There wain't nothin' here."

"**Vagabond**! Ruffian! Thug! Back away—in the name of the Duke!" a knight cried, **brandishing** his great gold mace.

"I mean no harm to ye idle rich," the old man said in a whiny tone. "I just be tellin' the laddie here some stuff, ain't it? Now I better be goin' now, there's business with the Gadians..." The man hobbled away, leaning on his cane.

"Well, as we were saying," the Duke began again, "I will give you seventy coins for a portrait of my wife, and another seventy coins for a portrait of myself."

"Yes, your Grace," Didoni said quickly.

"Knights! Clear the square of townsfolk!" the Duke cried. Within a few moments, the square was empty except for the Duke, the Duchess, Myles, Didoni, and the Duke's bodyguards. The Duchess lay down to rest as a **minion** fanned her and spread soothing oils on her white skin. The Duke was telling Didoni what he wanted on his portrait.

"Make me appear strong and majestic. I want no one to think that I am a weakling, like my soft elder brother, the King," the Duke said imperiously.

"Why not paint a suit of armor?" Myles suggested before he could stop himself.

"Yes! The lad has quite the idea!" the Duke exclaimed. "Paint me in a suit of shining plate armor, with nothing amiss. Make my eyes as sharp as an eagle's, and my nose straight and curved at the end. My lips I care for not—but make them solemn."

Didoni nodded.

"It shall be done of course, your Grace," Didoni said, already beginning to sketch on his canvas.

Didoni created the most powerful piece of artwork in all of Bulrox and beyond. The Duke looked so great and magnificent that it reminded Myles of God himself.

"Now those upstart lords in the Western regions will think twice about invading my land!" the Duke exclaimed proudly. "And now for drawing my wife."

Of course the Duchess wanted to be drawn pretty much the opposite. Her features were soft and gentle. Her nose was long and thin, but not curved at the end. She was to be drawn clothed in a burgundy kirtle with her golden hair tied back in a single braid.

"Thank you," the Duchess said when Didoni handed her the portrait. "It is beautiful."

"Tell your subjects," Myles burst in. "Perhaps they shall want some."

"A good idea, lad," the Duke said, laughing heartily and patting Myles on the back. Didoni, who had looked as if he was about to scold Myles, hastily shut his mouth.

"Well, best regards, your Grace," Didoni said, bowing. "And may God grant that we meet again."

"Yes, indeed!" the Duke exclaimed, shaking Didoni's hand in a warm grip. Myles was rather impressed by the **pomp** of it all.

Signaling to the men who had been carrying his litter, the Duke climbed in—and Myles never saw him again.

That afternoon, just when the heat was beginning to rise, Didoni and Myles mounted their donkeys and continued past Bulrox on a narrow, muddy path that would eventually lead to Crastitoles, a bustling city similar to Bulrox but larger. King Johann himself kept a summer villa there.

"*If* his majesty the King allows me to paint his portrait, or maybe the Princess's, I will be a human center of fame," Didoni exclaimed, throwing his hands high up into the air.

"I wouldn't count on it," Myles said. "You got the Duke, but that was probably because you were in the front of the crowd. In the crowd that awaits the King, knights will be in the front and back row of the crowd to keep peace if a person gets too rowdy and disturbs the King."

"Say 'his Majesty the King'! " Didoni whispered loudly.

"Why?" Myles asked.

"I don't want to be arrested and put in the stocks for not having the proper amount of respect for his majesty the King," Didoni said. At Myles's disbelieving look, he added irritably, "That does happen, you know."

"As if," Myles said under his breath. But the conversation was obviously ended.

The next morning, after a few more hours of riding (and Myles complained a good deal about that, as he was very stiff and sore from yesterday's ride), Didoni stopped the donkeys at a small hitching post and tied them up. He shoved some clean breeches, stockings, and a white shirt that was much too long for Myles into Myles's arms.

"Quick," Didoni said. "Change. And don't forget to say 'his majesty the King,' when speaking of his majesty the King." Myles was dressed in a few minutes.

"I would have you wash your hair and your face some," Didoni said crossly to Myles, "but that would make us late."

Myles saw many things at the gates of Crastitoles. One woman at the gates of Crastitoles was flirting with a guard, who looked rather puzzled. Another woman was complaining of a sore throat and that the herb stores did not open early enough for her to buy cumin seeds. Plenty of men were sitting unhappily in the stocks, some with runny noses. A tall man guarded the men in the stocks, blowing his smoke pipe at the same time. Suddenly, the peals of the great cathedral bell made all of the guards come wide awake. They jumped to their posts immediately. At the second tolling of the bell, the guards bowed and opened the grand door. Everyone ran in.

"Pass, sweet lady! Pass, good sir! Pass, wee babes!" the guards' cries rang out. If Myles had been gaping at the splendor in Bulrox, he was so stunned at the richness and beauty of Crastitoles that he kept his mouth shut.

"Make way for his majesty the King! Make way for his majesty the King! His Excellence! The anointed one! Aside, aside!" Knights ran in all directions. When the commotion had died down somewhat, Myles began shouting,

"Paintings! Portraits! By the most skilled and learned artist in the world, Didoni Marcelleni!"

"If you are not a fraud, come forward!" a knight commanded.

"Wayne, I will take care of it," the King Johann said from his litter. Johann, with Princess Anya at his side, stepped down. Didoni stepped forward and bowed. Myles did similarly.

"Hmm," Johann said. "I do not really need another portrait—but our court painter was fired just last summer and my daughter, Princess Anya, is receiving some inquiries about marriage. Some require her portrait, and I'm afraid that this year is not quite going well. I cannot bear to tax the people until they starve, so what I pay you will be rather meager. Actually, we can work out a deal. You can fill the job as court painter, and your apprentice can be my page."

"Of course! I am honored!" Didoni exclaimed. Myles would have protested against being the king's page, but he knew that he was in the presence of the King, so he kept his mouth shut.

That night, Myles and Didoni were put into separate rooms. Although the rooms were rather small for a king's palace, there was plenty of light and it was all very neat and clean.

From his room, Myles had an excellent view of the moat. Below he could see Johann taking one of his numerous walks, and Anya right beside him.

"Master?" a voice asked.

Myles spun around. A young maidservant, who looked terrified, took a step back. Myles immediately relaxed.

"Er…his majesty gave orders for you to eat," the maid said, putting the tray down on Myles's little coffee table. What the maid put down certainly looked appetizing, but, as Myles's father had always said, looks could be deceiving. Myles took a delicate forkful of some meat and almost spat the "awful stuff" onto the maid.

"Ugh! What is this?" Myles shouted.

"Er…well…it's snail," the maid said, quickly backing away.

"Snail!!!" Myles exploded. He choked down a mouthful of water and spluttered. The maid quickly dabbed at Myles's clothes with a napkin.

"Rachel?" Johann's voice came from the doorway. "Get the boy in his page uniform."

"Yes, your majesty," Rachel said, putting down the napkin and opening the door. Johann stepped in.

"I can see you didn't enjoy your food," Johann said grimly. "Yes, only for those who sit on the dais there is real meat. Even then, it is hard and tough." Myles had no idea what a dais was, but he thought that the king would think him ignorant if he asked. In truth a dais is a high table where the king, queen (she was dead), and princess sat, along with various high lords and ladies. But Myles did not know that, and resolved to ask Didoni as soon as he could.

The next morning, Myles awoke to find Rachel rekindling the fire. He found a new suit of clothes already laid out for him, and hastily dressed.

"His majesty the king would like to have you in his grand ballroom," Rachel said. "Your master, the artist, is already there."

"Thank you," Myles said, running out of the room. Of course he had no idea where the ballroom was, and at last he saw two grand double doors, one of which was open, he glimpsed Johann sitting on a grand golden throne under a dark purple awning. Didoni was sitting on a chair of honor next to Johann, his canvas already prepared. Myles almost laughed to hear the clickety-clack of Didoni's polished black shoes on the vast tile floor.

"Oh, there you are, lad," Johann said to Myles. "Come come, let's not waste time." Didoni barely looked up at his apprentice.

"Er, your majesty—" Myles began.

"Yes, you'll be wondering what you're doing here," Johann said. "Now you're to be my new page—Kirshley had to go to squire training last week. I wish that I could have a permanent page—boys take some getting used to." Myles had no idea who Kirshley was, but he guessed (and rightly) that he had been Johann's recent page.

"Anyways," Johann said, motioning towards a chair, "Sit." Myles sat.

"But first, I want you to meet somebody," Johann said. An old, twisted man entered the great double doors.

"Allow me to introduce Sir Roaad. Roaad, this is Myles," Johann said.

"*Retired* Sir Roaad," the old man croaked, leaning on a silver-tipped cane with many rubies jutting out from the middle. "My son takes on the family title."

"Ah, well, retired or not, Roaad, you're still up and a-talking, beating my poor pages black-and-blue with that cane of yours," Johann laughed wildly, clutching the arm of his throne. Myles could see nothing funny about Johann's words, but he attempted to make a fake laugh. It sounded horrible, and everybody stared in his direction.

"Enough," Johann said finally, stopping the awkwardness. "Let's get on with some serious business."

"Right," Roaad said, nodding his head and running a hand through his bushy hair.

"What?" Myles asked.

"It's all right, lad. Oh, and, I didn't get your name," Johann said.

"Myles," Myles said.

"Myles! Ah, a good name for a sturdy boy like you," said Roaad, nodding approvingly. Myles was rather surprised at Roaad's compliment. Back in the cottars' village, he had been called puny. It was true that Myles was small for his age and did not have broad shoulders and arms with muscles sticking out. But if a knight called him sturdy, perhaps he was!

Training as a page was harder than Myles had expected it to be. Roaad tried to be gentle with Myles, but it was not easy with a new page. After all, Myles was not even of royal blood. Roaad had discovered this after he had asked who Myles's father was. Myles most dearly wished he could escape from court life. He was being served ox meat now, but it hardly tasted any better.

One day, as Myles was exploring around the palace, wandering near to Didoni's room, he noticed that Didoni was not in his room and that his chest was open. Myles tiptoed in, hardly daring to breathe. He took the paints out, then the paintbrushes, and finally, a canvas. He looked in the mirror.

"Why don't I paint myself?" Myles said out loud. He thought it a rather good idea, and started at once. In two hours, about, he had created a masterpiece. It looked exactly like Myles in the mirror. It was at that moment Didoni returned.

"Myles!" Didoni clutched the doorknob till his hands turned white. "What...what?"

"You never let me paint," Myles said hastily. "That is what a master is supposed to do for an apprentice—teach them the trade."

"Oh, dear," Didoni sunk into his couch. "Myles, what have you done?" Didoni spoke more to himself than to Myles.

"I have created this," Myles pulled his creation from behind his back. Didoni glanced at it for a few seconds.

"It is beautiful," Didoni finally admitted. "But you have disobeyed me, and for that I am very displeased and disappointed."

"You never taught me to paint," Myles said. "You were supposed to teach me the trade. And here I am, stuck as a page with the king, all to your benefit and not to mine."

"You would still be in that tiny little hut had I not taken you in as my apprentice!" Didoni's voice was filled with anger. "You ungrateful wretch!"

"You are supposed to teach me to paint!" Myles exclaimed. "You have been neglecting your duties!" Finally Didoni had to give up. He rose from the couch.

"Perhaps I have," Didoni said, somewhat calmer, "but that does not change the fact that you have disobeyed me. An apprentice is supposed to obey his master."

"You have never told me not to wander near your things!" Myles exclaimed. "You have never said not to go into your room!" Didoni had to admit this was true.

"However," Didoni continued slowly, "about this page business. It is as much to your benefit as it is to mine. You have a clean bed, a clean room, and a good place in the court. You were a starving half-orphan when I took you, and now you complain."

"It is a good position, yes," Myles said. "But I want to paint. I want to wander in the outside world."

"You are my apprentice, and therefore bound to me," Didoni said sharply. "I do not give you my permission to leave."

"I could run away," Myles said, although his voice was unsure. He did not like the prospect of running away. Two years before, when he was only ten, a young boy named Fenn had run away. The next day, three men going fishing found his body, covered with snow and rain. And at least the palace had good heating.

"Myles," Didoni pleaded. "You must reason with me. The very idea of running away is doltish." Myles bit his lip. It was true. After all, he did have a good position. He had good food (with the exception of the ox meat), a good room, and he was never cold or tired. But still...

"I will leave," Myles said. "If you beat me, scold me, do anything to me, you cannot change my mind."

"I can see that you will not give up," Didoni said wearily. "Go, and take my blessing."

The next day, after packing, Myles took his leave. Didoni accompanied him as far as the gates.

"From here, just take the left path. Go straight for two miles, and turn right. There you will be in Benat. Past there, you can choose your path," Didoni told Myles.

"I shall, master," Myles said, hoisting his haversack onto his shoulders and waving back to Didoni.

It felt lonely riding without Didoni. Myles sighed and rested his head on his donkey's rough neck.

"I bet you miss your mate, too, old fellow," Myles said to the donkey. Amazingly, the donkey nodded its head. Myles assured himself that it was just a coincidence, but he made the sign of the Cross at the same time. Suddenly, twenty men leapt out of the tree tops, with burning sticks in their hands. Myles gave a start.

"He jus' be a laddie," Myles heard a bored voice say. As the men neared, Myles peered closer and noticed that the men all had a strange symbol on the middle of their bare chests. **Flagons** containing who-knew-what were tied to their waists with thick leather belts.

"Grab him, anyways," someone said roughly. "The chief will hold him up for inspection." Myles felt himself being grabbed by his collar.

"Stop, in the name of King Johann, under the grace of Jesus and God!" Myles shouted, regaining his senses.

"King? We ain't believe in no king, nor no snotty princesses! By the grace of Jesus, indeed! Ha!" the men shouted. With horror, Myles realized that these people were Gadians, people who were considered inhuman due to their refusal to believe in Jesus and God. They raided villages, killing and kidnapping. Myles desperately felt around in his haversack for his knife, which Didoni had given him. He finally touched the end of the blade, slid the knife out, and tried to look as threatening as possible. The men brought up knives also, large ones that Myles blinked at with surprise.

"The boy is armed, but he won't stand long!" A great man thundered, stepping out from behind the trees. "Get him!" Myles suddenly found himself battling one man after another, flinching when somebody would kick out at him.

"Let me take care of him. I'll show you how to really get somebody," the man said. He rushed towards Myles and threw him down from the donkey. Myles screamed with pain, but he could do nothing. His ankle was sprained very badly.

"Tie him up!" the man commanded. The men rushed to do as their leader bid them. Myles bit the men as well as he could, but finally one of the men threw a rope into Myles's mouth.

"Now that's a good sign of leadership, Growr," the leader said. A few of the men snorted. Growr glowered at them. Myles was dragged deeper and deeper into the forest (where Didoni had warned him on no circumstances to go) until the men finally stopped at a particularly sinister tree.

"May the race of the Gadians live forever," the leader, Iyvin, said.

"And may our leader's sons and grandsons and great grandsons multiply to form our destiny," the rest of the men chanted in reply. Myles listened to all of this, afraid that it was some kind of ritual to execute unfortunate prisoners. But he was quite wrong about this. Iyvin, despite his roughness, was usually very kind to young boys and had never killed one of them. He usually tried to turn their hearts against Johann, but only halfheartedly. None of the boys had ever dared go as far as **treachery**—everyone knew the price for that. But Myles did not know that, and was shuddering with fear. He even noticed that one of the Gadians was the patch-eyed man who had walked up to him while Didoni was painting the Duke.

"Ugh," he said as a snake slithered up the tree. "Disgusting things. I do hope they're not going to put that on me."

Despite the fact that Didoni usually drove him crazy, Myles couldn't help but think that the old man's presence would have been a comfort.

The Gadians dragged Myles into a dark hole, or at least what Myles thought was a hole. In truth it was a huge labyrinth of tunnels and underground passages. Iyvin, who was in the lead, kept on muttering "bring some light out, you lily-livered potbellies," but no light was brought out. Finally the men halted in a dark corridor.

"We're here, and untie the lad, dunce!" Ivyin's sharp voice drifted over to Myles's ears. Myles felt his cords being loosened and falling off, and he at once stretched out.

"Ah," Iyvin strode over. "A sight, is it not, my men? Well, let us not begin in foolish chatter. Let us begin in a feast!"

Iyvin was quite wrong in calling the men potbellies. He himself was an extremely obese man, weighing at the least five hundred pounds. His great tummy, which he patted often, hung a foot below his pants' waistline, and his chubby cheeks looked like a baby's. Myles watched all of this with interest. He was becoming more and more hopeful that they would not kill him and that perhaps he would have a way of escape.

"Now, for you, boy," Iyvin said rudely to Myles. "What are you called?"

"Myles," Myles said. He was sure that the Gadians were not going to kill him—after all, who would ask somebody's name if they were going to be executed anyways?

"Well, Myles," Iyvin said grandly. "You are ours to keep. Now come to the feast table."

But Myles refused to eat anything, mostly because of the tales of poison and enchanted liquids in the food which Gadians ate. Iyvin was very offended at this, and soon he said very angrily to Myles, "If you don't eat, I'll make you eat!"

"I submit not to the will of a barbarian!" Myles cried indignantly.

"Barbarians!" If there was one offensive name to call a Gadian, it was barbarian. Gadians were native to the land and had first settled it, although when King Johann I had come and settled the land, they were nearly wiped out. Barbarian really meant foreigner in a more nasty way of saying it.

"Boy! Boy!" Iyvin shouted, jumping up and down and knocking plates and bowls over.

"Chief!" The men were very nervous when Iyvin was angry like this. He would spill his wrath over everyone, especially those that disturbed him. "Chief! Er, Iyvina's here!" Myles was terribly afraid, and was relieved when Iyvin jumped down from the table. A girl entered the room. She was probably about fourteen, by the look of it. Iyvin immediately hugged her.

"Iyvina! My darling! What a pleasant surprise! What brings you to the men's place? Could I get you some wine?" Myles rightly guessed that Iyvina was Iyvin's daughter. After all, she did have the dark black hair and black eyes. Only she was very thin, like Myles.

"Wine would be good, yes, father. But I have much to tell. Johann, the so-called ruler, is riding across the plains. If we can remain hidden, we may be able to launch an attack," Iyvina said.

"You cannot!" Myles cried out, immediately biting his lip.

"Boy! You! Stop it!" Iyvin exclaimed to Myles, whirling around.

"The boy is right," Iyvina's lips curled into an eerie smile. "We cannot attack without using him first, can we?"

"No, Iyvina, we've talked about this before," Iyvin put in hurriedly. "Let's just plan our attack." Everybody put their heads together. Myles, seeing a chance, snuck past them. It happened that he stepped on Iyvin's foot at just the last second, so a great cry arose. Myles ran past them, but they were nearing. He put even greater speed into his running. Then with a splash he fell into cold water and his mind was an **abyss** of swirling darkness.

When Myles awoke he was surprised to find himself laid out on grass. There was a warm night breeze that was most refreshing. He found that his wet clothes were quite an annoyance, but the breeze dried them quickly.

"Myles!" It was King Johann! "What are you doing here?"

"My master gave me permission to wander the lands," Myles said hurriedly.

"And here you are, laid out on the grass dripping wet!" Johann exclaimed. "Do you not prefer life as a page?"

"No," Myles said, forgetting to say "your majesty."

"No! Well, at least come back to the palace to get some dry clothes."

"I must continue with my journey. But thank you for the offer," Myles said stiffly.

"Ah, well, then, I've seen that you've made up your mind. Have good luck!" And Johann was gone.

Myles made his shelter that day under the branches of a weeping willow. He was glad that he had slept there instead of out in the open, as there was a thunderstorm. Unfortunately, when Myles peeked out, he realized that the stream was undoubtedly too high for him to cross.

"Oh, fie!" Myles muttered to himself. "I just might as well have stayed at the palace with Didoni! I rather find myself missing the old bat. It's raining, there's thunder, and there's no way I'll be able to get to the other side of that horrible stream!" But as it so turned out, it was only a typical night of grumpiness.

The next day was quite a beautiful day. The sun was shining, casting its rays of lights everywhere and almost blinding Myles. The stream had lowered somewhat, although it was still not shallow enough to cross.

"Those Tyrs up in the North are lucky. They have those handy reed boats," Myles muttered to himself. He wandered around until he finally found a shallow spot in the stream he could wade across. When he emerged from the water on the other side, he was drenched and in a very bad mood.

"Curse those Gadians for leading me off the path!" Myles muttered, as well as various swearwords.

When Myles finally started on the path leading to Aroda, a holy city, he bumped into an old man who was wearing a dark burgundy hooded cloak. The man also happened to be walking to Aroda.

"Excuse me," Myles stammered. The stranger pulled back his hood. He was an old man, with long, unwashed gray hair. Myles guessed that the man was making a **pilgrimage** to Aroda, to see the holy **relics** of Saint Orada.

"It is a trivial matter, lad. My fault," the man said. "Allow me to introduce myself. I am Friar John, of the Franciscan Order." Myles immediately realized that he should have known this easily. It was obvious —the friar's gray **habit** was the symbol of the Franciscan Order.

"Well, er," Myles stood there stuttering. He was in a rather an awkward position. Neither knew what to say.

"Well, let us be off to Aroda," John said merrily, taking Myles's hand. "You're going there, I presume?" Myles nodded.

"Well, I have a few friends there. I'm sure they would be glad to give you some shelter for the night—I've heard that the inns there are filthy and serve terrible food. So let us not waste time," John said.

"Thank you kindly," Myles said, who could not think of anything else to say. So, after being much delayed, Myles and John set off.

A grand cathedral overlooked all the buildings in Aroda. It had a great massive bell that tolled each hour. There were no gates to protect Aroda, nor any guards. It was a very friendly place, with folk chatting and exchanging the latest gossip of the day. Fishmongers sold slimy fish and who-knew-what to laughing women, while grim-faced men wheeled carts loaded with bread and other goods around, bargaining about prices with cooks. It was very much like Myles's own home in North Yurxl.

"Come, come into Saint Orada's Cathedral," John muttered, making Myles come out of his daydream. The cathedral was very splendid, with its gold statues and great paintings. There were long tapestries with golden crucifixes, and a pair of steps encircling a platform led up to the archbishop's smooth wooden pulpit. The archbishop, however, was absent from the platform; praying in the back of the cathedral.

"Ah, Brother John!" A gallant voice rang out. "You have arrived at last, and with a youngster at your side! Have you given up the holy life and retired to a life of luxury? Is the boy your faithful servant?" Laughter broke out. The archbishop looked on with a disapproving look on his wrinkled face, although Myles noticed that he had just a hint of a smile on his withered gray lips.

"No, Brother Thomas! I met—well, what is your name, lad?" John said, turning to Myles, rather embarrassed.

"Myles," Myles said, fidgeting nervously.

"Well, I met Myles on the path to Aroda. Myles, this is Brother Thomas, Brother Augustine, Brother George, Brother Edmund, Brother Julian, Brother Stephen, and of course, Archbishop Peter," John said. Myles's head was in a jumble. Brother who? Brother Jumund? No...Brother Steorge?

"Anyways, I'm hungry," John announced. "Let's see if Mother's got anything."

"Mother" actually happened to be a tall woman by the name of Glorienne with a gray wool dress and a much-stained apron. She ran an ancient inn by the name of "The King's Bed." John and the rest were immediately seated.

"Only good inn in Aroda," John said to Myles, taking a mouthful of leek soup and wiping his face on the threadbare tablecloth.

"The others look horrid," Myles said, chewing on some sourdough bread.

"Yes. I particularly would not like to go to that Green Eyes Tavern. It looks extremely uncivilized," John said.

"Less luxurious buildings are not to your liking, John, eh?" Thomas joked with a grin.

"Luxurious indeed!" John sputtered. "Why—why—how dare you suggest such a thing!"

"Er, could I please have some more bread?" Myles asked awkwardly, nibbling on the edge of his crisp herring.

"It shall be done! The lad is quite right! We do need some more food and drink!" Stephen exclaimed. Myles was immediately served a fresh loaf of bread, along with a small dish of olive oil and vinegar. Glorienne proudly bragged that she had made the bread herself, "with not the help of any of those kitchen **sluggards**."

Though his lodgings were pleasant enough, Myles soon tired of the monks. Unfortunately, everybody wanted him to stay. One day Myles could bear it no longer, and packing his few possessions, slipped down from the window. He landed down on the ground with a thump and ran away. He had no sense of direction, and found himself always doubling back to check. Finally he got onto the South Trail and continued along the stream. He crossed the shallowest part, going back to where he had been captured by the Gadians. Only this time there were no Gadians in sight. Finally on the path leading to Branwole, Myles collapsed onto the ground with exhaustion. His eyelids soon became droopy and he fell asleep within seconds.

When Myles woke up, he was much rested and ready to continue walking. He breathed in the good scent of the beautiful roses that grew along the path, stopping to rest at each one.

When Myles arrived at Branwole, he made it just in time to run into the city before the gates were shut with a clang and a new group of knights took their nightly shifts. It was completely dark in the streets except for the dim light from a sinister building labeled "The Traveling Man." It was the lowest-rated inn in all of Branwole, and

Myles did not quite **relish** the idea of staying there for the night. Unfortunately he had no choice. Although Myles was not afraid of the ghosts and spirits who were said to haunt the streets at night, the nightly curfew prohibited any folk from being outside past eleven. He gulped down his fears and timidly entered The Traveling Man.

"Hi! Robert, we've got a newcomer!" A loud voice shouted across the small room. Myles took a step back.

"Come, lad," said a boy to Myles. "The room on seventh floor is open." Myles stepped back and suddenly realized that the entire inn was constructed of eight rickety rooms, one on top of the other. The topmost room was balanced on four thin sticks, one of which was rotten.

"Lad!" The boy tugged at Myles arm impatiently

"Are you coming or not?" Myles could do nothing but gape at the boy, who merely shrugged.

"You'll be wanting food, boy?" the innkeeper, a short, stocky man, shouted over.

"Yes," Myles said gratefully.

"Well, then, ya gotta work for it. Robert, show him to the kitchens," the innkeeper said, pounding his fist on the counter. Myles was dragged away to the back of the inn, where he was made to chop carrots.

"Do that and you'll get some bread and coffee," the innkeeper commanded. Myles nodded, so great was his hunger.

"Good. Now to work," the innkeeper said.

After about an hour of chopping, Myles was sent up to his room with a loaf of crusty rye bread and a cup of awful black stuff mixed with water, which was said to be coffee. It was very bitter and Myles poured it out of the small window after only a few sips.

"Ugh," Myles said to no one in particular. "That stuff is awful." Although nobody responded, he felt contented that at least *someone* had heard his remark. Talking to himself always made him miss Didoni. Yawning, Myles fell back onto his bed and was soon overtaken by sleep.

Myles was awakened late in the morning by a deep, melodious voice.

"Who is it?!" Myles exclaimed, jumping around and waving his sword.

"I come with tidings of his majesty King Johann," the voice said back. Myles jumped up, pulled his breeches over his night shirt, and flung a few dirty rats by their tails at the window. Finally he opened the door. A tall, slender man with dark black hair stepped in, his fine brown boots not leaving a single trace on the floor. He wore a tattered hooded cloak of dark violet which dragged behind him, and the gold pocket watch hanging from his thick leather belt was the only thing that suggested he was of noble birth.

"Er, why don't you sit down?" Myles asked awkwardly.

"You may not remember me," the man sighed, rubbing his thinning hair absentmindedly. "I am your companion of old, Sherwin. The news I bring is urgent."

"Sherwin!" Myles cried, jumping up and knocking his earthenware mug from the table.

"Yes, it is I," Sherwin said, smiling halfheartedly.

"And how did you come to earn that magnificent watch?" Myles asked, eyeing the pocket watch suspiciously. Sherwin immediately stuffed the watch into his canvas hunting pouch and repeated as if he had not heard Myles,

"The news I bring is urgent."

"Oh dear," Myles said, sighing. "I do rather think that I've had enough to put up with that awful innkeeper. But blast on." Just then the innkeeper stormed in, his bulging face red.

"Boy," he snarled, "it's late in the morning, and you've just missed breakfast." Sherwin sprung to his feet.

"If we are not welcome here, we will leave immediately," the boy said, his freckles looking redder than usual. Myles could have sworn he saw Sherwin's hand move to his belt, where a very sharp dagger was tied.

"No, no, you can s-stay h-here," the innkeeper stuttered, quickly backing away.

"That rids us of that troublesome fool," Sherwin said, settling back into his chair. "Now I must tell you of my grim news. The King Johann, Lord bless his soul, has caught it."

"What is that?" Myles asked blankly.

"My, your years with the artist have made you ignorant! Do you not remember?" And then Sherwin leaned so close that Myles could feel Sherwin's breath on his face. Myles suddenly had a fleeting image of wailing women and putrid corpses being dragged away. And then he remembered. It was a memory he still did not want to remember. Hardly daring to face that the King himself had caught the deadly sickness.

Myles took a deep breath and asked Sherwin, his voice shaking, "King Johann has caught the..." He hardly dared to say it. But he forced himself to. "The Hebre?"

Sherwin grimly nodded his affirmation. "Unfortunately, it is so."

Sherwin offered to accompany Myles, and he gratefully received the addition of Sherwin's company. Myles left in the early afternoon, running to keep up with Sherwin's long strides. Townsfolk barely glanced at them, merely going on about their daily business. Myles inhaled the cool, fresh air, and waved to the regular surly passerby. However, he noted that Sherwin was obviously disturbed. He was frowning, and often fumbled around in his hunting pouch for something that never seemed to be there. Finally Myles felt it was his duty to step in.

"Sherwin?" Myles asked timidly one night when they were sleeping under the protection of a broad oak tree. "Has anything been...bothering...you lately?"

"No, nothing," Sherwin muttered. But Myles knew that there was more to it then just that.

Myles was awakened in the early morning by the chirping and twittering of a couple of blue jays, who flew around Sherwin and himself excitedly. He groaned, rolled over, and tried to go back to sleep. He was roused by Sherwin, who had started a fire and was munching on some meat.

"Get up, lazybones, or else the day will be wasted before you know it," said Sherwin brightly, seeming to have forgotten all of the troubles of the previous day. When Myles did not respond, Sherwin poked Myles's ribs with an unusually sharp stick.

"Oi!" Myles shouted with rage, jumping up. "That hurt, you know!" Sherwin almost tumbled over backwards with laughter, clutching his chest. Myles pulled on his breeches, still muttering angrily. When he was fully dressed, he took a piece of meat from the fire and popped it into his mouth. He scalded his tongue accidentally, swearing all the more.

When Myles had finally contented his stomach, Sherwin took his arm and they started off on the path, singing an old milkmaid's ditty merrily again. He **skulked** around the borders of the farmlands, often bringing back mutton for supper. Myles suspected that he had been stealing from the shepherds' flocks, but he thought it best to keep silent. In the early afternoon Sherwin was back to his usual moodiness again.

It was a hot summer day that Myles suddenly blurted out to Sherwin,

"Why are you so unhappy…these days?" Sherwin turned to face Myles, and Myles noticed that a long, red gash ran down the side of his face. He took a step back.

"There are many things that I am displeased with," Sherwin said bitterly. "But amongst them are my fears of the Dark Horror."

"Him?" Myles cried. "And I did think that he was locked away in the old monastery quite safely!" He could imagine that gigantic gray wolf lurking in the shadows of a mysterious forest, and shuddered.

"Yes, he *was*, I'm afraid. But he recently escaped, and is returning to his old home. Along this path, I'm afraid," Sherwin said grimly.

"I don't think I particularly like thinking about that," Myles said, his voice shaking.

"And all the more reason to think about it. The Dark Horror has a taste for human meat, you might remember?" Sherwin smiled slyly. Myles groaned.

"Now I do very well wish I were with Didoni!" he exclaimed. "Safe within the walls of that nice palace, eating that putrid horsemeat!"

"There shall be many things you wish for," Sherwin said. "And I do agree that this journey will be long and perilous. But I am sure that when this comes to an end, you will be thankful."

"Sherwin, do you like to paint?" Myles asked suddenly.

"Yes, I **dabble** in it. I watched the artist, and I nicked a canvas or two and tried it out myself," Sherwin said **dryly**.

"Do you have any canvases or paints or brushes right now?" Myles asked excitedly.

"No, I'm afraid not—who's that?" Sherwin jumped up, drawing his dagger.

"You fool!" Myles cried, laughing. "Why, it's only Didoni!" And indeed it was—a Didoni clad in silver mail. He was only recognizable by his twinkling gray eyes, which were hidden somewhat by his bushy eyebrows. Myles immediately ran over to greet his master.

"What are you doing here?" Myles asked, staring at the rich mail.

"I have come to bring you back to where you will have safety," Didoni said firmly. "The Dark Horror lurks near, and it is my duty to see to your safety. And who is this, may I ask?" Didoni gestured to Sherwin.

"An old companion of mine from the cottars' village," Myles said quickly. "His name is Sherwin."

"Well, then, make sure that both of you reach home safely," Didoni said.

"What do you mean, home?" Myles asked, fear rising in his stomach. He never wanted to return to the smoky cottar's house!

"Well, King Johann has granted me a pleasant little stone cottage near the ocean, and I am glad to teach you there," Didoni said, taking off his gray helmet to reveal his large smile.

"Really...teach me?" Myles asked, hardly daring to believe it.

"Yes, teach you the technique of the brush, the quality of the paints, and anything else you want to learn," Didoni said.

"Sir...would you mind if I joined you also?" Myles turned around and looked at Sherwin in surprise.

"No, no, of course not! You're free to come!" Didoni exclaimed.

"Oh, and I meant to ask you," Myles said quietly, "Why did King Johann give you that cottage?"

"I've been promoted to the rank of a marquis!" Didoni cried joyfully. "By the law, the king has to give the marquis housing and a sum of ninety- four thousand gold coins a year!"

And so Myles, leaning contentedly on Didoni's shoulder, with Sherwin in front of them, made their way to the little stone cottage. Didoni opened the low wooden door, stooped under, and took Myles's hand.

"Come in, come in!" Didoni cried. Although it was a little dim at first, soon Didoni had opened all of the shutters.

"You know, I think that I feel like I'm really at home," Myles remarked, glancing out the window. Although life was always unpredictable, Myles somehow knew that he would always be happy.

Why Use Good and Bad When Excellent and Appalling Are More Precise?

Expanding Vocabulary

Thanks to the Harry Potter series, more and more kids are reading. However, with the distraction of TV and video games, many of today's kids are still hindered by a limited vocabulary, unable to express themselves to the fullest extent. Writing with a limited vocabulary is like playing a guitar that only has three strings. It gets old quick.

Omnipotent. Snide. Sinister. Did a seven-year-old really write this? Aside from the obvious achievement of publishing her first book at age seven, Adora's vocabulary may be the one thing about her that astonishes people most. Adora sees language in much the same way a talented musician looks at music. Though you can play a perfectly good song using only a few simple chords, there are certain moods and nuances that cannot be expressed without learning subtler and more complex combinations of notes. She sees words as magic things, things that sparkle and shimmer and shine. Her joy in a new word is almost tangible.

How does Adora learn these words? She gains new words every day through her reading and her use of the dictionary and thesaurus on her computer, but when we began to help her hunt for new words, she accelerated exponentially.

When choosing new vocabulary words, it helps to throw in a couple of wild cards to emphasize the zaniness of language. Not every selection should be a future SAT word. Include some outlandish choices regardless of the fact that your child may never really have the chance to use *omnifarious* in a sentence. The point is to keep things fun. Adora is fascinated by both piracy and wizardry, so we usually pepper our lessons with related words or sentences. *Scurrilous, dregs, skulk, ominous, maraud.*

Though effective, writing sentences to practice new vocabulary is not enough. It's crucial for kids to put new vocabulary into immediate use in one of their creative projects. This way they can see how changing a single word can have a dramatic positive effect on something that they are already invested in. When Adora is working on a story, we challenge her to see if she can incorporate some of the day's new vocabulary.

Having an impressive vocabulary alone will not make a good story, but mastering new vocabulary words is satisfying for most kids, and illustrates an important point about writing: you have the whole world at your fingertips. *You* have the chance to make this sentence precise, original, and memorable. *You* can improve upon the commonplace. When you're writing, *you* have the power. It's *your* choice, and the resources are right at your fingertips.

 ## Interview and Tips from Adora

Joyce: Why do you think vocabulary is important?
Adora: I think vocabulary is important because I don't want to use crappy vocabulary.

Joyce: (laughing) What would be an example of that?
Adora: For example I could say "Mary walked along the street. The street was plain." That would be an example of crappy vocabulary. But I could use drab as a substitute for plain, because drab sounds better. Mary walked along the drab street.

Joyce: Why does it sound better? Is it more specific?
Adora: Exactly. Like yoghurt can be plain, but it can't be drab.

Joyce: What do you do if you can't think of a better word?
Adora: Sometimes I use the synonym option on my computer, but if I don't find anything good I'll look it up in the actual dictionary.

Joyce: So do you get a lot of enjoyment out of using advanced vocabulary?
Adora: I feel regular, common and normal. I don't feel accomplished, achieved, or advanced.

Joyce: Your readers are astonished by the amount of vocabulary you use in your stories, how appropriately are these words being used? How are you able to do it?
Adora: Writing these words in my stories helps me remember them. I love using new words in my stories—it spices up my stories. Some words I just can't forget.

Joyce: What would you suggest to other kids to do to increase their vocabulary?

Adora: I would suggest reading lots of advanced-level books. Although you may not understand the plot perfectly, you can look these words up on the dictionary and learn many new words. It's more fun than just reading the dictionary page by page, anyways. If you use them in stories and regular conversations with your friends and family you'll get used to them and enjoy them.

 ## Tips for Parents and Educators

Humor is a great tool when teaching vocabulary. When using words in sentences and asking students to follow suit, make your sentences silly or tailored to your student's particular sensibilities—this keeps the lesson from getting tedious. Use your own name or the names of people they know. Put the familiar in an outlandish context, or vice versa.

Websites like Dictionary.com and Microsoft Office Encarta dictionary are good resources for kids to pick up new vocabulary and use them in their stories. Encourage your child to be different and adventurous when it comes to using vocabulary. Support your child's desire to use unfamiliar and different words in speaking and writing.

 ## Give It a Spin

If writing sentences gets old, ask your student to write a creative paragraph that shows (as opposed to tells) the meaning of the word. For example: Write a dialogue between an *egotistical* person and a constantly *ingratiating* person. Write a list of things an *omnivorous* creature might eat. Write a *scathing* review. Write about an *arduous* journey that ends in a *bucolic* scene.

Find a literature website (www.literature.org/authors), pick an author you like, then copy and paste your chosen text into a Word document. Have your child rewrite the text by selecting synonyms or antonyms for the original vocabulary.

The Spoiled Prince

In the brightness of his **lavish antechamber**, Prince Garrick **scornfully** tossed aside a beautifully gold-**embossed** leather-bound book.

"Peasant's trash," he scoffed to the trembling **minion** who had presented the gift.

"B-beg p-pardon, y-your sup-superior h-highness, I n-never meant no h-harm," the servant stuttered, stepping back and tripping over an ornately designed china pitcher.

"As if you expect me, the intelligent and the clever, to believe that," Garrick said **disdainfully**, staring at the servant with contempt.

"I s-shall b-bring another b-book at your behest, your highness," the man said, kneeling at Garrick's feet.

"Pah!" Garrick exclaimed, kicking the book absentmindedly. "I have no mind for boring, unexciting **epics**! Bring me my gelatin, a well-cooked sunny-side up egg that has a round yolk with heavily sprinkled sugar, two three-pound chocolate bars, a loaf of pumpernickel bread with perfectly red jelly, and crystallized sugar drops! And also bring my **carmine** robes and scepter! And don't forget my extra sugared tangerines!" At that moment Queen Hortensia entered. She was an overly plump, pimply faced woman who always liked to wear frumpy purple dresses with unusually low bodices.

"Sweetie plum!" she cried when she saw Garrick. "I just contacted

VOCABULARY LIST

lavish – bountiful, extravagant, over-the-top
antechamber – a small room leading into a larger room
scornful – feeling or expressing contempt for something
embossed – decorated with a slightly raised design or lettering
minion – a slavish follower of someone generally considered important
disdainfully – showing contempt or scorn for something or someone
epic – a long series of events characterized by adventure and struggle
carmine – a deep purplish red color
mortified – ashamed or humiliated
brisk – cool and energetic
incompetence – lack of skill
discernable – visible
vellum – fine parchment or animal skin
ramshackle – poorly maintained or constructed, about to fall down
leered – a look that suggests unpleasant intent
drab – dull, lacking color and shine
pompous – self-important
impersonate – to pretend to be another person, to mimic

that incompetent tailor, and he is to weave your new week's *adorable* wardrobe!"

"The regular perfumed carmine robes trimmed with mink fur, short gold satin tunic with jewels sewn in, green hose, white belt, long black velvet tunic for important occasions, yellow hose, gold belt, medium red tunic, white hose, green belt, hunting cap, hunting shirt, hunting trousers, and black welvet hunting jacket with brown belt?" Garrick said rapidly, counting on his chubby fingers (In case you don't know, welvet is a mixture of wool and velvet used for Garrick's royal family).

"Yes, sugar plum," Hortensia said, beaming. "And we've also made two new additions—for affairs of state, blue satin tunic with black belt, white hose, and for jousting matches, to watch, of course—green tunic with blue hose."

"Good. I did think that I needed some new clothing for that kind of thing," Garrick said in a bored tone. "Now I want to eat—be off with you, servant, and bring back my food!"

The Seven Good Protector Fairies of Jarrod (Garrick's kingdom) nervously glided to their usual meeting place in the Fairies' Forest.

"That Garrick is getting terribly spoiled," Ailyra, the wisest of the fairies, remarked, the bright twilight reflecting off her crystal necklace. "Did you see the way he treated that poor man?"

"It'll be the downfall of Jarrod, I predict it," Anya, her identical triplet

VOCABULARY LIST

ambitious – having a strong desire for success
henceforth – from now on
pious – reverent, devout, serious about morals and religion
rapier – a slender sword (often double edged) with a sharpened point
uncouth – poorly mannered
graveness – seriousness, somberness
emerge – to appear out of or from behind something
barbarous – uncivilized, cruel
poultice – a warm damp preparation put on the body to relieve pain or improve circulation
scrawny – unpleasantly thin
undertones – quiet subdued tones
carp – a large freshwater fish
malevolent – harmful or evil
grate – the bars in front of a fireplace, a word sometimes used to describe the fireplace itself
hearth – the floor of a fireplace that extends into a room
obscured – clouded, darkened, made difficult to see
yeomen - a loyal worker or a farmer who cultivates his own land
utter – to say something, to emit a vocal sound
sly – skillful, cunning, not straightforward

sister, said, burying her white face in her hands.

"Indeed it shall if nothing is done," the fairies' leader, Wyddfa, said **slyly**, a twinkle in her black eyes. The dim sky reflected off her dark locks. "It is still early enough for him to change." She had a reputation for being the craftiest fairy of them all, if not the prettiest.

"What are...oh...indeed..." the fairies all drifted into deep thought, twisting their shining curls.

"We could steal him away and raise him *our* way," Miria suggested.

"Perhaps," Wyddfa said, a smile on her pink lips.

In the morning, as usual, Garrick had his forty-two personal maids dress him (in his new short gold satin tunic with SUPERIOR ONE embroidered on it and a long carmine train) and then walk him into the Breakfast Hall, where the King Errold and Queen Hortensia were already seated at the head and foot of the table.

VOCABULARY LIST
nimble – fast, light on one's feet
chaos – a state of disorder
unconscious – loss of senses, unaware
opaque – the opposite of **translucent** - generally used to describe something that would normally be translucent, such as glass or water.
tarry – linger, stay too long
wistfully – longingly
mahogany – a type of hard reddish brown wood
pillory – a wooden frame used to prevent a prisoner from moving their head or limbs
barreled – moved at high speed
chiffon – an extremely light, thin fabric
haughtily – proudly, coldly, with an attitude of superiority
acquaintance – someone you know, but don't know very well

"Garrick, my lad!" Errold exclaimed gruffly, hastily wiping his mouth with the silk napkin which lay at his side. "Come to your seat!" He gestured to the thick gold chair which was at his side.

To the servant who was eagerly awaiting his order, Garrick commanded **haughtily**, "Bring me my gelatin. And my hardboiled eggs heavily sprinkled with sugar, as well as strawberry chocolate crepe, two waffles, one with honey, the other with whipped cream, sweet bread pudding, classic chocolate cake, crystallized sugar grapes, and some white buns with shredded cheddar."

"At least have some tofu to help your attractive face, dear," Hortensia wheedled.

"NO!!!!!" Garrick bellowed, jumping up. He was enraged at the thought. "THAT'S PEASANT'S STUFF!!!! HOW DARE YOU

MAKE SUCH AN IDIOTIC SUGGESTION, WHY—" He was cut off by a servant, who said politely,

"Your highness's breakfast?"

"What about bacon strips and fried palace mouse with chocolate syrup?!" Garrick shouted, jumping up.

"Your highness did not state that he wanted any bacon or fried mouse," the minion said, reddening slightly.

"Well, get me some!" Garrick exclaimed. "I'm underfed, weak, and famished!" Suddenly, King Errold's eyelids started drooping unexpectedly. Errold's head lolled to one side and he started snoring, his mouth hanging open.

"What the—" Garrick began. He was shocked to see Queen Hortensia also fall into slumber, with her unusually large nose in the stinky tofu and her short, reddish hair in the jelly dish. Garrick himself began to feel drowsy, and soon he was peacefully snoring like the others around him.

When Garrick woke up, he was astonished and also quite **mortified** to find that he was laid on a simple straw pallet, in a dim, dusty room with a thatch roof.

"WHAT IS THE MEANING OF THIS!!!" he shouted. "WHOEVER STARTED THIS SILLY PRANK IS—" He could no longer hear even his own words, due to the fact that his voice had degenerated into sobs. When seven fairies flew in the open window, he was so amazed that he stopped bawling immediately.

"Now, boy, you'll be quiet!" the fairy in front (who was indeed Wyddfa), rapped him on the shoulder with a long wand that seemed to have formed from midair. The other fairies clustered curiously around Wyddfa to have a look at this Prince Garrick (although they had done so many times from afar).

"We know," Ailyra began, very grandly, "that you are the Prince Garrick, heir to the throne of Jarrod, unless your parents suddenly decide to abdicate in favor of Regan of Northwick whom none of us would like as a possible candidate. We also know," and here she gave Garrick a piercing stare, "that you have been very wicked to your faithful minions, and ungrateful for your uncalculated wealth."

"And we are aware of the fact that you would make an evil ruler if you were allowed to rule. We are going to change you, and you must listen to us in every way," Anya added sternly.

"Let us begin now," Miria said brightly, and tapping Garrick's fine clothes with her wand, she muttered a word of command and suddenly Garrick was not wearing a shimmering satin tunic but a filthy plain wotton (wool and cotton mixed together, only for commoners and peasants) tunic, a worn brown leather belt, and uncomfortable wooden clogs.

"You must make all the food you eat, wash all the dishes you use, and clean up after yourself. You will harvest the crops and cut the wheat with the other farmers. You must be kind to others and charitable to the less fortunate," Wyddfa told Garrick seriously. Garrick could only stare at her open-mouthed.

That night Garrick had no dinner. He threw a fit after the fairies Andromeda and Arimthea reminded him that he would have to make his own food. That night he cried silently, tears running down his already tear-streaked face.

"They shall be sorry they did this to me!" Garrick had exclaimed, pounding his fists on anything within his reach.

The next day the fairies forced Garrick to join the farmers in the yearly wheat harvest. Although he had a sharp scythe with which to cut the wheat, he cut with much difficulty and the farmers sniggered at his every minor mistake. They found it particularly amusing when he dropped his scythe, horrified at the corpulent slug that was sliming its way over the handle. The fairies (invisible and inaudible to the other folk) made the slug vanish with a quick charm and hastily flew away. Garrick dragged his tool up to the next stock of wheat and clumsily chopped it down.

"Not like that, laddie, like *this*," one farmer said braggingly, lifting up his scythe with one skillful movement and cutting a large bunch of wheat.

"I know!" Garrick cried with frustration, attempting again. He was cuffed soundly on the ear, by a ruddy, red-faced man.

"Now don't let me hear you talkin' like that again, disrespectful youth," the man said, frowning. "You're not of their stock, I can see. New boy?"

Garrick, who had no idea what the man meant, burst into tears, dropped the scythe, and ran as fast as he could back to the hut.

Wyddfa, Miria, and Ailyra were waiting for him. Each held a basket full of different colored berries.

"You must wash the bugs and dirt off of these berries," Wyddfa said sternly. "Then you may eat them." Garrick was horrified to see that each berry was covered with particles of dirt, little pill bugs and ants crawled along the round surface of the fruit.

"But—" Garrick began.

"There is a well of clear water one mile away from here in the village," Wyddfa said sharply. "We shall now leave you." And with a flick of her wand, she and the other fairies had disappeared.

Garrick lay on his straw pallet crying for a few minutes, but he soon realized he was famished and decided to take the baskets to the well. After all, hadn't he looked upon the village women when they washed the fruit? It was simple—just duck the basket underwater and all of the dirt and bugs would float away. This plan was foiled by a sign that read: THOSE WHO LET DIRT FLOW IN THIS WELL WILL BE PUNISHED. So he ended up hauling a heavy bucket of water to the hut, where he dipped the berries in the water, sunk them, and rubbed them. Finally all of the dirt and bugs were gone.

"Now you may eat!" Wyddfa cried, suddenly appearing at the window and quite frightening Garrick. Miria, who was directly behind her, carried a small block of moldy goat's cheese.

"NO! I shan't eat that, I shan't, and I shan't!" Garrick wailed, knocking the cheese out the window. Miria retrieved it at once.

"Ungrateful little wretch," Wyddfa said menacingly, moving dangerously closer to Garrick's face. And for the first time in his life, Garrick was slapped hard on the face.

"WAAAA!" Garrick cried like a baby. He rolled over to one side, knocking over a crude wooden stool and a rattling oxcart.

"He needs to be taught," Miria pleaded to Wyddfa.

"The problem with you, Miria, is that you are too soft. Use your inner eye. Can you see what will happen if this boy is allowed to rule without changing his ways?" Wyddfa asked sharply, suddenly turning back to Miria and brandishing her wand in the frightened fairy's face. Miria nodded slowly, backing towards the wall.

"Good," Wyddfa said, her black eyes flashing. "For if he is allowed to continue his ways, you will not even exist as a legend." From the corner, Garrick wailed again.

"Be quiet, wench!" Ailyra shouted, her sparkling wand transforming into a sharp, glinting sword. Garrick screamed in fright.

Wyddfa silenced him with a hand to his mouth. Although the fairy's hand looked small and delicate, Garrick felt as if he had been hit by a heavy plank of wood.

"If you refuse to do this, I shall enlist you as an apprentice to the village's baker," Ailyra said coolly, and right before Garrick's eyes, her sword (or wand, Garrick could never tell) disappeared, and she took the form of a regular village woman. She wore a long apron which was much stained, and a blue-and-white checkered kerchief was tied about her head. Wyddfa nodded her approval, and followed after Ailyra and Garrick, invisible. Miria stayed in the hut.

The village baker was a plump little man with a small round head. His bald top shone in the bright light of his hot bakery, and his hands were always covered in flour and bits of dough. Sugar clung to his stained apron, and salt dotted his patched brown shoes. He always took in as many apprentices as his small house would hold, and was overjoyed to see Ailyra and Garrick.

"Come in, come in, quite charmed to see you both, I suspect you'll wanting a sample of my new blueberry bread?" the baker said merrily, already reaching for a plate piled high with small blueberry bread squares.

"Yes, of course," Ailyra said, taking one piece and popping it into her mouth. "Delicious. I assume you would be wanting a new apprentice, ever since your old one—Curver, I believe—left your shop."

The baker's merry smile faded as he said grimly, "Ah, Curver. He became the leader of a shady gang who terrorized the shops at night. Came to a bad end, that one—drowned in the fishpond." He made an effort to laugh. Garrick's face paled.

"But of course you will accept this boy? I believe he's been pampered by the…high society, one might call it, so I need him to learn the basics of your trade," Ailyra said, fixing her stare on the baker.

"Yes, of course, my dear!" the baker cried, jolly once more. "Yes, I just need a fee of about twenty coins." Ailyra reached into her apron pocket and pulled out a small pouch.

"Here you are," she said, dumping the glittering gold contents into the baker's hands. His eyes widened as he stared at the coins.

"Of course, of course! What is your name, anyways?" And he peered at Garrick.

"Garrick," Garrick said between sobs.

"Homesickness, I expect," the baker said **briskly**. "Not that it's really a problem; I expect I'll fix him up in a week or two."

"Good. Now, just to make sure, here's an extra ten coins…" Ailyra poured more coins into the amazed man's hands. "Just be careful…"

When Garrick had wiped away all his tears on his tunic's frayed sleeve, the baker led him away to a small, hot room in the back of the bakery. Wood was blazing under a small brick oven, which contained three loaves of rye bread. Great amounts of sticky batter clung to the sides of a green mixing bowl, and yet there was still a sufficient amount inside the bowl.

"Just shake these poppies into this batter while I stir," said the baker, rolling up his sleeve. He took a wooden spoon and began to stir the mixture. Garrick saw a small tin pail labeled "POPPIES" next to the oven, so he grabbed it and poured the contents in the batter.

"No, no, no!" the baker cried, wringing his hands. "Not like that! Slowly, slowly, pour it in! And now I shall have to buy another packet from Monstraue's, how expensive!" Muttering on and on about the **incompetence** of new apprentices, the baker flung the batter out the window.

"Call me 'sir' when you address me, anyhow," the baker said stiffly, shaking his head as he stared at the wasted dough.

"You!" he finally cried to Garrick, who trembled. "Get me a few cups of flour from that bin there—and make sure you don't spill any!"

Garrick, not wanting to face the wrath of "sir" again, took the cup that the red-faced baker handed him and scooped a fair amount from the bin which he lugged out of the cupboard.

"Good, now," the baker said, evidently pleased. "Just put this much into this bowl, add a biddle bit of yeast…just a pinch, here we go…crack an egg or two, the ladies like it that way…" Garrick had a hard time following these instructions, but he did as best as he could. The baker stood near, often peering over through his cracked spectacles.

"There, that's good," the baker said when Garrick had stirred for at least fifteen minutes. "Put it in here, put a damp towel over it, and leave it to do its magic!"

"What do you mean?" Garrick asked, puzzled.

"Rise, of course!" the baker cried. "Now, to take the loaves out of the oven!" He took a long, paddle-shaped stick from the corner and cautiously stuck it in the oven. It **emerged** with a golden-brown loaf.

"Perfect! Just smear that with butter, will you?"

"Of course," bragged Garrick. "I can do anything." Just then a sparrow flew in the open window, twittered, and pooped right on Garrick's silky golden curls. Garrick yelped, tossing himself about and trying to rid himself of the dung.

"Here," the baker said quickly, pouring a pail of cold water over Garrick's head. Garrick yelped again, jumping up and jamming his head in the pail. He tugged on the pail, quite angry.

"Well, here's the butter," the baker said airily. "Just smear it heavily over these two loaves. I'm getting the last loaf out." Garrick took a block of butter from the cupboard and smashed it into the bread. The butter immediately melted, drenching the bread in oil.

"Do it delicately there, boy," the baker said absentmindedly, turning around. "And put some more on..." Humming a tune, he took the third loaf from the oven and dropped it on a plate.

"Oh, gold fig trees," Garrick muttered angrily under his breath as he rubbed the butter on the hot loaf. "This is a kitchen maid's work."

"Finally, you're done," the baker said, sighing. "There's a lot of work to put up with—what's that?" The sound of tingling bells rang in Garrick's ears. A young girl, with a snub of a nose and small, pursed lips entered, her mother following close behind. For some reason Garrick felt as if he knew her. It was possible, actually, for she was attired in fine crimson velvet.

"Oh dear," the baker said in a low voice. Garrick watched as he ran to the front of the shop and hastily hung a "CLOSED" sign on the door.

"Er, I'm very sorry, madam, but these are not business hours," the baker said, looking rather flustered.

"I just need one butter loaf," the woman said in a shrill, high-pitched voice. "Four coins."

"Fine, fine!" the baker exclaimed, handing the crisp golden brown loaf to the woman. "Now please leave!" Garrick suddenly knew why the people had seemed familiar to him. The girl was his second cousin's half-sister! They had only been introduced once, the cause of Garrick's confusion.

Morning's bright yellow sun faded into somewhat darker orange, and the heat slowly lowered. Garrick shivered as a breeze blew in the window.

"Looks like we're done for today, then," the baker said, glancing outside.

"Yes, sir," Garrick said, remembering just in time to call the baker "sir."

"C'mon," the baker said, throwing his purse of jingling coins over his shoulder and leading Garrick out across the cobblestone street.

Months passed. Garrick improved in his baking skills, and soon was at the level of a Master Baker. When the baker was sick or had other obligations, Garrick ran the shop. Gossip ran around the village about "the wee fellow who runs that bread shop." Even the Grand Magistrate heard word of it. Although Garrick had learned to be a responsible baker, he still believed that all others were his inferiors. At night he would lie on his pallet and wonder why he had ever ended up with such a common lot.

One early night as Garrick was rounding the corner to the baker's familiar house, Wyddfa suddenly appeared in front of him.

"Next," she told Garrick, "after you get some sleep, we will be going to the stonemason." Garrick slept for about nine hours. He joined Wyddfa, who was waiting at the hut, and walked for about a quarter-mile. When the two emerged from the pathway, they found themselves staring at an impressive stone structure. A crude wooden door was attached crookedly to the building by three leather hinges. Inside, a tall, slender man with hairy arms was hammering at a gray stone.

"Mory!" Wyddfa cried at once. "I have brought you an apprentice!"

"I want ten coins, a pig, and four figs," Mory said, putting down his hammer and gazing at Wyddfa.

"Your wish is granted," Wyddfa said. With a loud squeal, a pig walked in, followed by four rolling figs. Ten coins dropped from a cracked lantern. Garrick stared open-mouthed.

"So?" Wyddfa asked, stomping her foot impatiently. "Are you taking him or not?"

"Yes, yes, of course," Mory said, hastily pocketing the figs and the coins. The hog, as if by mental command, ran into a small pigpen to join the other pigs. Mory took a small knife from his belt and handed it to Garrick, along with the leather sheath.

"There you are," Mory said to Garrick. "It shows that you're part of the trade."

"Good!" Wyddfa cried. "Well, I'll leave you two to do your things."

When Garrick's eyes finally adjusted to the dim light of Mory's workshop, the old stonemason showed him various types of rocks and interesting gemstones.

"Quartz—very popular with the ladies. The boys like to use it for friendship stones," Mory began.

"What are friendship stones, sir?" Garrick asked. Mory snorted.

"Don't call me sir, Mr. Know-It-All," he said, turning to face Garrick. "And I'm surprised that you don't know what an F.S. is. To show their friendship, one boy will give another boy a quartz stone, probably carved in one crude shape or another."

"Oh," Garrick said, although he hadn't really been listening.

"Ah, topaz!" Mory cried, taking a rough blue-green rock from behind his anvil. "Used especially for good luck amulets and healing potions!"

"Er, I thought that amulets were…rather out of date," Garrick said, squirming uncomfortably.

"Out of date! We are still using them today!" Mory glared at Garrick.

"Oh then," Garrick said, not being able to think of anything else to say.

"Opal!" Mory cried, holding up a tiny, round gem. "Used especially for bridal gowns and veils! Symbolizing purity, it is also put in women's rings." A knock on the open door startled both Garrick and Mory.

"Come in, come in!" Mory cried, quickly shoving the stones behind the anvil. A tall man with bulging eyeballs and a large egghead entered. His patch of yellow hair flopped about as he walked.

"Mory," he slurred, taking a gulp of grog from a cracked flask, "the old bonesetter needs a sharp rock."

"I'll charge ye later, Olaf," Mory said as he threw the man a pointed gray rock. "Just be sure to send Sorrel with four coins!"

"Thanky." Olaf gulped down some more grog and ran out of the shop, teetering on his reed sandals.

"And now I must show you how to carve a stone," Mory said, winking at Garrick. "Take out your knife." The boy unsheathed his tool, staring at it.

"We want to start with big rocks first. They're the easiest," Mory said wisely, taking a large quartz from behind the anvil and scraping at its side. Soon it had a sharpened point. "You try."

Garrick took a large topaz and attempted to cut it. In one fleeting moment, the knife slipped on the rock and Garrick barely pulled his hand away in time.

"Dolt! Why in the name of Jesus did you have to ruin a perfectly fine stone!" Mory shouted angrily, examining Garrick's finger. Finally satisfied, he took the topaz and made a small chip in the corner of the rock.

"See?" Mory asked snidely. "That's how you do it, of course, if you have the knowledge."

The next day Garrick was most unpleasantly awoken by the sound of heavy stomping. He rubbed his eyes and looked around.

"You, boy!" A soldier in a blue tunic pointed at Garrick with his pike. "Do you know anything about the whereabouts of Mory the Stonemason, hereby accused of theft?"

"He should be in his room," Garrick said stupidly.

"To his room, then!" the soldier cried. Garrick could only stare as the haggard stonemason was dragged down the hallway bound with thick splintery ropes.

After Garrick had dressed, he was not quite sure what to do. He had seen Mory taken to the village prison, a dark, dirty, and sinister place. Although Garrick could have gone back to the hut, he felt as if something were tugging at him to take Mory out of jail. Garrick reached into his tunic's pocket, unaware that he had done so, and was surprised to find that he had a great quantity of money. The coins he pulled out were of a strange bronze variety and were inscribed with ancient runes, but he had no time to ponder their origins. He ran down the hill to the heavily guarded prison, where he a surly-looking soldier met him at the gate.

"Your pass?" the soldier asked in a bored tone.

"I have enough money to take the wrongly accused stonemason out of prison," Garrick said, stiffening.

"Hold out your coins," the soldier commanded. Garrick threw the coins at the soldier's feet.

"I will fetch him for you," the soldier said. Moments later, Mory emerged from the dimness of the bars. He looked around, as if expecting to see someone, until finally his glance rested on Garrick.

"Why, Garrick!" Mory cried with amazement. "It was you who took me out of jail! A former apprentice whom I disliked set me up to be taken away for a crime I did not commit. I am surprised that you would bother about an old man who was thought to be a thief and a robber!" Although Garrick was staring down at his clogs, he could have sworn that he saw the fairies for one second flying above.

The days passed. Finally Garrick won his Certificate of Mastership and left the stonemason. Anya accompanied him to a small cottage on the outskirts of the village.

"This is the village school," Anya said. "Here you will be the teacher's assistant, doing small chores and the like."

"Aren't you coming with me?" Garrick stared at Anya.

"The teacher is expecting you. She'll know," Anya said briskly, disappearing with a wave of her hand. Garrick sighed and trudged up the hill. He carefully opened the creaky door and peered around the cottage. A dim lantern hung from rotting beams, its flickering flame letting off rays of light. Crude wooden desks and benches were jammed closely together. There was hardly any room to walk in the cluttered classroom. At a larger desk in the front of the room, a young woman was busy scribbling on a sheet of **vellum**. She looked up as Garrick entered.

"Ah, Garrick!" the teacher cried. "I'm very glad you're here. My name is Eleanor. Please call me Ella."

Garrick stared down at his shoes.

"Just begin with stocking the fireplace up with fresh wood, sweep the floor, and clean the desks." Eleanor looked pleadingly at Garrick.

"Oh, er, of course," Garrick said, rather confused.

"You can begin with sweeping the floor," Eleanor said brightly, handing him a broom. It took only a few minutes, so Garrick piled the fireplace up with wood and lit it. Next came the cleaning of the desks. The boys and girls tended to be untidy, so Garrick busied himself by collecting the textbooks which were scattered across the benches and desks.

"Could you please help me sort the books out?" Eleanor sighed. "I'm afraid the children made rather a mess." Garrick nodded and brought the books over to Eleanor's desk.

"Let's see...this is Cory's borrowed edition...Willie's...ah, this belongs in the cupboard," Eleanor murmured, putting a thick brown book in a small wobbling cupboard. Two shabby textbooks, labeled "Cory's" and "Will" were placed aside. Eleanor put two sheets of vellum on a desk (two students would share one desk), two quills, and an inkstand in between. She did the same on the other desks. When Garrick had finished the rest of the job, a loud whoop was heard outside the cottage.

"Oh dear," Eleanor said softly. "The older boys are coming back from the harvest." A large, husky boy ran in the cottage.

"Mornin', Miss Ella!" he called out. Eleanor blushed.

"Tayme, this is my new assistant, Garrick," Eleanor said quietly. Tayme stared at Garrick.

"So—would ya like to come out for a round of Hot Potato?" Tayme asked, grinning.

"No, actually, could you please tell the other boys and girls to come in?" Eleanor cut in quickly. Tayme nodded and ran to the entrance, hollering,

"Hey, fellows! Time to come in!" There was a great shout, a stomping, and a stampede of children pouring in. Little rosy-cheeked boys immediately jumped in the back seats, near the **hearth** if possible. The girls ran as fast as their long smocks would allow, always choosing the most well-lit desks. Eleanor raised her hand for silence. Not a single word was heard.

"I would like to introduce my new assistant, Garrick," Eleanor said firmly, placing a hand on Garrick's shoulder. "If you have trouble and I am with another pupil, you may ask him for help." A few of the younger boys squirmed.

"Today we will start on Arithmetic," Eleanor said, striding forward. "For the older boys: begin with 2. 4 x 5. 0. Younger boys: start with two plus eight." There was a hasty dipping of quills and a scribbling on vellum.

"Garrick, please collect the answers," Eleanor whispered. He swaggered forward, swept the sheets off with one quick move, and handed them to Eleanor.

"Willie!" Eleanor cried, looking up at a small, curly red-haired boy. He bit his lip.

"Your answer is wrong," Garrick said superiorly. Willie hung his head, staring down at the rotting wood of his desk.

"Garrick, why did you have to do that!?" Eleanor hissed. To Willie she said kindly, "You're just off by one. The answer is ten." The little boy smiled.

The class ran on. Writing was next. A young girl broke into tears at the prospect of having to write one page about life in the village.

"Now, Sorrel dear, don't cry," Eleanor said, glaring at Garrick, who was sniggering.

"But—but—" Sorrel sobbed, wiping her puffy eyes as a wet drop landed on her wrinkled vellum.

"Would you like to write yours on the chalkboard?" Eleanor asked generously, handing Sorrel a stub of chalk.

"Y-yes," Sorrel said happily, drying her tears immediately. Garrick sat down in Eleanor's chair, bored.

"Garrick!" Eleanor cried sharply as she noticed the boy out of the corner of her gray eyes.

"I was just sitting down," Garrick said, irritated.

"Well, perhaps you could have been more courteous by asking me first," Eleanor said in a huff. "Please move." Garrick rose haughtily from the chair, barely glancing at Eleanor as she resumed her place.

Reading the essays was great fun. Eleanor invited some of the best authors to present their writings in the front of the cottage, while Garrick read excerpts out of other ones at Eleanor's desk. Garrick embarrassed many of the writers by laughing out loud.

"Here, listen to this," Garrick guffawed, and said in the most snobby voice he could manage, "Today was bad. We had too do boring things. Ellynor was mean. Schol is hard." The writer reddened.

"Garrick, will you please stop it?!" Eleanor's voice was on fire now. The schoolchildren backed away in their seats.

"Fine, fine. Just a bit of a joke, that one," Garrick said, smirking superiorly.

Class finally ended at six o'clock. Eleanor scolded Garrick for teasing the children and then stomped off. When everyone was gone, Anya appeared.

"You did badly, Garrick," she said sternly.

"The whole lot of those children are commoners and peasants! Why should I, a noble prince, pay any attention to those inferior peoples?" Garrick shouted.

"They are not your inferiors," Anya said firmly, pressing a hand on Garrick's shoulders. "They are superior to you in many ways."

The remark stung. Garrick kicked at a rock, crying angrily, "They have nothing to teach me! They are not of high birth!"

"Watch your words," Anya said quietly. Garrick could not sleep the entire night.

The next day Garrick was polite and did not talk much. He felt guilty as the children stared at him piercingly, and knew it was entirely his fault.

Day by day, he steadily improved, until finally he gained Eleanor's trust and the schoolchildren's friendship.

Garrick's days as a teacher's assistant finally ended, and Miria told him that he was to be apprenticed to an herbalist.

"She knows what she is doing," Anya added hurriedly. "Just don't try to mess up her collection of potions." Garrick frowned. An herbalist, who was probably bound to be superstitious! How low was he going to have to sink?

"Her name is Glenn," Miria continued. "She is learned in the lore of plants and herbs."

"Let us go," the young fairy said finally, taking Garrick's arm and leading him out of the hut to the village.

Glenn's Healing Herbs was a small, rickety shop with broken windows and a **ramshackle** porch. The owner, Glenn herself, was a hunched-over, withered lady who leaned heavily on a gnarled stick.

"Pleased to see you, pleased to see you!" she croaked merrily, straightening her short red kerchief from which one long braid emerged. The brown shawl which hung to her waist was patched and faded, but it held the sweet aroma of many flowers. A pair of cracked spectacles hung crookedly on her brown nose.

"Here is your new apprentice," Miria said, gently pushing Garrick into Glenn's warm arms.

"Good to meet you, my boy!" Glenn cried, hugging Garrick tightly. "Now come into my shop…" Garrick barely noticed Miria disappearing.

As he entered, Garrick stared in awe at the bubbling flasks stored on the top shelves. Jars full of green, slimy stuff were stored in the bottom shelves, while jugs full of different-colored liquids dotted the middle shelves.

"Ah, you're interested in my Herbal Essences, eh?" Glenn asked croakily, hobbling over towards the shelves. Garrick took a step back.

"Er," he said, not sure of what exactly to say.

"Now don't be afraid of old Glenn, m'dear, I just need you to help me get a few ingredients for my newest potion," Glenn said, waving a small piece of yellowed parchment in Garrick's face. "You'll find these in the Forgotten Forest." Garrick snatched the paper and dashed out of the herb shop. He wasn't *exactly* sure where the Forest was, but it simply wouldn't do to let on that he was less knowledgeable than his subjects by asking Glenn.

It was easy to find his way around the little village. Garrick knew where the church was by its great bronze bells, and the dairy by the mooing of the cows. At the edge of the village, two paths led into large, brambly thickets. Garrick guessed that the first was the Fairies' Forest, it being bright and merry. The other was dark and sinister, with glinting yellow eyes that were barely discernible peeking out from every single tree. He gulped, somehow knowing that it was the Forgotten Forest.

As he entered the Forest, Garrick looked down at the list which he was clutching so tightly. A messy scrawl read:

Rootworm (don't step on!!!)

Laurel Leaves

Maple Bark & Sap

Spider Web Thread

Handful Dark Dirt

Three Pinecones

Quart Stream Water

Garrick had no idea what rootworm was, why in the world the old herbalist wanted spider web thread or dark dirt, and most annoyingly he had a mosquito bite on his foot—a most inconvenient place.

"Oh Hellgates," he muttered, pushing back a bush of thorns and crawling through the undergrowth. Long, gnarled roots emerged from the ground as the circle of trees grew thicker and thicker. Garrick began searching for some of the ingredients. He found sap and bark easily enough, and took a few pinecones from a frightened squirrel. However, Garrick had no idea what rootworm was. He was about to turn back in the direction of the stream when he tripped on a hard root. The root, as if it were a snake, slithered slowly to Garrick and coiled its body around the boy's foot. He lay transfixed with fear, unable to move. The pain grew sharper and sharper. Suddenly Garrick regained his senses and yelped. Thinking that he heard an answering cry in the distance he shouted again, reassured.

"Heeeeeelp!" Garrick cried. The villagers, led by Garrick's voice, hastily crawled to the spot where he was trapped. A young redheaded girl kneeled down and drew a flashing knife from her thick leather belt. She slashed wildly at the root, also ripping Garrick's tunic to shreds.

"How'd you get trapped by a rootworm, foolish youth?" she asked, staring at him with dark black eyes.

"I had no idea that this fairly innocent-looking plant would harm me," Garrick said, irritated.

"You had no idea!" the girl cried. "To think that you wandered the path of the Forgotten Forest not knowing what lay ahead!"

"Come, Dianna!" Garrick turned his head as a sharp voice called out.

"Well, you might as well get up," Dianna said, tugging on Garrick's arm. He pushed himself up, very annoyed. As the villagers began to drift away, Garrick gathered the rest of the things on the list (excluding the rootworm).

Garrick burst into the dark herb shop at about midnight. The herbalist limped down from a wobbling bunk.

"I did think that you'd never come out of that dreadful wood," she said crossly, lighting a taper and opening a cupboard. "What do you have?" Garrick put the ingredients on the table. Glenn scanned them.

"You're missing rootworm!" she cried shrilly. "Didn't I clearly state I wanted rootworm!"

"I almost got killed by a rootworm and you want me to get some!" Garrick shouted with anger, smashing his fist on the table.

"Oh dear," Glenn said, softening somewhat. "I didn't think that it would go to that point. I must check your leg." Garrick rolled up his ragged pants. Large red welts glowed in the candlelight.

"Deary me," Glenn muttered, taking a jug of ruby wine from one of the shelves. "Drink this. It'll help you sleep. The operation I'm going to perform is bound to be painful. Hopefully you won't feel it." She shoved a teaspoonful of the bitter alcohol into Garrick's mouth. He began to feel drowsy, and his eyelids drooped.

"There, that's it!" Glenn encouraged him. "Just try to make

yourself go to sleep!" Although Garrick's fingers and legs felt numb and asleep, his mind still worked as actively as ever. As Glenn wrapped a damp bandage around his leg with grains of crushed popperwart, he imagined the fairies hovering above. While he imagined this, Glenn tightened the bandage and tied more lengths of damp linen around his leg. Then she made a small cut in Garrick's skin with a rather dull knife, split the cut open, and rubbed some strong wine around and in the injury. When the wine was almost all gone, Glenn rubbed a small quantity of lard around the cut.

"There, that should disinfect his blood," Glenn muttered, unrolling his bandage. The welts were barely **discernable**, much to Glenn's satisfaction. Garrick awoke just when Glenn was finished with the operation.

"Am I dead?" Garrick asked sleepily, sluggishly lifting an arm.

"No, of course not, you great sluggard!" Glenn cried, laughing. "I just finished the operation, and you're fine!" As Garrick drifted into his peaceful slumber, Glenn wearily climbed up to her bunk.

The next day was bright and sunny. Boys played games in the cobblestone village square, while girls sat skipping stones and chattering by the millpond. Glenn sent Garrick to the market to buy some rosewater and hibiscus petals, as well as four carrots, a block of cheese, and some fresh fish.

"The fishwife, Martha Barlyns, is on good terms with me for curing her babe once of the fever," the old herbalist explained briskly, pressing a few coins into Garrick's palm. "Just tell her my name and ask for some fresh trout." Garrick nodded, took the basket, and dashed out the door.

"Oh and don't forget I need a length of wool!" Glenn shouted from the doorway. Garrick waved to indicate he had heard and ran along the path.

The market was a busy, bustling place. Garrick stared in awe at the sharp, shiny knives a sword smith proudly displayed. He sniffed the sweet-smelling saffron and peered into the large billowing pavilions. With a sigh, Garrick remembered his duty and turned away from the grand pavilion.

Garrick's first stop was at the weaver's. Katie Webster was a sharp, brisk lady, and operated her business quickly and conveniently. As Garrick had feared, she was not at all happy to see the boy at closing time.

"Name your price!" Katie snapped, shoving a long roll of **drab** gray fabric into Garrick's face. Not quite understanding what the weaver meant, Garrick stammered,

"Er, I have about eight coins…" Katie stomped her foot.

"Not that, dolt!" she shouted, waving her fist. "Name a suitable amount of money which you can give to me in return for this wool!"

"Oh, er, t-three c-coins then," Garrick stuttered. Katie grabbed the coins, biting them to make sure they were genuine, and scribbled something on a pad of paper.

"Your receipt," she said irritably, handing the paper over. "Now go, and Lord help you if I catch you here again!" Garrick scrambled away with the wool as fast as his legs could carry him and stumbled onward to the fishwife. Plump and ruddy faced with her short hair tucked up into her brown cap; Martha Barlyns was just as Garrick had imagined her.

"Ah, what can I help you with today?" she cried out to Garrick as he arrived in front of the booth.

"Please—I'm here on Glenn's orders—I need some fresh trout," Garrick said, panting. It was the first time he had ever said please, or at least the first time he remembered doing it.

"Glenn, the old lunatic!" the fishwife exclaimed, throwing back her head and letting out a roaring laugh. "Of course you're her new apprentice! Here you go, little one!" She handed Garrick a fairly large fish wrapped in thin paper. He accepted the package gratefully, waving good-bye to Martha as her dim shape faded into the distance.

Getting the hibiscus petals and rosewater was not nearly so easy. Garrick walked about a quarter mile before he finally found the right booth. The man who was selling the rosewater and petals was extremely grumpy, it being almost nighttime, and agreed to sell Garrick a half-cup of rosewater only after the boy had given him five coins. As Garrick turned around to look at the hibiscus petals, he realized that he had no more coins. The seller **leered** at him.

"Don't have any more coins, do you?" he asked, advancing dangerously closer to Garrick. "I suppose you don't want to give coins to me?" Suddenly, the seller pounced on Garrick, ripping Garrick's tunic.

"Heeeeeeeeeelp!" Garrick shouted, waving his arms and legs wildly. A crowd of village men ran towards Garrick, brandishing pitchforks, burning torches, and even planks of wood. Women and children cautiously emerged from the small huts, the women jumping back when they realized they were standing in the midst of a brawl.

"Yaaaaah!" the little boys cried, running out of the doorways, banging heads with porridge pots and hot pans. The small girls, their skirts tucked up, led great ferocious dogs to the battle. The animals barred their teeth, clawing madly at the man who had attacked Garrick. Finally the attacker was dragged off to the jail and Garrick trudged off towards Glenn's shop.

Glenn's face was very solemn as Garrick told her the story.

"I am afraid that the man you encountered was none other than a low-down thug and robber," she said, applying a **poultice** of ground orange zest to Garrick's arm. "You must be cautious around the market."

"I—" Garrick began angrily, attempting to rise. Glenn gently pushed him down.

"You must have rest," she said quietly, pulling a thick quilt over Garrick's shivering body.

The next morning was miserable. The sky was covered in a blanket of fog. Gloom hung over the village. The first raindrops were heard in early morning, plunging Old Joe's bonfire into smoke. Garrick was amazed at the number of ill and wounded folk who trudged through Glenn's doorway. The old herbalist busied Garrick with little tasks, like measuring the ruby wine, wrapping bandages, and handing out elderberry cordial to reduce the pain. One old man, who was carried in by his wife, was badly burnt on his foot, having accidentally fallen into a fire. A deep gash ran through his chest; blood spurted out as Glenn examined it gravely.

"No tonic shall cure this wound," the herbalist said grimly. "The least we can do is let him die in peace."

"No!" Garrick cried. He bit his lip as Glenn glanced back at him.

"Garrick is right," Glenn said finally. "We must save this man."

"H-his n-name is J-Jonathan," a woman said between sobs. "M-my h-husband."

"Leah!" Glenn exclaimed. "Don't be so unhappy. We'll do something, I'm sure…" Her voice trailed off. Garrick peered up at the shelves. He carefully lowered a jar full of crushed pearl. He stood on his toes and carefully lowered a jug half-full of rosewater. Mixing the two together, he added olive oil, rose hips, and dragonseed powder. *I really hope this will work,* Garrick thought as he poured a pint of buttermilk into the mixture for good luck. *I've watched Glenn make her remedies...*

"Glenn," Garrick said, tapping the herbalist on the shoulder. "I've made something I think might help Jonathan." Glenn looked at Garrick's hopeful face.

"I suppose you could try rubbing it on the wound," she said, sighing. "I must get to the other patients."

Garrick carefully applied the lotion onto the moaning man's bloody chest. As if by magic, Jonathan's skin slowly closed up around the wound, leaving no trace of the injury but a few trails of blood. Garrick was hit with the enormity of what he had just done.

"You must be an angel sent by the Lord!" Jonathan's astonished wife cried, falling to her knees and kissing the hem of Garrick's tunic. "No other mortal could cure my Jonathan!"

"Garrick, I free you from your apprenticeship," Glenn cried, striking Garrick's shoulder with her wrinkled finger. "You have shown me that you are a worthy healer!" There was a great cheer from the crowd and the clinking of glasses. Men and women alike toasted to Garrick's future, while Garrick stood, surprised, in the middle of the room.

The Knights of the Cavalry were the ancient unit guarding the Magistrate and his family. Andromeda, who was Wyddfa's daughter, led Garrick to the thick stone walls of the fort, which encircled the village.

"You will be training as a squire," Andromeda said softly. "I trust that you will be a loyal companion to the Knights." With a quick wave of her hand and a coquettish smile, Andromeda leapt into the air and disappeared.

After waiting for a few minutes, Garrick bit his lip, walked forward, and knocked timidly on the magnificent, towering wooden gates.

"Friend or foe?" a deep voice called, although Garrick could already hear the unlatching of the gate.

"I am a friend!" Garrick called back. The gates swung open on their shiny iron hinges. Garrick gasped at what he saw. Tall knights dressed in full chain armor and wielding gleaming bronze lances rode on majestic war stallions. Glinting helmets were set on their heads, with red plumes sweeping over their necks. Captain Vincent Mercivelle rode in front of them, outshining them all in his gold chain armor and silver helmet.

"Lad!" the Captain called. "Be you Garrick?" Garrick bowed his head.

"Yes, I am Garrick," he said, shielding his eyes from the glint of Mercivelle's lance.

"You have been given to me as a squire," the captain continued **pompously**, "and although you are young of age, I am confident that you shall serve the Magistrate and the Cavalry dutifully. To begin with you must take an oath of allegiance along with my men." A knight dismounted from his horse and kneeled on one leg. The rest of the Cavalry followed suit, until finally Garrick was surrounded by kneeling men. Feeling that he was supposed to do likewise, Garrick dropped awkwardly on his knee.

"On the Stone of Sir Modyford, I swear to serve the Magistrate, my Captain, and my comrades as long as I live, and if I betray my company may the Lord crush me dead under his mighty hand," the Knights recited, with Garrick murmuring as much as he could hear.

"Rise!" the Captain thundered. The Knights rose, Garrick following suit.

"Garrick," the Captain said, turning to the trembling boy. "Recite the oath by yourself."

"I—I c-can't, sir," Garrick stammered, shaking.

"He cannot!" Mercivelle roared. "He cannot! He is a simpleton among wise men!" The Knights jeered and guffawed with their captain, not daring to do otherwise. A few gave Garrick sympathetic looks, but that was about all.

When at last the general clamor had died down, Vincent raised his hand, which was sheathed in a white silk glove.

"There is a youngling amongst us," he said, more softly this time. "We must all take part in teaching him. He must learn the way of the warrior. But he must start, as I did," and here Mercivelle looked pointedly at the crowd, "with humble beginnings."

That night Garrick could hardly sleep at all. He tossed in his narrow bunk, occasionally banging his head on the hard wooden sides. He slept with the rest of the squires, who were all at least twelve or thirteen. Two particularly large squires reached over Garrick's bunk, their piggy eyes glinting menacingly, and snatched Garrick's flickering candle. With a cry of alarm, Garrick jumped up from his bunk. The Knight Sentry immediately ran in, and finding Garrick out of bed, cuffed Garrick soundly and retreated to his position.

The next morning Garrick overslept and was given nothing but a small bit of soggy toast for breakfast. As he passed through the drill line he was taunted by the squires and scolded sternly by an officer. Their first lesson, it seemed, was based on the art of the sword.

"You must hold the sword just like *this*," Officer Alan said pompously, displaying his "perfect" grip on the sword's shining hilt.

"But—sir—I don't have a sword," Garrick said timidly, as the squires leered.

"Use this one," Alan said carelessly, tossing him a rusty blade with a broken hilt. "Now, let us continue…who can tell me who Sir Thomas Modyford **impersonated** during the War of Eighteen Battles?" Immediately the crowd of squires raised their hands. Garrick took a step back.

"Garrick!" Alan cried sharply. "Tell me, whom did he impersonate?"

"I—I'm n-not sure, sir," Garrick stuttered awkwardly.

"Why, fool, he impersonated Launitnoc Maladies!" Alan bellowed. "In the Battle of Continual Seidalam, Modyford disguised himself as the infamous Lieutenant Maladies!" Garrick hung his head. The other squires jeered.

"That will conclude our exams for the day," Alan said abruptly. "Raise your swords." Garrick could barely lift his, but he followed the other squires as well as possible.

"Not like that!" Alan roared, slapping Garrick's face. "You must have a dignified posture and a grave, solemn expression!"

"Alan, I must borrow the boy for a moment," Vincent Mercivelle said smoothly, emerging from the fort. "I will have a…little discussion, as you might call it." Garrick shuddered.

"Come, Garrick," Mercivelle said heartily, laying a heavy hand on Garrick's shoulder. "I must talk with you for a second." Garrick, somewhat relieved that Vincent was at least sparing him humiliation in front of the squires, followed the Captain as fast as he could.

"I understand that you are behind in classes," Mercivelle said once they were out of earshot. Garrick twitched nervously.

"I completely misunderstood your intentions when you first came to the Cavalry," Mercivelle said, bowing. "I thought you to be an **ambitious** village youth with a taste for swordsmanship. And for that, I must humbly beg your pardon." Garrick stopped short. Here was the captain of the most famous military unit in all of Jarrod apologizing to a peasant! It suddenly dawned on Garrick that he wasn't a peasant. He was a prince. *The* prince. He was the heir of Jarrod.

"I realize," continued Mercivelle, taking up his stride, "that you are not a common village boy. I know you are somebody more—inside." Garrick's eyes welled up with tears. He had never felt so much joy and happiness at one time.

"**Henceforth**," said Vincent, drawing his sword from its gleaming scabbard and striking Garrick lightly on the shoulder, "You shall be Sir Garrick."

Garrick's first battle came unexpectedly. For decades the roguish Bumblinks of the Northern Lands had been plotting to invade Jarrod by way of the Serpent Sea, which divided the vast hinterlands. Although Jarrod had excellent military geniuses who knew all about army tactics, hardly anybody knew about sailing. A few sailors from the First Civil War remembered tidbits of their old drunkard days, but that was it. Garrick was surprised when he first glimpsed Crystal Dock—the miniscule vessels submerged in the cluttered shipyard were leaky and infested with vermin. The only large ships tied to the dock were clumsily built and hard to steer. One large ship would require at least one hundred and fifty men, many of whom would lose their lives due to the ship's faulty design.

"Why is Jarrod's navy not grander?" Garrick asked Mercivelle, who was staring out at the water. The aging captain sighed.

"We have no skilled shipbuilders," Vincent said grimly, pushing aside a lock of thinning hair. "This is the best they can make." Suddenly there was a cry from the fort's newly-constructed watchtower.

"The Bumblinks have been sighted! The Bumblinks have been sighted in the Serpent Sea!" the watchman called. The bells in the cathedral tolled loudly. Women fell to their knees, praying **piously**. Men grabbed daggers and slashed about wildly, raising the call and alerting the entire village. Mercivelle grabbed his **rapier** and shoved Garrick aside.

"You must evacuate," Mercivelle said, his forehead creasing with worry. "If you are captured by the **uncouth** Bumblinks, say nothing."

"No!" Garrick cried. "I shall remain by your side as long as your heart beats!"

"An act of loyalty, I see," Mercivelle said, smiling despite the **graveness** of the subject. "Do as you will. I shall not blame you if you run."

The Bumblinks were not long in coming. After hearing the tolling of the cathedral bells and the cry of the watchman, their only choice was to attack Jarrod with an open battle. They thought it was possible they would still be the victors if they had speed on their side. Garrick felt sick in the stomach, but he said nothing. When the first Bumblink war cry was heard, Garrick excused himself to change into armor. Once he was fully dressed, Garrick emerged from the fort. Mercivelle wore nothing but a short tunic and padded trousers. His knee-high boots shone black in the burning sun. Garrick stared in awe at the captain.

"There they are!" Mercivelle exclaimed, pointing his long finger to the far distance of the rolling waves. "I can see their **barbarous** red flag!" Garrick shuddered under his armor. The Bumblinks did not at all sound like a very nice civilization.

The first war cries were heard about twenty minutes later. Garrick sprang to his feet, as did Mercivelle.

"We shall fight to the death!" Mercivelle cried valiantly, raising his sword. A small Bumblink opponent, wearing nothing but a loose baggy white shirt and tight black pants, barred his teeth and ran forward. Vincent dodged the attack, circling the Bumblink to intimidate him. None of the Bumblinks expected Garrick, a mere boy, to attack. When the chance was ripe, Garrick snuck up behind a row of Bumblinks and slashed through their line.

"They shall seek revenge for the death of their officers," Mercivelle wearily wiped sweat from his brow. "We need more recruits."

"There are none," Garrick said hopelessly. "The Bumblinks' numbers are great, and your men are busied with fighting."

Mercivelle glanced at the village, cupped his hands around his withered lips and cried, "People of the village! Come, do not be cowed by the unthreatening Bumblinks!"

That did it. Men, women, and children raced out of every corner, armed with knives, daggers, pitchforks, thick rolling pins, and cutting boards. With fierce war cries, the men pounced on the Bumblinks. One woman banged a pot over a Bumblink's head and dragged the Bumblink inside her house. The enemy was caught by surprise, sandwiched between their two opponents.

"Why is the leader not surrendering, when the battle has almost crowned us its victors?" Garrick asked, slashing a Bumblink combatant. Mercivelle suddenly fell, revealing a Bumblink behind him.

"Captain!" Garrick cried with terror, heaving the heavy man to the side while pointing his sword at the Bumblink. Mercivelle groaned, clutching his arm. The Bumblink leered and did an imitation of a chicken. With a cry of rage Garrick severed the Bumblink's head from his body. Victorious, he stomped on the Bumblinks' bloodless carcass. Glancing around to make sure the coast was clear, Garrick dragged Mercivelle to the hospital tent. To his surprise, he noticed Glenn busily rubbing creams and poultices onto injured knights' wounds.

"Glenn!" Garrick cried, pointing urgently at Mercivelle. "You must cure the captain!" Glenn ran to Mercivelle's side.

"He still lives," Glenn said. Garrick noticed she looked unusually grave. "But only just. His breathing is ragged." While Glenn bent over Mercivelle, Garrick ran to help the other knights, hastily bandaging major wounds and quickly treating minor injuries.

Looking out the window, Garrick noticed that the largest Bumblink had fallen, sorely wounded in the thigh. An enraged cry arose from the Bumblinks. They raced forward, waving their swords blindly. The Knights easily trampled them with their snorting stallions.

Although Mercivelle had won, many lives had been lost. Some of the best knights were killed or badly wounded, while others were taken prisoner. Mercivelle's wound was healing slowly, but he could talk to Garrick and the other knights.

"You put up a great show of loyalty, Garrick," Mercivelle said as the other knights gathered around him. "You are a worthy knight."

Next, Arimthea, Wyddfa's niece, took Garrick to the village orphanage. It was a small red brick building with a creaky door and a leaky roof. The shivering children, who were huddled inside, near to the flickering fireplace, wore stained rags about their feet and itchy wool tunics. Even the girls had to make do with the tunics. Arimthea disappeared, leaving Garrick to knock on the battered door.

"Come in!" a weary voice called. Garrick cautiously peered in.

"And do close the door behind you!" A small, plump lady emerged from the corner. Her gray hair was hastily tied up in a bun on top of her head, and her pale cheeks showed signs of worry.

"Do come and help these children, they've just lost their parents in a Bumblink attack over in the far West," the lady said briskly, taking Garrick's hand and shoving him towards the orphans. "Try cheering them up a bit."

"They look as if they're in need of food." Garrick stared at the **scrawny** orphans. "Maybe there's something you could feed them?"

"I'm so sorry, dear," the lady said, covering her face in her bony hands. "Today we finished off our last stores."

"Mama!" a small girl cried. "I want bread!" The lady sighed, and turning to the girl, she said sweetly,

"You'll get some later, Millie." Turning back to Garrick, she spoke in low **undertones**.

"It's a little habit the children have, calling me Mama. I feel so attached to them," the lady confessed. "By the way, you may call me Dame Abigail."

"Er…Dame, I have a bit of money," Garrick said, again miraculously producing weird coins from his pouch, "maybe I could go to the market and buy them a bite to eat?"

"Oh, would you?" Abigail asked, brightening.

"Of course I will," Garrick said, glancing sympathetically at the orphans. "I'll just…jog down there." Garrick waved good-bye to Abigail and was off to the market. First he bought a loaf of bread, a block of hard yellow butter, and some large **carp**. Garrick found one more coin in his pouch, so he purchased some fresh red strawberries. The sky had begun to darken, so he hurried towards the orphanage.

"Good, good, you've brought some food!" Abigail cried delightedly when Garrick set foot on the doorstep. "It's simply wonderful…" she leaned down and kissed Garrick on the cheek. He reddened slightly.

"Millie, you may have your bread now," Abigail said, generously handing a good-sized piece to the little girl. The other orphans were fed until all had full tummies. Garrick watched them with satisfaction as dusk began to fall, sighed sleepily, and fell into a deep slumber.

The next morning he was awakened with a hard kick in the ribs.

Garrick groaned and rolled to his side, only to receive another kick. Finally accepting that it was impossible to sleep, Garrick rose sluggishly.

"Good, you're awake, and it's about time, too." A squat little mean-faced man stood above Garrick. His brown overcoat was buttoned tightly over his rotund belly. "Those spoiled brats over there are begging me for food. Naturally I gave them a good slap on the backside, but they started crying. *You* go over there and see what's wrong with them. I'm only here on short notice. Old Abby should come back in a few hours. By then, I'll be away at the tavern! Ha!" Garrick was openmouthed with surprise at the man's cruelty. How dare he do such a thing to unfortunate little children??? Little did Garrick realize that he had once been unkind and thoughtless like the **malevolent** man.

"Hurry up with it, too. I can't spend all my time in this smelly little place of an orphanage," the man said, sniffing. Garrick, wanting to be rid of the man as soon as possible, hurried to the cold **grate** where the orphans were seated.

"H-he p-put o-out o-our f-fire b-because h-he said w-we w-were s-spoiled l-little b-brats," Millie sobbed, wiping her tears on her already soaked tunic sleeve. Garrick was hit with rage.

"Come on!" he cried urgently, tugging on Millie's arm. "We must make that wicked man sorry for his evil deeds!" A cheer arose from the orphans.

"Whaddya doin', spoiling those brats mo—" the man stopped short as he noticed the hatred in the orphans' eyes. Garrick took a step towards him, his eyes glowing angrily like fire.

"Look—kids, I d-don't mean any harm," the man stammered. "I'll just be off, then!" He dashed hurriedly out the door.

"That gets rid of that stupid lout," Garrick said, busily rummaging around in his pouch. "Now where's Dame Abigail?"

"She can't come every day, you know," a tall, gangly boy with red freckles and dark reddish hair said quite regretfully. "She has to make money. I'm Oliver, by the way."

"I thought that the orphanage did make money!" Garrick exclaimed, dropping his pouch with surprise.

"It used to," another boy muttered. "That awful man you saw— Felix, or Ogre, as we call him—was the greediest man in all of eternity."

"I could imagine it," Garrick said, gritting his teeth.

"He would charge eighty or eighty five coins for little girls like Millie, one hundred and fifty coins for small boys like Trevor here, and two hundred coins for big boys like Oliver and I. Plus a fifty coin fee if we wanted to sit by the fireplace. There was a city council, and everyone agreed that it wasn't fair. So they brought Dame Abigail in to take care of the tramps, but Ogre wasn't giving up his chance for an easy money business that fast. He threatened to tear the building down unless Dame married him. He liked her, you see. Dame liked us so much she actually wedded that thick-lipped ninny," the boy finished off.

"Have you had breakfast yet?" Garrick asked, already fearing the answer.

"No, Ogre stole it away and stuffed his big mouth with it. I'd like to give him a fat lip," Oliver said angrily, shaking his fist as if an invisible enemy stood before him.

"Do you know when the market opens?" Garrick asked, glancing about. He had again produced coins from his pouch, of even more bewildering design.

"Maybe later," Oliver replied. "I don't know exactly when, but probably soon."

"Meanwhile, why don't we build up the fire?" the other boy asked, yawning. "No sense in talking if we're icy cold." Garrick, seeing the sense in this, piled the grate full of wood and started a small flame. The orphans gathered around it, deeply inhaling the hot air and leaning close to the warm hearth.

"If you're still wondering about the market, it should be open by now," the boy said carelessly. "Call me Jack, if you have a mind to."

Garrick stared out the window, eyeing the white sky critically. It was not raining, but a thick cover of mist and fog **obscured** the village. It would not be easy to find his way to the market, however close it was.

"I don't really like the weather," he said uneasily, turning back to the orphans. "But if you want to go, I'm sure I could navigate the market somehow." The children exchanged doubtful glances. Finally Jack spoke up.

"Oliver and I want to go," he said. "Millie and Trevor are chickening out, I suppose there's no way Betsy or Annie would want to come—"

"I am not chickening out!" The small boy who sat unnoticed by the hearth finally spoke out. "And neither is Millie!"

"Who votes yes?" Garrick asked. The young prince had often eavesdropped on the Baronet of Mallisque dealing with his troublesome **yeomen**, and considered himself experienced in these affairs. Three hands shot up. Millie and two other girls remained silent.

"Tie," Jack said lazily. "Now what?" Garrick opened his mouth to say something, but hastily shut it. He realized that he had never witnessed a tie between the Baronet's bothersome yeomen.

"I say we go," Oliver said, rising to his feet. "Might as well, anyways...Dame wants some turnips and a bit of cheese."

"No!" Millie squeaked, covering her face with her hands.

"What were you ever afraid of, anyways, Mil?" Jack asked casually, leaning back. "I don't suppose you thought the hawkers could tear their grubby fingernails into your soft little heart?" The little girl **uttered** a scream of fright.

"Cut it, Jack," Oliver said coldly, elbowing Jack in the ribs.

"Millie, he didn't really mean it," Trevor coaxed his little sister. "The hawkers are nice people! Maybe you'll get a peppermint from Miss Barlyns, or a bit of cherry pie from Robin, or..." His voice trailed away doubtfully. Millie shook her head.

"Well, it's obvious that if Millie isn't coming, someone will have to stay at the orphanage with her. And who will that be?" Garrick asked. There was silence.

"Er, well, fine, if nobody's going to stay, I might as well," Garrick said awkwardly, pouring his glittering coins into Oliver's hands. "Just don't take too long and make sure the turnips are good."

"You sound like an old mother hen," Oliver said, chuckling. The coins mysteriously disappeared in his hands.

"What!!!!" Jack cried, diving for the previously visible coins. Garrick stared with astonishment at Oliver's hand. Just then Dame Abigail came around the corner, her face lined with stress. Her eyelids drooped.

"My dear children," she said wearily. "I do hope you didn't make Felix angry."

"We did," said Oliver savagely. "He put out our fire, stole our food, slapped us, and called us spoiled brats." Abigail buried her face in her hands. Reaching into his pouch, Garrick drew out a hard, cold lump of gleaming silver. He gasped at it.

"My dear lad!" Dame cried. "Where in the village did you find that?"

"Er…" Garrick stammered, not sure what to say.

"Why do things just keep appearing in your pouch, anyways?" Jack asked slyly, advancing dangerously towards Garrick, his fists clenched into balls. "Suppose you…stole them?" He raised a fist. Garrick stepped back.

"Peace, peace!" Abigail cried shrilly, waving her hands in front of the two boys' faces.

"Let me deal with this, Dame," said Oliver, **nimbly** stepping aside and dealing an unexpected blow to Garrick's face. **Chaos** broke out in the orphanage.

"Stop, boys, this is really—" Dame Abigail stopped short as Trevor tumbled backwards and Garrick threw Oliver over her shoulder. Finally Jack was left with Garrick. Millie sat sobbing in a corner, while Abigail hitched up her skirts and tried to stop the fight. Garrick knocked Jack in the ribs, while Jack punched Garrick in the stomach. Finally Garrick seized Jack and kicked him to the ground.

"Now finally this dreadful ordeal shall be over," Abigail said, sighing. "You'll all need a soft bed and some sleep before we go off to the market." Jack moaned, blood dribbling down his tunic.

"Really, I don't see why you got into this fight in the first place," Abigail said, placing her hands on her hips. "Garrick, I'm ashamed that you would want to hurt the boys. Jack, you should know better than to accuse Garrick of something he would never do. As for you, Oliver—Where is Oliver?" Garrick turned and found himself staring at shattered windowpanes. Oliver lay on the sidewalk, cut and bruised but still alive.

"As for you, Oliver," Abigail said, continuing as if she didn't realize the boy was **unconscious**, "I wouldn't have expected you to side up with Jack and hit Garrick."

"What about Trevor?" Garrick asked suddenly. Millie let out a sob. They all turned to look where she was weakly pointing. Trevor lay slumped against the wall, his leg cut and his lip split. Blood poured from his nose.

"He's still alive," Garrick said shakily, trying to make himself believe it was true. Abigail pressed a hand to Trevor's chest.

"He still breathes," she said. "But we must find help, quickly." Garrick immediately ran for Glenn. His mind was racing as he flew into the herb shop. Glenn, however, was nowhere to be found.

"Glenn!" Garrick bellowed. "Glenn!" He pounded on her wooden dresser. Finally the old herbalist clambered down from her bunk.

"What now?" she asked briskly, pulling on her ragged shawl. "I do expect you got into a fight and here you are, with a black eye and a bruised arm. Just show me where the place is and I'll do my work." After Glenn had collected her various poultices and potions, Garrick anxiously led her to the orphanage. The place was in shambles. Trevor had been laid on a straw pallet with a thin blanket over his small body, but his breathing was fading. Every once in a while his breath would stop completely.

"Oh dear," Glenn said. "This is not at all what I expected. Hmm..." she began arranging her remedies on the floor, kneeling at Trevor's side.

"Hurry!" Garrick cried, jumping up and down with impatience. *This old woman is dealing with a matter between life and death!!! If only this stupid fistfight hadn't been started in the first place!! If only I hadn't taken that stupid hunk of silver or whatever it was from my pouch! Jack accused me, and I hit Jack or maybe it was Oliver, in the ribs! What Father would say if he learned I had sunk to their level!* "He won't breathe much longer!" Glenn ignored Garrick and took a small vial from her healer's pouch. She tipped the contents into Trevor's mouth, muttering,

"That should ease his breathing." Abigail let out a relieved sigh, smoothing Trevor's blonde hair back. Garrick sunk onto the ground, exhausted, and fell into a deep slumber.

He was awakened early the next morning by Dame Abigail's soft voice and the beautiful singing of the nightingales, which were staying out later than usual.

"Good, my dear, you're awake," Abigail said, tiptoeing towards Garrick as he yawned and rubbed his eyes. "Trevor couldn't be doing better; your friend the herbalist stayed all night, muttering strange pagan chants, wrapping all those wet bandages, and pouring glassful after glassful of odd tonics into the little boy's mouth. Why, there he is!"

Garrick turned and glimpsed Trevor out of the corner of his eye, limping about with his leg wrapped in a tight bandage. *Maybe we shouldn't have started this entire fight in the first place,* Garrick thought, biting his lip. *Jack and Oliver were wrong, but we could have resolved it somehow...*

Millie watched her brother with round eyes, tagging along and asking him questions. Garrick could not help chuckling at poor Jack's plight, for the older boy had been laid on a pallet with raw meat and ice covering his black eye. Oliver had been laid next to Jack, his arm wrapped in a clumsy sling.

"And now for you," Glenn said, tottering along to where Garrick was standing. "Lie down, that's a good boy. Let me see...hmm, no major damage done...I'll just fix that cut and be off."

"No, really, I'm fine," Garrick said, backing away. "I mean, why don't you heal Trevor or Jack or Oliver?" He glanced desperately at the three boys.

"I must cure you, little one," Glenn said gently. She laid a reassuring arm on Garrick's shoulder. "Do not worry. It will be short."

"Oh, fie!" Garrick exclaimed impatiently. "Do it, and be done with it!" Glenn chuckled, rubbing strong alcohol on his cut. Garrick winced. The injury stung, and the sting seemed to be seeping along to the rest of his leg.

"As for your bruise, there is nothing to be done about it but wait," Glenn sighed. "Just don't walk on it."

"I won't be able to do anything this week," Garrick grumbled, pushing himself up. "No chance of going to the market either."

"Have heart, laddie," Glenn said, rising from the ground. "I must be off, there's bound to be a line of patients by the herb shop."

"Bye, then," Garrick said weakly, waving to Glenn as she hobbled out of the orphanage.

When the foggy sky had cleared somewhat, Dame Abigail took Garrick to the market. Coins kept reproducing in Garrick's pocket, until finally they had bought fresh turnips and carrots, warm bread straight from the oven, and, as a special treat, clean red strawberries. Jack and Oliver were up and awake when they arrived, playing a game of checkers on a crude wooden board. They had forgotten all events of the previous day and showed no hard feelings towards Garrick.

"Hey, Garrick!" Jack called. "Want to play a friendly game of checkers?"

"Er," Garrick said nervously, staring down at his feet. "I'm not really sure...how to play." Checkers was not a common game in the palace, it being considered a roguish amusement.

"You don't know how to play!" Jack guffawed, tumbling over with laughter. "He doesn't know how to play, Oliver!"

Turning a light shade of red, Garrick retorted heatedly, "Well, I'm sure you don't know how to play…how to play…chess!" Jack stopped laughing at once.

"Uh…oh, um, that, it's…er…easy, really," Jack said casually. Hearing a quiver in Jack's voice, Garrick smirked.

"Stop it, you two!" Abigail cried. "The strawberries are ready!" Garrick dashed towards the tiny kitchenette. Jack ran after him. The sweet strawberries were piled high on a cracked plate. Trevor, Millie, Betsy, and Annie were already eating the juicy berries. Garrick had barely swallowed one strawberry when he was swept up into a multicolored vortex and deposited outside of the orphanage.

Armenia awaited him outside the orphanage. She greeted him kindly and took his hand in hers.

"Where are we?" Garrick asked in confusion. Although he had been dropped outside of the orphanage, the orphanage was nowhere in sight.

"I just did a little bit of magic to make it quicker," the fairy said, smiling coquettishly. "If you please, here we are." Garrick found himself staring up at a medium-sized wooden sign that hung from rusty iron hinges. Garder's Print Shoppe was painted neatly on the sign.

"Knock," Armenia commanded. Garrick did as he was bidden. He was answered by a short, plump man wearing a white vest buttoned over his round belly. A pocket watch hung from the man's vest's pocket on a gold chain and swung as he walked.

Armenia disappeared.

"I presume you are Garrick?" he asked curtly, nodding.

"Yes, sir," Garrick replied, attempting to look past the man's gigantic figure into the room beyond.

"Then come in," the man said shortly. "I am Ralf. Arithios! Show the boy to his workplace." The tall, long-limbed teenager who had been lying lazily in a corner made a face and finally swaggered towards the two. He turned to grin at Garrick, showing two missing teeth and one black tooth.

"Just come round here," Gilbert said, clapping Garrick on the shoulder and shoving him towards a desk on which a long row of metal letters was placed. "You have to set the letters to match Hugh's text. Now don't frown, it ain't nothin' hard."

"I expect, Arithios Gilbert Marson, that you will first teach the boy how to set the letters," Ralf said coldly, staring over at them. Garrick took a step back.

"It ain't a problem, Uncle," Gilbert said, grinning once more. "Now see, little fella, here's a letter, an' ye just gotta move it to make the words. D'ya know how to read?"

"Of course I do!" Garrick cried, stomping his foot indignantly. "Why, dare you suggest that I could be ignorant of books, you son of a swine, you—" He stood quivering with suppressed rage and fury.

"Chill, chill," Gilbert said, laughing. He patted Garrick on the back. "No hard feelings, nuh-uh."

"Mr. Ralf!" A clear voice called from the front of the shop. "New shipment of ink!"

"Northwick Special?" Ralf inquired sharply, peering over his cracked spectacles. "I won't accept it if not." Garrick could not help but remember his distant cousin, Regan of Northwick, and giggle.

"Yessir, indeed it is and no other," a slender redheaded boy emerged from the front of the shop, carrying a large package in his sunburned hands. "Ain't got no business with wee Master Regan, but me boss says if there was ever a book learner he's one. The little duke uses our Northwick Ink, might add for ye."

"Yes, yes, I know, Walter," Ralf said, waving his hand impatiently. "Just give me the ink and be off."

"If master pleases…?" Walter held out his hand as if expecting something, likely money. Garrick suddenly felt an urge to reach into his pouch and bring out whatever might be in there. He undid the pouch strings and took out a glittering silver coin. Walter stared at the coin hungrily. Garrick dropped the money into the boy's hand. Walter's fist closed around the coin quicker than Garrick could say "Jack Robinson."

"Thanky, sir!" Walter cried gratefully, and dumping the ink on a chair, scrambled out of the shop.

The afternoon was spent in the tedious job of setting the metal letters. Garrick was summoned from his task every ten minutes or so to look at Hugh's writing, collect the printed pages and bind them together, or correct any words that had been blurred. Occasionally Garrick would wander off into the back of the room, where Hugh leaned over his cracked parchment and peered over the **opaque** glass of his useless spectacles.

"Get back to work, boy!" Ralf would usually call on those times.

Ralf finally closed the print shop at dusk. Wearily Garrick followed him and Gilbert through the dark streets of the village to a small, respectable house on Merchant Corner. Pink roses lined the trellises, set against a pretty white background of painted boards. As was the town custom, the shingled roof was almost flat, with only the shortest of peaks. Light shone brightly through thin **chiffon** curtains. Garrick looked expectantly at Ralf and Gilbert.

"Do you think your mother will take me in another day while I...?" Ralf ended abruptly, turning to Gilbert. Garrick shivered as a cold breeze swept past the village.

"She won't be any more angry than she was yesterday," Gilbert said, biting his nails thoughtfully. Garrick stared at him.

"Then I suppose I'll risk it," Ralf sighed. He knocked twice on the great wooden door as Garrick fidgeted nervously. A gaunt woman opened the door. Her gray eyes, hair, and lips matched the dusty withered shade of her woolen dress.

"Oh, Gilbert, you did give me a fright. Ralf—" Here she put her hands on her hips. "I did expect that Hugh gave you the proposal for Greenbarrow. No mind. It's late and I don't want to be caught outside past the nightly curfew." Garrick took a step back as Gilbert strode through the doorway.

"And you, lad, who are you?" the woman asked, peering towards Garrick. "Ralf's new apprentice? He mentioned something about a new boy."

"Er, yes, ma'm," Garrick said, turning red and staring down at his shoes.

"Well, come in, and don't **tarry**," Ralf said sternly, pulling Garrick in as the woman closed the door. "Garrick, I would like you to meet Beatrice, my sister. You've met her son Arithios, my nephew."

"Oh—yes," Garrick said, rather stunned. Before he had been made aware of the family connection, he had never thought that Gilbert looked anything like Ralf, but as Garrick surveyed Gilbert's reddish-brown hair, his dark hazel eyes, and sharply chiseled nose, he could find many similarities.

"I expect you haven't had a decent meal yet," Beatrice said briskly, cracking a hard brown egg into an earthenware bowl and lightly sprinkling it with cilantro and salt. "Eat quickly. Rowena the Midwife from next door doesn't favor bright candlelight from neighboring houses. And Gilbert, you should be in bed." Garrick eyed the yolky slop doubtfully, twitching uncertainly.

"Ma, it ain't muggers' time," Gilbert whined, yolk dribbling down his chin. "I don't see why I ain't allowed to stay up like Neal! My friend," he added as Garrick glanced at him.

"Neal is differently disciplined, Arithios Gilbert Marson, and both your mother and I expect that you will react to our method differently," Ralf said sharply, raising his eyebrows. "Therefore you will issue no complaints." Gilbert was silent. Garrick stared at him sympathetically. When the young prince had lived at the royal palace he had been able to go to bed as late as he wished, listening to old Bard Rhem tell tales of the elder days and watching the court dwarves and jesters amuse the great ladies and lords.

"There's Rowena, glaring at me," Beatrice chuckled, shutting the drapes. "I expect she'll holler over any minute now." Garrick watched as she took the egg dish and scrubbed it thoroughly.

"Gilbert, go to your room. No reading, understand! Ralf, second chamber in the corridor on the left as usual. Gavin—no, Garrin—I mean Garrick—follow me," Beatrice said, taking Garrick's hand. He was suddenly faced with a labyrinth of endless passages and hallways, not to mention various rooms of many sizes. Some were locked and tightly shut, but others were wide open, displaying their neglected state.

"Here's where you'll be staying the night," Beatrice said hurriedly, pushing Garrick into a dimly lit entrance chamber. Solid, thick log walls that were chinked with dry mud prevented any of the chilly night breezes from entering, while small windows near the decorative ceiling allowed the bright light of the stars to come through.

"Thank you," Garrick said, but his gratefulness was met with silence. Beatrice had gone, and he was alone.

Garrick slept peacefully that night. As soon as he had undressed and wearily covered himself in thick woolen quilts and blankets, he immediately fell into a deep slumber.

He awoke to find a bright fire blazing in the hot hearth, with a basin of hot wash-water beside his bed. Garrick was pleased to discover a clean pressed wool tunic laid out on his bed, as well as sturdy black shoes and a fresh washcloth. After scrubbing himself and changing into the tunic, he skipped downstairs. Beatrice was waiting for him with a slice of somewhat burnt toast and rapidly melting butter.

"Eat quickly," she said coldly, hardly glancing at Garrick as she swept the floor with a long broom. "Ralf does not tolerate tardiness, and Gilbert prefers apprentices to be strictly punctual." Gulping down the remains of his toast, Garrick grabbed his shoes and dashed out the door.

As Garrick had feared, Ralf was not at all happy at Garrick's lateness.

"Go and assist Hugh," he said crossly, pointing to the back of the shop. "He needs some help choosing his ink, the ignorant dolt." Garrick trotted off to do as he was bidden, helping the bewildered writer select a suitable ink type. Finally Ralf called him over to set the metal letters.

"That mad writer Hugh has finally turned in an article," Ralf said grumpily, tossing a roll of cracked parchment aside. "Crazy, that man's manuscript." Garrick bowed his head respectfully, although he personally thought that Hugh's writing was most fascinating.

"Garrick!" Gilbert called from the front of the shop. "I need you to set the letters while I oil the printing press!" Garrick groaned, but Ralf pushed him towards the rack of letters.

"I've got most of it done, why don't you just organize it a bit more and we'll be set," Gilbert said, busily pouring ink into a small cartridge.

"I—what?" Garrick asked, his mouth hanging open.

"Just organize the letters a bit and we'll be ready," Gilbert said, looking up and spilling ink over the side of the cartridge. "Hurry up with it, too." Garrick sighed and went back to the tedious job of setting the letters. Finally he was able to rest his tired arms as Gilbert collected the last of the freshly printed papers.

"Get up, boy, and make yourself useful!" Ralf snapped, dumping a stack of book pages into Garrick's arms. "Take this to Friar Augustine the Bookbinder at Saint Christopher's Chapel." Garrick stared at Ralf, stunned.

"And be quick about it!" Ralf shouted, waving his finger in Garrick's face. "I can't tolerate laziness!" Garrick dashed from the shop and across the cobblestone street to the dimly lit chapel on Rural Row. Garrick froze with awe at its towering, sinister entrance.

"Behold the holy chapel!" A deep voice rang out from the darkness of the apse. Garrick shuddered. Suddenly an overweight monk dressed in a long brown habit emerged from the chapel. He had a bald patch on the top of his head that glinted in the candlelight.

"Welcome, welcome, I am Friar Augustine the Bookbinder," the fat friar said, laughing merrily. "More pages from old Ralf?"

"Er…yes, sir," Garrick stammered, unsure of what to say. "I have an entire stack."

"Just give them to me!" said Friar Augustine, still chuckling jollily. His face became suddenly serious as he accepted the pages. "And don't call me sir."

Augustine broke into laughter again as Garrick stared at him with surprise. He watched as the friar took an ornately carved plank of wood, measure it, and measure the printed pages. Augustine then took another beautiful plank of wood, and taking a long ribbon, tied the pages and the wood together.

"There," the friar said with satisfaction, handing the finished product to Garrick. "Tell old Ralf to send in a whole load of pages next time. I want to bind a novel." Garrick thanked Augustine gratefully and ran out of the chapel.

Garrick was given another task after giving Ralf the book—to stamp each page with Ralf's seal, a red outline of a howling wolf encircled with red ink. It was a very boring job, and soon Garrick was at the end of his rope.

"I won't do this any longer!" Garrick cried impatiently, throwing down the stamp. "I cannot and will not!"

"Since I have hired you, simpleton, I have had more trouble than help," Ralf said, angrily taking up the stamp and pressing it upon a page. "Go and sit in the corner until I find a useful job for you." Garrick stomped off indignantly and slumped down in a chair, his thoughts wandering from time to time on what life would have been back at the palace. A wicked voice in his mind reminded him *If the fairies hadn't kidnapped you, you would still be living a nice life at home.* Garrick hastily banished the idea and went back to thinking about the print shop. He could think of nothing but hate for Ralf, and quickly switched to imagining what Glenn was doing now. *Probably healing her patients,* he told himself. Still he could not forget the idea that she might be having a good time reading or resting.

"Boy!" Garrick could barely hear Ralf's gruff voice from the front of the shop. "Come and write what Hugh dictates!" Garrick hurried to where the writer sat, stretching his arms and yawning.

"Get up, you great lazy lump," Ralf said meanly, kicking Hugh in the leg. "Garrick is going to write for you." Hugh's eyes brightened as he sat up in his chair. Garrick quickly grabbed a roll of parchment and a quill.

"Alright, start," Hugh said dreamily. "There was once a young, beautiful princess by the name of Andorra. Her flaxen curls fell to her feet, shining at every angle. Suitors were entranced by her dazzling blue-green eyes and her fair white face with soft red lips and pointed ears. Her dresses were of finest quality, spun from gold thread and silver thread. Andorra's jackets were made of green dragon hides with bronze coating, which she wore all seasons. Her father, the mighty King Arandis, agreed only to give her to a wealthy suitor, for, as he said, the good of the great kingdom. At this Andorra fell to sorrow, for her lover was a young squire, poor, but courageous and valiant. Many suitors tried in vain to win her heart, but none succeeded. In a rage, the King declared that Andorra would marry the Duke of Yorlsbourgh, an old, withered man with many estates and long coffers filled with endless treasure. At this Andorra wept hysterically, but she gathered her wits and finally slipped down the castle walls to the open arms of her true lover, the squire Myron. They stole away in the midst of night and kissed under the sturdy branches of an oak tree. Then they parted with many a sad farewell and went their separate ways." At this Hugh stopped. Garrick stared down at the parchment guiltily. He had become so entranced with the story that he had forgotten to write anything down, save a few blurred words on the top of the page.

"Fool!" Hugh cried, slapping Garrick soundly. "You dim-witted bastard! You witless nincompoop! You doltish simpleton!"

By that time Ralf had emerged from the front of the shop, accompanied by two fairies Garrick knew well to be Wyddfa and Armenia. However, they had taken woman shape again and were walking like humans.

"This is your new apprentice?" Wyddfa asked Ralf, surveying Garrick as if she had never seen him before.

"Yes, and a bothersome one, too," Ralf said, bristling with fury. "He's been no use these days, lazing off and saying that this printing work is too tedious. I agree, but you must have patience, whatever trade you practice." Like Wyddfa, Armenia inspected Garrick from head to toe.

"Indeed, this idiotic moron has given me more trouble than I can cope with!" Hugh exclaimed, raising his fist. His eyeballs bulged from underneath his bushy eyebrows, his temples throbbing. "I demand that you take him away at once, Ralf, or I shall no longer remain in the partnership!" Ralf's face paled as he stared at Garrick. Finally Wyddfa broke in.

"I am aware that my niece, Armenia, has paid you a fee for you to take him in as an apprentice," she said smoothly, stepping in between the two bickering men. "You made an oath to keep him as long as the apprenticeship lasted. I gave you fifty coins for one year, as was each of his apprenticeships. Either you keep him, or you must refund my money." Ralf let out a long sigh. Clearly he was beaten.

"I see that I have lost this argument," he said, sighing again. "But, Hugh, my friend, be as good as to stay with me!"

"I refuse to stay under the same roof with such a fool and simpleton!" Hugh roared, storming out of the print shop, never to be seen again. Once his shadow had faded into the distance, Wyddfa spoke once more.

"If it is possible for Garrick to take Hugh's place as the writer, I will pay you thirty more coins," she said, taking a pouch from her thick belt. Ralf's eyes glinted greedily as he reached for the coins. Wyddfa immediately snatched them back.

"Do you agree that Garrick will be the new writer?" Wyddfa asked sternly.

"Yes, but he must continue with his other tasks as well," Ralf said defiantly, crossing his arms across his chest.

"Very well," Wyddfa said, smiling wryly. "I can see you will not give up."

Although Garrick had been promoted to the high position of a writer, he was constantly under the pressure of many things at once.

"Take this to Friar Augustine the Bookbinder!" Ralf would shout, smashing Garrick's finger. Or: "Dim-witted idiot! *That's* not the right kind of ink!" Possibly a stern "Don't touch that" or "that article is too abrupt."

Finally on one cloudy, rainy day when it was obvious nobody

would want to buy anything from the print shop, Garrick had a few hours of rest and relaxation to himself. Ralf was snoring next to him on a large fluffy pillow, and Gilbert was at Beatrice's house. There were no books to read at the printing shop, but Ralf had ordered Garrick to stay.

Ralf must be crazy, Garrick thought as he stared out the window **wistfully** towards Beatrice's house. *I do expect that Gilbert is having a right jolly time over there.* His eyes wandered back to the printing press, a large machine that took up the entire width of the inky desk.

"I wonder how that thing works," Garrick said aloud, feeling its shiny **mahogany** surface with his fingertips.

"Whaddya think you're doing, boy!" Ralf barked, jumping up from his pillow. Garrick shrank back guiltily.

"Never mind, you've just disturbed my pleasant little siesta," Ralf grumbled, shoving Garrick onto a hard chair. "Stay there. And *don't* touch the printing machine."

After a few hours, Garrick could endure it no longer and rose from his seat. Yawning, he rubbed his eyes and examined the printing press closely. The metal letters were set on a rack below the mahogany top, dripping with ink. Another rack holding clean white paper was balanced on two short wobbly beams that stretched across the low section of the press. The rusty handle on the side of the press was supposed to be cranked to lower the inked metal letters, pushing the ink onto the pages and therefore creating printed text. Garrick stared wistfully at the impressive machine. *If only I were allowed to try it,* he thought longingly, glancing back at Ralf's plump figure. *If only...well, Ralf is sleeping...No, it'd be too risky...maybe I could have a go.* Garrick slipped a long sheet of paper onto the rack, quickly arranged the letters to make GARRICK, and turned the handle. With a loud screech, the metal letters were lowered.

"Imbecile! Moron! Idiot! Bastard!" Ralf bellowed, springing up from his pillow. "How dare you play with such expensive material, you—you" Ralf's furious words were cut off by Gilbert, who entered the shop countless minutes before.

"UNCLE!!!" Gilbert shouted, stomping his foot. "I have the proposal for Greenbarrow! LISTEN TO ME!!!" By the time Ralf had turned his head towards Gilbert, Garrick had ducked underneath the safety of a large canvas blanket. He cupped his ear against the floor to hear every word.

"The proposal, eh?" Ralf's voice was somewhat softer, but Garrick could hear its furious edge. "Hand it over." Seeing Gilbert put a long, crackly scroll into Ralf's hands, Garrick peeked further over the blanket, interested.

"You, boy!" Ralf barked, turning to face Garrick. "I need to give you some proper punishment!" Garrick winced, already imagining himself in solitary confinement in a miniscule cell, his head and arms pinched in the tightness of a **pillory**.

The real punishment was not nearly so severe.

"You'll have to help Beatrice clean the table, wash the dishes, and cook dinner every day after you return early from the print shop," Ralf said grandly, sauntering towards the canvas blanket. "Then you'll have to do extra work at the print shop with absolutely no breaks. And next—WHERE IS THAT BASTARD!!!!!!" Ralf did not notice that Garrick had quietly slipped away, as quick as a cat, down the sinister streets of the village.

Panting, Garrick dashed towards the Memorial of King Eldon at the village square. He leaned against the smooth marble of the statue, breathless. Two great bloodhounds **barreled** out of an alleyway, followed by three other howling dogs. They stopped to growl at Garrick's feet, licking him and scraping his skin with their sharp teeth. They were chased away, to Garrick's amusement, by an undernourished kitten with round black eyes. The cat reminded Garrick distinctly of Wyddfa, with its sleek black fur and long erect tail.

"I wonder who you are, little kitty," Garrick said, stroking the graceful kitten. "I'm not sure why, but you remind me of Wyddfa…" His voice trailed off as he stared at the cat. Indeed, it was no longer in feline shape. There stood Wyddfa, straight and proud as ever, her long, sweeping chiffon dress shimmering brightly.

"Go back to the print shop," she commanded haughtily, waving her beautifully embroidered handkerchief. "Ralf is meeting with a few of his **acquaintances** at the tavern, and will not return until midnight. Obviously he will not recall your punishment, being drunk and dizzy. Oh, and I might say, your printing is shipshape."

"Thank you," Garrick said, gasping. Wyddfa was no longer there.

Being unsure of Beatrice's hospitality, Garrick slept in the print shop that night. He arranged a crude bed out of a few chairs and the spare canvas blanket. As the sky darkened, he formed a pillow out of a soft paperback book and fell into sleep.

The next morning Garrick awoke to coldness. It was again slightly overcast, with a drizzle of rain to top it off. Ralf was nowhere to be seen. *I wonder when Gilbert comes,* Garrick thought, peering out the window. *I hope it's soon.* His wish was answered by Gilbert himself, humming a jolly tune and swinging a bulging book bag.

"So you've got here early, eh, Garrick?" Gilbert asked, putting down his book bag. "How'd you leave without me seeing you?"

"I didn't, actually," Garrick said, rather confused. "I slept here last night."

"Oh, oh, I remember!" Gilbert exclaimed. "Ralf was very angry at you for something, I remember? What, did you try to work the old printing machine?"

"Yes—how did you know?" Garrick asked with wonder, staring at Gilbert.

"Once I tried that when I was 'bout your age," Gilbert said, chuckling. "Received a spanking and a lecture I'll always remember. Three hours, as I might remember, Ralf droning on and on about how I was supposed to obey him…then he went off and got drunk in the old tavern."

"Did you print anything successfully?" Garrick asked, raising his eyebrows.

"Not really," Gilbert said, chuckling. "I printed it decently enough, but I didn't realize that the paper was the wrong kind. And then a week later Ralf found it and printed it in our newspaper—the Village Weekly."

"I only printed my name," Garrick said enviously. "You started with an entire article?"

"Not my own," Gilbert said casually. "Hugh's. I printed it, though. And look, there's Ralf." Garrick turned to look. Indeed it was Ralf, barreling up the sidewalk.

"Uncle!" Gilbert cried. "Garrick arrived before you! Just a little joke," he added to Garrick in an undertone.

"You little whippersnapper! Telling me lies—what?" At that moment Ralf noticed Garrick.

"Why, Garrick!" Ralf exclaimed. "You came here earlier than me! My record is shattered!!!"

"We were just having a friendly little chat," Gilbert said carelessly. "Anyways, when are we going to start printing?"

"Right now," Ralf said, stacking a fresh load of white paper onto the printing rack. "Garrick, you do the printing today. I'm feeling a little dizzy..." He collapsed onto a worn settee and vomited into his hands.

"Well, what article do you have for us today, writer?" Gilbert asked jokingly, turning to Garrick.

"Er, this," Garrick said, pulling a short, unorganized article out of a cupboard. "It's...um...about the print shop." Gilbert scanned the page.

"Ugh!" Gilbert exclaimed, throwing the article back. "It's awful— Garrick, you really need to make your sentences longer, include more information, and get a little more organized!"

"Why!" Garrick cried impatiently. "Why do I have to correct it?!"

"Henceforth I will be your official editor," Gilbert said severely. "Now hand me that article!"

The edited version ended up like this:

Garder's *over one hundred*

Come to ~~the~~ print shop! We have printed ~~many~~ magnificent books! Lyrics, newspapers, and fairytales ~~are in here~~ *dot our shelves!* ~~Come to Garder's Print Shoppe~~! Garder's is the place you'll want to be!

"I did think that my writing was quite good," Garrick said sullenly, folding the article.

"Not good enough for the public to see," Gilbert said, chuckling. "I fixed the old thing up a bit. But you need to write some more—and longer sentences, alright?"

"Oh, fie!" Garrick cried with exasperation. "Why can't you be the writer?" Gilbert immediately took a step back.

"Oh-ho, never!" he exclaimed. "I'm not made for writer's stuff, not all morbid and poetic like Allan a Dale."

"I think if you spent your time writing instead of bossing me around everyone would think better of you, including Ralf and your mother," Garrick said sourly.

"You sound like my Auntie Georgiana," Gilbert laughed. "Always saying that if I did something useful to 'contribute to the society,'

Father would like me better. Anyways, that was before I started printing with Ralf. Even then, she wasn't very pleased. She didn't like Ralf much—she didn't really acknowledge him as part of the family."

Garrick frowned.

"But why don't you want to write?" he persisted, trying to veer away from the subject.

"We'll discuss that later," Gilbert said abruptly, turning away from Garrick. "First we need to print a few articles for the Village Weekly— maybe I'll compose a riddle or two."

"What can I write about?" Garrick asked, sighing. "There's nothing I can really do right now, you know."

"Can't you even make a decent joke?" Gilbert exclaimed.

"No," Garrick said, irritated. "But I'm sure you can't do everything, either."

"Well, at least I know how to make a *joke*..." Gilbert muttered. Garrick fumed.

"Boys, I'll be off for a game of d-draughts over at the t-tavern," Ralf slurred, rising from the settee. "P-print a lot..." Garrick quickly set the metal letters to form the text of his article and cranked the press. Gilbert sat next to him, scribbling busily on a piece of paper with his messy scrawl.

"How many copies of the newspaper do we need?" Garrick asked, peering over Gilbert's shoulder.

"Maybe five or six," Gilbert said carelessly. "Nobody really buys it that much."

"All the more reason we should make advertisements!" Garrick cried. "People would see how good Garder's is and come over to buy!"

"The people don't actually come over *here* to buy, silly," Gilbert said. Garrick was instantly annoyed. "A few boys from the criminal ghettoes south of the Cavalry's stronghold come here to work off their sentence."

"But don't they get paid?" Garrick asked with amazement.

"Sometimes," Gilbert said, shrugging. "Cheap labor, anyhow."

"Why, it's basic crime!" Garrick cried, stomping his foot. "People should get paid for their work!"

"Chill, chill," Gilbert laughed, whacking Garrick on the back. "It's not like we abuse them or anything. They consider themselves lucky not being taken before the executioner squad."

"Still, I don't see how little boys could commit crimes big enough to deserve these cruel sentences!" Garrick exclaimed, placing his hands on his hips.

"Usually it's a small offense," Gilbert said, tying a large stack of freshly printed papers together with a green ribbon. "Stealing a noble's handkerchief or whatnot. But the nobles go before a grand magistrate, and he usually gives in to their commands. By law the sentence for that is twelve months of labor. Nobody except for us wants to take in robbers, so they just come over to do our work."

"But what noble would be so cruel to do such a thing?" Garrick cried angrily, crumpling a piece of paper in his clenched hand. "I would like to challenge that royal coward to a duel!"

"Ssssh," Gilbert whispered. "There might be the tax collectors roaming about, and I'm sure that they'll repeat any...interesting...news back to King Errold."

"I don't care about any blasted tax collector!" Garrick roared. "Just let me voice my opinions!"

The seven fairies sipped glasses of steaming sugared coffee as they surrounded the Memorial of King Eldon. Wyddfa spoke first.

"I have informed Their Royal Majesties of Garrick's whereabouts. Soon their strongman will arrive at the print shop to take the prince back to the palace," she said, placing her goblet on the ground. "At promptly eight o'clock Garrick will arrive at the palace." Ailyra nodded in agreement.

"Indeed, it is a fitting time for Garrick to be sent back."

A tall, slim man clothed in a scarlet cloak with a bright silver brooch pinned to his cloak entered the shop. His iron breastplate glinted in the candlelight of the print shop. The man seemed strangely out of place in the untidy shop, and yet Garrick thought he remembered something about him.

"Your highness, come with me," he said, taking him roughly by the arm. "By the orders of his royal majesty King Errold and her royal majesty Queen Hortensia, I am to take you back to the palace. There we hope you will forget your brief mingling with peasants and commoners."

"It wasn't brief!" Garrick cried, trying to break away from the soldier as he dragged Garrick out of the print shop. "And I will not at all forget my life in the village!"

"As his prince wishes, then," the soldier said, grinning. As the two made their way past the lush green cornfields and crops, the sun began to sink for the coming of a new day. And so concluded the story of the formerly spoiled prince.

What Are You Cooking Up?
What Your Story Is About

Theme: *the essential meanings of the story that can be expressed directly or indirectly.*

It's not an easy task to get a child to articulate the theme of the story he or she just wrote. This shouldn't cause any concern. It's cause for celebration when children simply enjoy the process of creating stories. When their love for writing has firmly been established, we can slowly steer them towards more abstract thinking. After all, theme is not as tangible as plot. To convey a theme requires a mature understanding of the potential underlying meanings of day-to-day life.

Adora could exploit the basic tenets of dramatic tension and imagine an entire culture before she began to really understand the concept of theme. Many children experience difficulty in grasping abstract concepts like theme unless they directly relate to concrete examples, like, for instance, their own writing. Through their own writing, they can begin to make the connection between the abstract and the concrete. In *The Spoiled Prince*, Adora had an excellent plot that expressed a deeper theme, but she wasn't aware of the connection until her writing tutor and I asked her some questions to lead her to connecting the abstract idea to the actual plot. She feels much more confidant and enthusiastic about her story now that she understands the underlying meaning it embodies. If you feel your child is sufficiently enthused about writing and confident in his/her abilities, you can gradually begin asking questions that lead towards more in-depth work.

 Interview and Tips from Adora

Joyce: Why is it a challenge for you to come up with the theme of your story?
Adora: I always forgot what it means.

Joyce: What kind of themes do you often write about?
Adora: Good overcomes evils, journey is more important than the destination.

Joyce: Do you think about the theme when you write or do you just enjoy the writing process?
Adora: No, I just enjoy the writing process.

Joyce: Do you think about your story when you write, or just focus on the plot?
Adora: I just focus on the plot.

Joyce: How important is the theme to your story?
Adora: The theme is very important to my story but usually I try to get the plot planned out before really focusing on the theme.

 Tips for Parent and Educator

Many times when a student starts to write a story, he or she doesn't have a defined theme in mind. It's perfectly fine to wait until they are finished with a story before you discuss possible themes with them. When you read stories with your student or child, ask them questions in a friendly, non-threatening, and encouraging manner. Your student and child will gradually direct their thinking and creative process towards a more complex and deep theme beyond the simple plot line.

 Give It a Spin

1. Write down five themes that stand out from the movies you saw and books you read.

2. Find a theme you like and write a story plot to demonstrate the theme.

3. Change the theme in one of your favorite fairy tales story and change the plot accordingly.

4. Write a story and go through your story to find out the theme.

5. What are the themes expressed throughout the Harry Potter books?

6. How could you use your setting to emphasize your theme?

7. In a story your main character should be different at the end of the

story than he/she was in the beginning. How does the way your character changes reflect the theme of your story?

8. What are the themes you have discovered in your own stories?

9. If you could choose any themes for your story, what theme would they be?

10. What themes have influenced your opinion and views on life the most?

Uncontrollable Magic

"**A**rani, you goat!" This irritated cry came from Anders, the village shepherd boy, as he jumped up from his resting place on the Big Rock. Anders's sharp hazel eyes followed the playful goat for a distance. "Come back here!" Sighing and throwing down his long yew staff and shepherd horn, Anders ran after the mischievous goat. Casting a few troubled glances at the rest of the herd, Anders ran towards the rocky crags of Mt. Thaed, blocking the goat's path. His shoulder-length brown hair flopped in the breeze.

"Arani, Arani," Anders said, panting. He waved his long arms wildly, unaware of the cliff edge behind him. "Don't try to run off again." The goat grinned, as well as a goat could grin, and rammed his horns on a low branch of an oak tree in reply. Anders took his staff from the ground and watched with pleasure as the goats enjoyed their daily meal of

dewy grass, occasionally nibbling on a daisy or two. The shepherd boy suddenly felt a tingling seep through his veins and out through his hands. He yelped and leapt backwards as a pale green light shot out from his fingertips. Immediately the magic died down. The goats surrounded him, licking him with their rough tongues in concern.

"What'd I just do that for…?" Anders muttered to himself, although he well knew the reason. From what he had overheard from Auld Marina the Storyteller, when boys came of age at fourteen, they were granted a magical gift from the supreme god Darius. It was an ancient but well-known myth. People claimed that those who could not control their power would eventually die as the magic sapped all their strength. Anders quickly banished the idea and tried to concentrate on watching the goats eat. It was a difficult project—his active mind was **prone** to wandering back on things he did not wish to remember. As a gray-bearded stranger wearing a long, dark robe strode past him, Anders wished more than ever that he was not thinking about his uncontrollable magic. Suddenly, the stranger turned back as if startled and, raising his dry, bony hands, cried, "*Kazadoom!*" Dark blue shot out of the man's fingers. Anders shuddered as the man said the word. He felt as if there was a strange coldness enveloping his body.

"Boy," the stranger said to Anders, suddenly serious. "Are you aware that you are in the possession of magic?"

"What?" Anders asked, jumping up from the rock.

"You were invisible to me when I walked past you," the man said, his brow furrowed. "I first suspected nothing. But when I noticed the ring of goats without a shepherd…there was a problem. If you are unwillingly invisible, there are only two options—either you cannot control your magic, or another mage is holding you captive under an invisibility spell. However, if a person wishes to make another invisible, he will have to remain visible himself. Therefore I came to the conclusion that you cannot control your magic."

"No—really—I don't have any magic," Anders said anxiously, stepping in front of his goats.

"I am aware that you do have magic," the man said, smiling crookedly. "Therefore, you must come to study with me."

"But who shall take care of the goats!?" Anders exclaimed, standing in front of the goats protectively.

"They will take care of themselves," the man said smoothly. "And if you wish to know my name, I am Aelfdane, Shaman of the Warring Tribes."

VOCABULARY LIST

coffer – a box or chest used to store valuables
severe – stern, serious, harsh
shaman – sage, a priest who uses magic to heal the sick
vary – differ, be different
preposterous – ridiculous, outrageous
selfless – someone who puts others before themselves
curtly – briskly, briefly, snappishly
intently – fixated, absorbed, paying close attention
ornate – elaborately decorated
sneer – a look that mocks or suggests contempt
inappropriate – not suitable or fitting to the occasion
burnoose – an Arabian style hooded cloak
marauded – to raid for plunder

So began Anders's studies. He was joined by two other boys, Enad and Minivar, whom he utterly **despised**. Enad, a short, stocky boy with short red hair and a **bombastic** manner, was an annoying braggart. The shaman continually gave him detentions for lack of attention and intelligence in class. Minivar was almost exactly the opposite. He was tall and long-limbed, not unlike Anders, with long black hair and pale skin. He was sly and crafty, always spending his silence in plotting **malicious** tricks.

"Minivar, tell me, what power do amulets have over fate?" Aelfdane asked, passing by Anders's desk with a sweeping of his long robes.

"None, sir," Minivar said, pushing back his chair superiorly. "Amulets cannot hold the might of the Supreme Ones. If they choose to ignore the wearer, the amulet will have no use and can possibly turn against the wearer." Enad made a face as Aelfdane nodded.

"Precisely," the shaman said, conjuring a large picture on the wall. "Magic amulets can be ignored by the great gods. However, if the minor gods favor the wearer, their charms combined will turn fate to the wearer's advantage." Minivar stared **arrogantly** at Anders, his black eyes glinting wickedly. But Anders's eyes were not focused on Minivar's **menacing** pupils. The young shepherd boy's eyes were focused on the girl who had just entered the large tent. She was tall, and fair, with long golden-reddish curls running down her back. Her nose was long and pointed, like Anders's, and her face was sunburned on the side. She wore a dark crimson tunic belted tightly around her slender waist and sandals strapped about her ankle.

"Rowena!" Aelfdane cried. "We're very glad to see you!" Rowena smiled, revealing a dimple on the side of her mouth. "As I am to see you, Master Anewor."

"Now it's Aelfdane," the shaman said abruptly, raising his hand. "After the Great Battle, Anewor seemed too...too gloomy a name. It was cursed with bloodshed and despair."

"I can understand your plight," Rowena said, smiling wryly. "Father wished for me to change my name also, but I told him that my mother had named me Rowena and I would remain so for as long as I live."

"I bear the mark of a man who has seen too many terrible things in a lifetime," Aelfdane sighed, turning to Anders. "Might I introduce my new student, Anders?" Rowena smiled again, holding out her hand.

"I'm pleased to meet you, Anders," she said softly, shaking Anders's hand daintily. Minivar stared at her haughtily.

"And what do I get, cousin?" he asked, his eyes now concentrated on Rowena. "Surely more than a shepherd boy of low birth."

"You deserve no more and no less, Minivar," Rowena said, staring at Minivar with obvious dislike. "You and I have met before."

"I am directly related to you, Rowena," Minivar said with contempt. "It is obvious that I deserve more respect than the doltish Enad." Rowena turned away from Minivar.

"I trust you are doing well," she said coldly, not bothering to put out her hand to Enad.

"I am Minivar, son of the great Minivat, son of the omnipotent Minivab, Warlord of the Lion Clan!" Minivar cried with **indignation**. "Why do I not receive the proper amount of respect!?"

"Yeah, Mini Vats of milk," Enad muttered, ignoring Rowena. Minivar turned red with fury and raised his hand. Anders, fearing a fight, immediately ducked under his chair.

"Let there be peace!" Aelfdane cried, raising his hand. Streams of dark blue shot out of his fingers, surrounding Minivar, Enad, and Rowena. Anders watched with awe from under his desk. After leaving them in frozen positions for a few moments, Aelfdane lifted the spell.

"Rowena and Anders, sit in the front of the room. Minivar, Enad, to the back," the shaman ordered. "Anders, you'll have to borrow a textbook." Anders nodded, biting his lip.

"Rowena, you brought your things, I'm sure," Aelfdane said, giving Rowena a penetrating stare.

"Yes, Master Aelfdane," Rowena said coolly, reaching into her bundle. "I have a spare textbook also, if Anders wants to have one."

"That's very kind of you, Rowena," Aelfdane said shortly. "Would you like to accept Rowena's gift, Anders?"

"Yes—thank you," Anders said, gaping as Rowena passed him a small, thick volume.

"All please skip to Chapter Two, Page Forty-Five." Aelfdane said, rapping the desk with his ruler. Anders flipped through the pages, often peeking over Rowena's shoulders, until he found Chapter Two. By then Aelfdane was already reading from the fourth paragraph, so Anders hastily scanned the page as Aelfdane continued, "The War of the Wizards took place mainly in Jarrod, long before our time. The reigning monarch was at that time King Eldon, a wise and caring ruler. However, he was not gifted with magic as most boys are, from the start, being too weak to wield the power. Therefore he dedicated his time to good deeds and much reading, all of which would help him in his later years. By the time he had passed his sickly state, it was too late for him to receive a gift of magic from the great god Darius. When neighboring mages from the vast **hinterlands** beyond learned of Eldon's lack of magic, they gathered armies and marched to Jarrod, storming Jarrod's main strongholds and fortresses. As for Eldon, he sent the most skilled wizards out to meet the enemy sorcerers. He wanted to weaken the magic powers of his opponents and then drive them away with real weaponry. Who can tell me who was the victor of the War of the Wizards?" Rowena immediately raised her hand. Minivar did likewise.

"Rowena," Aelfdane called, ignoring Minivar.

"Nobody won," Rowena said rapidly. "After besieging King Eldon for many years, the enemy drifted away to their homelands."

"Quite true," Aelfdane said, nodding in approval. "Anders—were you listening?" Anders turned red.

"Yes, sir," he said **meekly**, staring down at the floor. Enad sniggered. Minivar stared at him smugly.

"Then let us proceed," said Aelfdane, turning a page. "Skip to Chapter Six, Page Ninety, please. Anders, begin reading."

"Queen Hil-Hildegard of Jarrod," Anders began, pronouncing the long name with much difficulty, "was the cleverest sorceress of her time. She could create earthquakes at a distance of one hundred miles. She could move boulders countless feet away. Most importantly of all, she was a magic mapmaker. Great philosophers and scientists sought her great magic maps for their experiments. Her maps were unlike any of those ever seen in the realm of magic. They showed a person's every single movement, depending on who you wanted to see. Hildegard—"

"That's enough," Aelfdane said abruptly. "Minivar, read the next paragraph."

"However, many nobles were **skeptical** about Hildegard's abilities. Being the first feminine ruler since Queen Alexia, townspeople were reluctant to support the young princess. More than fifty percent of Jarrod's population formed parties who wished to uphold the existing **oligarchy**. Others wanted her younger stepbrother, Jacque, Prince of Moy, to become ruler. But Hildegard was a powerful **orator**. She **entranced** the townspeople with her soft, gentle words, and her oaths to protect Jarrod and make it great. She was elevated to the throne a month later," Minivar finished off with an unattractive curling of his lips.

"Precisely," Aelfdane said, nodding curtly. "Rowena, continue."

"Hildegard's map played a gigantic role in the War of the Wizards," Rowena read smoothly. "With her maps, they could see enemy locations and spoil any plans of surprise attacks. Hildegard made one great map that wielded even more power than the others. And it was stolen."

"That concludes our reading for the day," Aelfdane said stiffly. "Please line up in the front of the room." Enad swaggered forward, followed by Minivar, Rowena, and lastly Anders.

"To communicate with each other, mages must concentrate deeply," Aelfdane said, closing his eyes. "You must think of the wizard you are trying to communicate with and put your effort into breaking through the barrier of the mind." Rowena and Minivar closed their eyes. Enad blinked stupidly. Anders stood still, confused.

"Breathe in deeply," Aelfdane said, inhaling and exhaling. "Send your telepathic messages to each other through relaxation and concentration of the mind."

"Sir—Master Aelfdane—I don't think Anders has it quite yet," Rowena said, opening her eyes. Anders reddened.

"Oh—Anders—maybe you should try to do something a little bit simpler," Aelfdane said, coming out of his trance. "Rowena, could you please teach him the Stretching Spell?"

"Yes, of course," Rowena said, taking Anders's hand. "Come on, we'll have to go outside."

The weather was hot and dry. Rowena cut a thick branch from an oak tree, set it down, and laid her hands on it. With a flash from Rowena's hands, the branch had stretched to four times its original size.

"Here, you try," Rowena said, handing the branch to Anders. "The magic will flow through your body, onto the branch." Anders clumsily attempted to spread his magic to the branch, failing dismally. The branch backfired and hit Anders in the stomach. He stumbled back, groaning with pain.

"Hmm...that does sometimes happen...I wonder if you should try a simpler spell..." Rowena mused, taking the branch away. "How about an easy flying charm?"

"No, really, uh, Rowena, I think I need a rest," Anders said, moving towards the tent entrance. "Excuse me."

"Stop!" Rowena cried, grabbing his arm. "First you have to learn. It's really not hard—I'm sure you can do it."

"I wouldn't be so sure about that, Ro," Enad drawled, sauntering towards the two. "Anders can't even do an easy charm —"

"For that matter, neither can you," Rowena said heatedly, her black eyes flashing. "And *stop* calling me Ro!"

"All I was trying to tell you was that maybe you would want to choose your company more carefully," Enad said loudly, jabbing Anders in the leg. "This shepherd boy has limited magic powers and has no great cities to inherit when he comes of age. My grandfather's place as warlock of the tribe is secured, as well as my father's title of tribe treasurer. My money and inheritance is strong. As for—"

"Is money and inheritance all you care about?" Rowena demanded, eyes narrowed. "At least Anders's first thought isn't about his wealth!"

"Quite true, cousin," Minivar said silkily, striding towards Rowena. "Enad often finds it difficult for his small intelligence to pierce his thick skull. As for Anders, he belongs nowhere but with the goats." Hot fury overtook Anders.

"I'm just as good as you!" he shouted angrily, jumping up. "Why can't you treat me decently?!" Green fire shot out of Anders's hands, hitting Minivar squarely on the nose. Blood spurted out of Minivar's wound.

"Stop!" Aelfdane commanded angrily, emerging from the tent. "Minivar, to your healer. Rowena, Enad, review Chapter Two of the textbook. Anders, I want to have a talk with you." Anders bit his lip nervously. *Whatever he's going to tell me,* he thought, *is not going to be good.* When the two were out of earshot, Aelfdane turned to face Anders.

"You must learn to control your magic," he said **severely**, wagging his finger in Anders's face. "If you are not more conscious of your power it will overtake you. You may end up hurting people."

"It's not my fault!" Anders cried, stomping his foot. "Minivar has his prejudiced notions about low birth, high birth, and the whole lot of **balderdash**! Enad is always trying to convince Rowena I'm no good and that his **coffers** are filled with gold and silver! And—" He was about to say "and you always blame me for things that Minivar and Enad started" but he stopped abruptly. It would be disrespectful to talk of the shaman in such a way.

"What about Rowena?" Aelfdane asked calmly. "Does she annoy you?"

"Not at all!" Anders cried. "By far she's the kindest maiden I've ever met!"

"I suspected as much," Aelfdane said, chuckling. "Rowena was born into a strict law-abiding family, her father being the Grand Chieftain of the Warring Tribes and her mother being the daughter of a wealthy Eastern landlord. Trained at an early age to be kind to all people, she always ignored the barrier of rank.

"She seems to favor you," the **shaman** continued. "Her mother, alas now gone, always liked the peasants and the commoners, and Rowena seemed to follow after her." Anders stared down at his feet nervously.

"Sir…perhaps might I be able to practice my magic…alone?" he asked timidly, not daring to look upon Aelfdane's face.

"I'm not so sure about that," Aelfdane said gravely, stroking his long gray beard. "The main point of magic is to be able to practice it in the presence of others. And I'm not sure if there is enough spare time in which you can practice. Of course, you can try, but I would advise you to limit your time. In some cases what you learn in privacy you will forget in group classes."

"Could I please just try?" Anders asked hopefully, staring up at Aelfdane's face.

"I'm not preventing you," the shaman said, chuckling again. "But if you're forgetting everything you learn in privacy, you must stop it."

From that day on Anders practiced his magic in his private tent. Soon he had mastered the Stretching Spell, the Flying Charm, and telepathy. Rowena praised him for every triumph, much to Anders's pride. There finally came a day when he had surpassed even Minivar in the magic arts.

"Practicing in private does seem to help you," Aelfdane agreed one pleasant day when they were taking a stroll on the Western banks of Lake Gnivom. "It seems to **vary** with different people. Minivar, for instance."

"I don't really want to talk about *him* right now," Anders groaned, stopping as they neared the lake. "I though this is supposed to be a *peaceful* walk."

"You must learn to negotiate with other sorcerers," Aelfdane said sternly, splashing water onto his bony hand. "If none of the mages in the entire realm could communicate without starting an argument we would have an epic war." Anders made a face.

"I *know*," he said, sighing. "But I just don't feel like talking about Minivar right now. I hope he has an early summer vacation."

"Possible," Aelfdane said, smiling wryly. "Minivar's father often sends for his son, for Minivar's family takes many lengthy breaks. Ah…perhaps we should be starting back." Anders bent down to touch the cool surface of the lake and followed Aelfdane back up the steep path leading to the tents of the darkening field.

Anders awoke early in the morning to find that his wrap-around quilt and his tent was soaked with rain. Minivar, Rowena, and Aelfdane slept peacefully in their dry blankets, not bothering to open their eyes. Enad shared Anders's misfortune, also being a novice in the arts of magic.

"I don't see why I, son of the most important man in my clan, can't have a nice warm blanket!" Enad cried with fury, stomping his foot. Anders stared at him flatly.

"The grass is greener on the other side of the hill," he said dryly, repeating a saying he had often heard Auld Marina say. "Be content with what you have."

"Scolding me doesn't help!" Enad cried, jumping up. "Get me a nice hot meal!"

"I think you overuse the word 'nice'," Anders said coolly, edging away from Enad. "A synonym would be better."

"How dare you mock me, you son of a goat, you inferior person!" Enad fumed with rage.

"I am no more inferior than you are," Anders said coldly. "Aelfdane is awakening, so ask him to prepare your breakfast." Slowly he moved towards the snoring shaman, watching Aelfdane's every intake of breath.

"Just tap on him," Enad said carelessly, bringing his fist down on Aelfdane's wrinkled face. The shaman groaned.

"No!" Anders cried, stepping back. Enad pushed Anders forward.

"Aelfdane, I'm afraid that Anders took it into his hands to wake you," Enad said loudly, pushing Anders aside. "But now at least that you're awakened, I can have a proper breakfast."

"Is this true, Anders?" Aelfdane asked sternly, rising from the ground. Not wanting to start an argument, Anders bowed his head in respect.

"I'm too tired to inflict any punishments on anybody today," Aelfdane sighed. "Maybe I'll just forget about it for now. We might as well take a course in making our own breakfast." He smiled weakly. Anders stared at him.

"That's **preposterous**!" Enad sputtered, falling backwards into the wet grass. "I, the son of the great tribe treasurer, do my own labor! Why, it's—"

"He's only jesting," Minivar said coldly. "If it had been otherwise, my reaction would have been similar to yours." Aelfdane nodded.

"However, I would be pleased if you could learn to conjure food out of midair," he said, stepping out of his purple nightshirt. "For now...*Fatheron*!" Anders gawked at Aelfdane as four silver plates appeared on the grass, followed by cutlery and a warm loaf of bread. Minivar immediately stepped forward and examined each of the plates carefully. Finally he selected a flawless silver platter with a sweet, pleasant aroma. Next Enad stepped forward, only to be blocked by Rowena.

"I am the daughter of the Grand Tribe Chieftain," she said haughtily, choosing a medium-sized plate with a slight dent in the middle. "It is my right to take my pick before you." Enad made a face but made no attempt to go past Rowena's slender body. When she moved aside he grabbed a gleaming plate. Finally Anders was left to take his dish.

"I suppose I'll just have this one, then," he muttered, picking up a tiny plate with particles of dirt and breadcrumbs covering its surface.

"You have shown to me that you are the **selfless** one, Anders," Aelfdane said, stepping forward. "For that, let me do this—" Shouting a word of command, the plates were switched around. Anders was left with Minivar's plate and Minivar with Anders's. Rowena had Enad's and Enad had Rowena's.

"That solves our...little problem," Aelfdane said, scooping large helpings of lentil soup into separate bowls. "You might be surprised to learn that since we shall not need plates at all, these moves were useless. Rowena, some tea?"

"No, thank you, Master Aelfdane," Rowena said **curtly**. "I would enjoy pumpkin juice, however." Anders stared as Aelfdane handed him his bowl of soup.

"Isn't there any shepherd gruel?" he asked, gaping. "I mean, er, it's what Auld Marina made all the time—"

"Did I not claim that he was unaccustomed to your teachings, Aelfdane?" Minivar asked coldly. "Now only shall you believe me. He is unfit for magic."

"Never will I believe you unless he proves himself unworthy," Aelfdane said abruptly. "Do not judge a land by its color. Do not judge a man by his birth." Anders turned red.

"I'm not quite a man yet...er...sir," he said, bowing his head. "I'm still a boy, aren't I?"

"Your youth is not everlasting," Aelfdane said firmly. "You are now twelve, and therefore you have entered into the world of an adult. You must take on the life and duties of a man."

"I'm sure I was eleven or ten yesterday," Anders managed to say, shaking.

"Then perhaps today is your birthday."

Rowena nodded.

"Aelfdane may be right. It is our custom to honor those who are born on such days," she said, reaching into her pouch. "Luck is it that I have a gift for you in my pouch...here." From the small brownish sack she wore belted around her waist Rowena drew out a shiny gemstone. Because of its dark blue color, Anders knew it to be a sapphire. Anders stepped back with astonishment.

"Accept it," Aelfdane said gruffly, pushing Anders forward. "It is a gift from the heiress of the Warring Tribes." Anders watched with fascination as Rowena slipped a small knife from its string on the belt.

"Take this also," she said, handing the two presents to Anders. "May they grant you luck on your adventures, wherever you roam." Anders was out of words.

"Thank you," he said gratefully, pocketing the sapphire and tying the knife to his belt as Rowena had done. "I will remember these gifts forever." Rowena nodded and turned away.

The entire morning was spent in a curses lesson. Aelfdane demonstrated how much damage a temporary curse could do, therefore making a permanent curse all the worse.

"Anders, could you please tell me the inventor of the Perpetual Curse?" Aelfdane asked pleasantly.

"Er, Indrajit the Crafty," Anders said with difficulty, looking down at his textbook page. "I think."

"Correct," Aelfdane said, looking up from his desk. "However, it was Indrajit the Clever, not Indrajit the Crafty. Not much difference. So…let us continue with our lesson." Rowena raised her hand.

"Master Aelfdane," she said, looking down at her textbook. "I believe Anders was reading it correctly. It does say Indrajit the Crafty. Perhaps…?" Anders stared at his feet.

"Hmm…" Aelfdane mused. "You are right, Rowena. It does say Indrajit the Crafty. But I am positively sure that it was Indrajit the Clever who invented the Perpetual Curse."

"*Indrajit's son, Indrajit the Crafty, followed in his father's footsteps. He made revisions on the Perpetual Curse and hired several slaves for his various magical experiments,*" Rowena read. "I suppose that's the root of our confusion."

"Er, sir," Anders began. "It doesn't say that in my textbook." Rowena peered over his shoulder.

"You're right," she said with wonder. "Only a powerful wizard could have performed a successful Sentence Switching Spell. And I think Aelfdane put a magical barrier around the tent."

"You *think*," Aelfdane said grimly. "Unfortunately, I didn't." Minivar leered wickedly, his black eyes glinting menacingly.

"The least we can do is try to find hints as to who the culprit is and where he went," Rowena said gravely, staring at Aelfdane. "We should split up."

"Yes, Rowena, you go with Anders. Minivar, Enad, together," Aelfdane ordered, pointing out towards the horizon beyond. Anders shrunk back. "If one of you sees something, shout." *I'll need my knife more than ever for this,* Anders thought gloomily. *Great Gods, we'll need a lot of luck.*

As afternoon faded into dusk and dusk into midnight, Anders plowed his way through a large thicket of brambles. Rowena crawled by his side, followed by a small procession of spiders.

"Great Gods!" Anders cried with pain as his hose ripped on a thorn bush. "If you weren't with me I would have bolted back ten miles!" Rowena smiled weakly.

"Six or seven more miles to go till Indra," she said, taking Anders's hand. "Port city." Anders groaned.

"I hope they'll have a bite to eat there," he said darkly. "I'm feeling particularly ravenous." Suddenly, a wild howl broke out, followed by loud growls and barks.

"Indra werewolves," Rowena whispered, clutching Anders's hand. Anders gulped and felt his mouth turn dry. He muttered faintly, falling forward.

"Be quiet!" Rowena hissed, grabbing his arm. "If we're lucky we'll escape with a few broken limbs!" Anders shuddered as the howls came closer.

"Don't draw your knife!" Rowena whispered, dropping to the ground behind a humongous oak tree. "Werewolves are immediately attracted to anything shiny!" Anders vomited onto the turf. Out of the corner of his eye, Anders could see a hefty werewolf coming closer.

"We're really in for it now," he muttered under his breath. "Great Gods." Another wild howl broke out. Sniffing the ground on which Anders and Rowena had trodden moments before, an entire pack of werewolves slunk past their hiding spot. Anders held his breath, hardly daring to breathe. When the werewolves were finally out of sight, he rose.

"Don't!" Rowena cried, pulling him down. "They're not gone yet!"

The lead wolf pricked up his ears and advanced towards Rowena and Anders with a wild cry. The rest of the pack followed **intently**. They closed around the two, licking their chops hungrily.

"Draw your knife!" Rowena screamed, throwing a stick at the wolves. "Hurry!" Anders grabbed his blade and slashed ruthlessly at the animals. Dodging an attack, he grabbed Rowena's clammy hand and hoisted himself up onto the lowest branch of the gigantic oak tree.

"I-I've g-got to g-get to the n-next b-branch," he panted, wiping sweat from his forehead. The werewolves had surrounded the tree trunk and were yapping loudly.

"Go away!" Rowena cried, raising her hand. Streams of white fire shot out, hitting the pack directly. The wolves let out wild yelps.

"Good one, Rowena!" Anders shouted, jumping up with excitement.

"Don't! You'll lose your balance!" Rowena cried, trying to grab Anders's hand. It was too late. Anders clung to the bottom branch, wriggling and writhing in his attempt to climb up.

"Ropia!" In answer to the spell, a long coil of rope immediately appeared in Rowena's hands. Anders pushed himself up.

"Catch on!" Rowena shouted, throwing the rope down for Anders to catch. With the agility he had mastered in his years as a shepherd, Anders leapt onto the firm rope and waited as Rowena hauled him up.

"Gods, you're a heavy load," she gasped, wiping her hands on her tunic.

"Didn't I feel the same when I had to bring you up here?" Anders asked, grinning. "We're equal, then." The werewolves had drifted away in search of easier prey, and even Anders, with his keen eyes, could see nothing on the plain below.

They met up with Minivar and Enad an hour later in Indra. Aelfdane was questioning the city magistrate about the whereabouts of a certain powerful mage. Anders wanted to go with Aelfdane, but Rowena immediately disagreed.

"He'll be busy talking with the magistrate," she said, turning to Anders. "I'm sure he wouldn't wish to be bothered, and after all, Enad does need…a little help." Minivar turned away arrogantly.

"But shan't we be safer if we're with Aelfdane?" Anders asked meekly, quivering. "Er, after the werewolves and all…" Rowena placed her hands on her hips.

"Normally I wouldn't speak to you like this, Anders," she said, her eyes flashing, "but sometimes you just have to master your fear!"

Sighing, Aelfdane stared at the magistrate.

"You're sure you didn't see anyone strange entering the gates?" he persisted, leaning forward.

"We keep strict records on the gates," was Indrajit's cold reply. Aelfdane sighed again.

"I can see that I will squeeze no information out of you today," he said, raising his staff. "But perhaps a day of drinking will loosen your tongue."

"I drink not," Indrajit said. "It is improper for a ruler to drink."

Anders followed Rowena through a series of winding alleyways and passages, Minivar and Enad bringing up the rear.

"Isn't Aelfdane going to be out by now?" Anders asked breathlessly, offering his hand to Rowena as she bent down to inspect a large footprint. "I mean, it's already midnight and everything—"

"Do me a favor and try not to talk!" Rowena snapped, turning to look at him. "It's getting hard to see and we need to concentrate!" Anders hung his head.

"Stupid, stupid," Enad jeered. "Stupid Anders, stupid Anders!"

"Shut up!" Rowena cried, turning around. "Just because you were born with wealth and an inheritance doesn't mean you have the right to taunt Anders!" Enad glared at Rowena.

"He's lower than me," he said sourly, kicking Anders. "He's only a peon."

"I am not!" Anders cried. "If you want to tease me, do it in privacy! I don't want to hear your blabber ringing in my ears every time I try to relax!"

"I hope you are aware of our nightly curfew?" A smooth, cool voice called out from the shadows. "All men, women, and children must be inside their dwellings by nine o'clock." Anders shuddered.

"Show yourself!" Rowena cried, pointing her finger at the shadow. "If you refuse, I will use magic force!" A tall, angular man stepped out from the shadows. A steel helmet with a short red plume was set on his head, a purple cape billowing out behind him. He wore an elegant brocade doublet and wielded a fine diamond sword.

"We are newcomers to this area," Rowena said, crossing her arms, "and we know of no curfew."

"Know of no curfew?" The man chuckled, his bitter laugh steely cold. "Know of no curfew?" he repeated again. "That is impossible. Everyone within ten miles of Indra knows of our strict rules, made by our ruling oligarchy."

"We are not within ten miles of Indra," Rowena said coolly. "We dwell in Dyrn, where the lush grass grows fair and sweet."

"Dyrn." The man laughed again. "Barely a city, I've heard. What tidings do you bring of…Dyrn?"

"None until you step aside," Rowena said icily. "We must continue on with our quest." Still the man barred the way, his muscular arms blocking the only narrow escape.

"Guards!" the man cried, suddenly flinging off his cape and doublet to reveal a suit of armor. "Come to my aid! Four mages stand before me!" With wild cries, men brandishing broadswords and daggers leapt into the alleyway.

"To the jail for lawbreakers!" the tallest cried, waving a great white flag. "To the jail!" Anders shot fire at them, but a pike man grabbed him. Enad had been taken first, but Minivar and Rowena were still fighting. Finally Minivar collapsed with exhaustion and Rowena's magic died down. They were dragged away to the city prison, a miniscule, filthy place on the outskirts of Indra. Being tired and weary, Anders fell asleep almost as soon the guard grabbed him. Rowena did not fall asleep so fast and started gnawing at the slippery glove of her captor. Finally her eyelids drooped and she fell into slumber. Anders and Rowena were put into one cell, Minivar and Enad into another. At first, Anders was somewhat comforted that he had been put next to Rowena, who could probably easily free them with her magic. He was disappointed to note her closed eyes, but soon fell back asleep himself.

The next morning Anders was awakened by a knock on the door of their cell. Not wanting to wake Rowena, he stayed silent. Without warning, the door burst open and Aelfdane walked in.

"So I see you roamed about past Indra curfew?" Aelfdane chuckled, untying the ropes that bound Anders and Rowena tight. "I need your help finding Minivar and Enad's cell. This labyrinth of dungeons is too big for a weary man like me to wander."

"I think they're two cells away from us," Anders said, frowning. "But I don't remember very well." Rowena groaned, rolling over in her sleep.

"You can get up now, Rowena," Aelfdane said kindly, nudging Rowena in the side. "We're going to find Minivar and Enad." Rowena sprang up.

"They should be in the room next to us, but I'm not sure," Rowena said, tossing the ropes into a corner. "I wonder who that man was. And who rules here, anyways?"

"Lords and magistrates," Aelfdane said. "All very stern and power-hungry. Indra is the only city in the entire realm to have a curfew." Anders rose from his sitting position.

"Shouldn't we go now?" he mumbled. "Er, if you want to…" He stared at the shaman nervously.

"Yes, we are, indeed, wasting time. Let us set off," Aelfdane said, opening the cell door. "Minivar and Enad must be bursting with impatience."

As Anders had guessed, Minivar and Enad were held in the cell next to them. They were both angry and indignant over being forced to wait for about thirty minutes to be rescued.

"Why did you have to rescue the shepherd boy and a *girl* first?" Enad demanded, blocking Aelfdane's path. "I'm much more important than them both combined!"

"Silence," Aelfdane commanded. Enad shut his mouth hastily. "Just hold onto my hand—*tightly*, Minivar—and here we go." Anders felt as if he were being pressed between two very narrow walls. Suddenly he was dropped into his tent back at Dyrn. Rowena stood next to him.

"What was that?" Anders asked, gaping at Rowena. "I mean…the thing we just went through."

"That?" Rowena asked. "It was a Transportation Spell. I haven't mastered it yet, but my father was famous for his ability to move from one province to another like a flash of lightning."

"Who is your father, anyways?" Anders asked curiously. "From all I've heard he's the head of a tribe."

"Not just *a* tribe!" Rowena cried, jumping up. "The Warring Tribes of Dyrn! They defend their ancient homelands and beat back invaders. He's their grand chieftain Aldberht Belghard."

"Aldberht Belghard," Anders repeated, savoring the sound of the name. "He sounds like he's noble and courageous."

"Oh, indeed he is!" Rowena exclaimed emphatically, picking up a pebble and throwing it towards a large boulder. "Even if he has the lesser army, he'll charge at the enemy, ambush, and attack. But he's got advantages in both ways—his massive army is equipped with modern weapons and commanded by brilliant generals. Even the privates in his army are fed four times a day, drilled nine times a week, and have decent beds. The generals live in grand-" Anders was growing bored.

"I think it's lunchtime," he said, patting his stomach as it let out a long rumble. "That is, of course, if you're hungry."

"I'm feeling particularly voracious," Rowena laughed, taking Anders's hand. "Come, let's go see what Aelfdane's prepared for us."

The next morning it was dark and foggy. Rowena had been suddenly called home by her father, Ald, for some war ceremony, and Minivar and Enad had been sent away to work as apprentices for the imperial wizard. Anders was left alone with nobody to talk to, nobody to play with. He even missed Minivar's leering face and Enad's taunts.

The weather turned worse. One rainy morning a few days later, Anders entered Aelfdane's tent and noticed Aelfdane looked unusually grim. He was surveying a letter, his eyes scanning the parchment gravely.

"What's wrong?" Anders asked, plopping down onto the ground.

"Rowena has been kidnapped," Aelfdane said gravely. "By bandits in the Desert of Dyrn."

"WHAT!" Anders sprang to his feet, immediately unsheathing his knife. "This must be a lie!" He fell down, gasping.

"It is only too true," Aelfdane said, burying his face in his hands. "With all my magic powers, I can do nothing to save her. I am an old man. A young rider would be needed to overtake the swift bandits of the desert." He looked at Anders meaningfully.

"I shall do it or die trying!" Anders cried, raising his knife. "By Darius, I swear that I shall do it!"

"Make no oaths before you set out," Aelfdane warned, raising his hand. "Foolish bravado was often the ruin of many a valiant mage. Plan your path carefully."

"I must have the swiftest horse in all of Dyrn," Anders said rapidly. "Otherwise there will be no hope."

"Take my treasured steed, Aurick," Aelfdane sighed, making a snapping noise between his fingers. Almost at once there was a great galloping. A snorting white stallion appeared, his hooves shaking the soft earth of the camp. At once, Aurick bent down to nuzzle Aelfdane's hand. Anders stared in awe.

"Take him now," Aelfdane said, fastening a glittering saddle to Aurick's sleek back. "Ride hard." Anders could barely make himself mount the magnificent animal as it stood majestically.

"Go on," Aelfdane said, pushing Anders up into the saddle. "He will take you many miles." Anders nodded and gave a jerk of the reins. With a loud neigh, Aurick galloped into the foggy mist.

Anders rode through the Desert of Dyrn for three hours nonstop. Gasping for breath, Anders finally stopped at a large boulder. Dismounting, he collapsed onto the huge rock. Aurick's eye flashed in the brightening sunlight. Anders stared at him, shielding his eyes from the bright glare of the rising sun.

"I-I t-thought it was s-supposed to b-be foggy," he panted, stroking Aurick. A voice inside of his head scolded him.

Of course it isn't! he thought. *Don't you remember anything Aelfdane told you? The Desert of Dyrn is the only place that has sunlight all the time!* Aurick whinnied impatiently, rubbing Anders with his side.

"I know you want to go," Anders sighed, hoisting himself up onto Aurick. "I suppose we can't delay any furt—" He was cut off by the sound of galloping hooves in the distance, perhaps twenty seconds away. Aurick reared up, throwing Anders off balance.

"Aurick!" Anders cried as he fell into the scorching sand. "Help!" But Aurick had already sprinted off towards the rider, his golden mane flying in the wind.

Anders opened his eyes to see Minivar, seated on a grand brown horse. It was not nearly so magnificent as his own horse, and Anders was pleased to see Minivar's staring jealously at Aurick.

"If you are looking for Rowena, go away," Minivar said abruptly. "I am brave and gallant. I shall take the quest."

"Am I not as brave and gallant as you?" Anders asked, mounting Aurick. "Am I not as well armed as you? I shall take up the quest, whether it goes against your wishes or not." Minivar scowled and galloped on. Anders soon overtook him and rode ahead.

As he glanced back, Anders noticed Minivar riding behind him. Three men drove dusty packhorses with great bundles tied to their backs further into the swirling sands of the desert. Anders sighed and patted his stomach, suddenly realizing how hungry he was. Aurick slowed to a trot, sensing his master's weakness. Minivar's mount stopped abruptly.

"Too cowardly to continue?" Minivar **sneered**, kicking his horse absentmindedly with his sharp silver spurs. "Too cowardly to continue?"

"I'm not cowardly," Anders said, frowning. "I'm only resting."

"Excuses are for cowards," Minivar said, waving his hand impatiently. "I have no time to listen to such prattle." And with that, Minivar galloped forward. Anders gritted his teeth.

The brightness of afternoon soon faded into the darkness of evening. Anders stopped by a tall cactus and dismounted. Minivar was by now many miles behind him. Sighing, he brushed himself off and lay down on the ground. Aurick watched him, his sharp eyes alert.

"It's been a long day," Anders said aloud, sifting the warm sand through his fingers. "Tomorrow can't be much different." Aurick whinnied in reply.

I wonder what Rowena's doing right now, he thought. He could just barely make out the smoke of Minivar's fire drifting to the clouds. With a smile, Anders fell into slumber.

"Let me go!" Rowena cried as a heavy man grabbed her from behind.

"Be quiet, little missy," the man said, holding his grubby hand to her mouth. "Or else you'll wish you'd never spoken."

"Let her go, Aldus," A taller man emerged from behind a cactus. "*They* want her back alive."

"She's going to be a problem, Baldred!" Aldus barked, drawing a dagger from his gray baldric. "You're not the only boss around here, you know!" Rowena shuddered, tugging at the cord which bound her.

"Just don't injure her!" Baldred shouted, shaking Aldus. "If I see a single mark on her, you'll be punished!" Aldus scowled, but he made no protest. Baldred turned to Rowena.

"Get up," he ordered, jabbing her in the side. Rowena was about to point out that she couldn't get up while she was tied from hand to foot, but Aldus pushed her up and kicked the horse, which galloped forward with a neigh of terror. Aldus grinned wickedly and jumped up onto the saddle beside Rowena. Disgusted with his smelly breath and blackened teeth, Rowena looked away.

"One hundred miles till Aeldra," Baldred said, turning back towards Aldus. "Look sharp." Aldus grunted and pulled a cigar from his pouch.

"Don't smoke that!" Baldred exclaimed, wincing. "It smells— awful!"

"Come on," Aldus wheedled, putting the mossy cigar to his lips. "Just one go."

"Oh fine," Baldred sighed, plugging his nose. "Just don't get anywhere near me." Rowena wished she could have had the freedom of her arms as an odoriferous green substance drifted out of Aldus's cigar.

"Phew," Baldred said, fanning the air in front of his nose. "That is one stinky cigar."

"You weren't even breathing!" Aldus exclaimed, raising his fist.

"Well still, it's foul…" Baldred's voice trailed off as the shining rooftops of a city came to view.

Anders groaned. What time was it? Finally he remembered. Rowena had been kidnapped, and it was his duty to find her.

"Ugh," Anders groaned again, leaning against Aurick. "I should have brought something to eat." Aurick did nothing.

"I'm feeling particularly sick today," Anders said, mounting Aurick. No sound or movement came from the horse as Anders jerked the reins.

"What is wrong with you!?" Anders cried, losing his patience. He kicked Aurick. "You're as still as stone!" *Stone!* That was it! Someone had snuck into his camp and performed a spell on Aurick that turned him to stone. If only Anders knew how to break the spell...

"Kazadoom!" Anders tried, pointing his finger at Aurick. Nothing happened.

"Dalrennia!" he tried hopelessly. Aurick did not move.

"Verdgmagon!"

"Need a little help?" Minivar sneered, coming up behind him. "I don't suppose you ever thought you could overcome my great power."

"It was you!" Anders cried, clenching his fists.

"Indeed it was I," Minivar said, advancing closer. "And only I know the magic that shall break the spell." With one last effort, Anders shouted,

"Ahasfer!" It was a spell that came out of nowhere. Aelfdane had never taught it to him—it simply came to Anders. Aurick gave a great neigh and sprinted forward, kicking Minivar squarely in the stomach. This time Minivar would not give way to pain.

"Come out and fight like a man!" Minivar cried, drawing a broadsword from an **ornate** copper scabbard.

"No, I think I'd rather skip," Anders said, and with that, he leapt onto Aurick's back.

"Coward!" Minivar cried with rage, racing after Anders. "Cowardly dastard!" But by then Anders was far, far away.

Rowena was tossed down from the horse into the arms of another man, taller than both Baldred and Aldus, with sharp, sunburned features.

"She is not as I expected," the man said silkily, his eyes glinting penetratingly from under his black hood. "You *have* been taking good care of her?"

"Aldus found it an amusing sport to disobey your commands, my lord," Baldred said, bowing very low. "However, I did my best to discourage any **inappropriate** behavior." Aldus spat at Baldred's feet.

"Baldred exaggerates, lord," Aldus said loudly. "I—" The man in the black hood narrowed his eyes.

"You have *not* been molesting her in any way?" he asked, staring at the two men in turn.

"No, Lord Cadarn," Baldred said hastily. "We would not think of it."

"Good," the hooded man said. "Take the girl and lock her in my uppermost tower. I will have a talk with her afterward."

"Let me go!" Rowena shouted as she found herself being dragged away to a high pinnacle. "My father shall have revenge!"

"Your father won't think about having revenge, now that we've kidnapped his little girl," Aldus laughed, hoisting Rowena up onto his shoulders. "But for now you must remain imprisoned." Rowena groaned.

Anders stopped Aurick amid a swirling sand dune. It was almost impossible to navigate one's way through the blinding sand, so Anders rested for a while beside Aurick. The sound of Minivar's horse's hooves could no longer be heard over the whirling circles of sand, so Anders guessed that Minivar had stopped also.

"This desert is so unpredictable," Anders sighed, straightening the **burnoose** Aelfdane had given him. "Yesterday it was calm and today it's like a sea of swirling sand." Aurick nodded serenely, swatting at a fly with his long golden tail.

"Finally a chance to ride on," Anders said, remounting Aurick as the sand cleared. Galloping on, they could just barely make out the glinting rooftops of a desert city.

"Hurry, Aurick!" Anders cried, urging the horse on. "Rowena might be trapped there!" He was not far from the truth.

Aldus threw Rowena onto her crude wooden bed. It was one hard mattress and a few faded covers put on top the wooden bed frame. Scrawny rats and other vermin scurried about, putting their filth into the thin sheets. Although Rowena felt nauseated at the sight, her weariness overcame her and she drifted into sleep.

Anders peered into the keyhole of the city gates, interested. The streets, dark and sinister, could barely be seen through the narrow hole. *I hope Rowena's not trapped in there,* he thought as he stared at the streets. *I would certainly be scared.* A tall tower stood high above all the rest, the striking point of a large gray stone castle. Two guards stood at attention in front of the great doors of the castle, their sharpened pikes at the ready. It was beginning to grow dark, and Anders felt tired.

I suppose we must go in here, Anders thought, testing one of the entrance gates to the city. *At least they'll have something to eat and drink.* He led Aurick through the shadowy streets up to the castle. The guards did not even glance at him. Anders stood waiting at the entrance, unsure of what to do. If he simply walked in, he might be cut down by the guards. But every minute he wasted on talking would give him less time to search for Rowena.

"Boy!" one of the guards suddenly barked, pointing his pike at Anders. "What be your name?"

"Er, Anders," Anders said, staring nervously at the pike.

"You wish admittance to the castle?" the other guard said, his voice deep and melodious. "Where is your pass?"

"What pass?" Anders asked, confused.

"To enter this fortress, one must have a letter or pass issued by Lord Cadarn of Darkness," the guard said, crossing his pike with the other guard's. "If thou does not bear one, thou will not pass."

"But why can't I go in and just have a look around?" Anders asked, moving forward. The guard raised his pike. As though sensing Anders' wishes, Aurick charged forward, knocking both guards onto the ground. Anders leapt up the stairs and into the castle foyer.

"Someone is tracking us," a low voice hissed next to Rowena's ear. Rowena immediately stiffened, cupping her ear to the bed. She could hear pounding footsteps, getting closer and closer.

"*Anders,*" she breathed, hardly daring to believe it.

"Hurry!" Cadarn exclaimed, running to the window. "Bar the doors! Someone has taken our trail!" Baldred and Aldus immediately ran to carry out their master's orders. Cadarn sprinted towards the watchtower, alerting the bowmen at once.

"Set your longbows!" he commanded, surveying the dark plains beyond the city. "I can see a dim shape approaching the castle!"

"But—Sire—it shall be impossible to find a good aim in this darkness," the captain of the archers protested, dropping his bow onto the balcony ground. Cadarn spat at the captain and dealt a blow to his face.

"Cowardly dog!" the angry lord sputtered, kicking the captain. "How dare you question my commands!? Leave your absurd counsels in the back of your mind and bother me no more with foolish babble." The captain nodded, trembling with fear.

"Let that stand as a lesson to all of you bowmen!" Cadarn shouted, turning to the frightened shooters. "Shoot straight and true—I hear hooves approaching!"

Panting, Anders dashed up a series of winding steps. Rowena's prison couldn't be much further. Aurick stood waiting in a richly ornamented hallway, chewing on some decorative grass. Anders took a sharp sword from its place on the wall and tested it against a gold mirror. The glass shattered into tiny shards.

"I'll be right back," he promised, stroking Aurick as the horse kicked the glass aside. "I just need to rescue Rowena and bolt out of this place." Aurick nodded, licking a long golden tapestry with his rough tongue. Anders smiled despite the dire situation and scrambled up the steps.

Rowena listened to Anders's footsteps, each pounding a shimmer of hope for her. Aldus and Baldred were in very bad moods and shouted at Rowena in turn as a stream of pale green magic flowed up through the floorboards.

"Ye damn bitch," Aldus swore, gritting his teeth. "Curse ye."

"Stupid lass," Baldred said, raising a fist. "If it weren't for the lord's orders I would have pounded you into mincemeat." Rowena bit her lip nervously.

"She is to be hidden!" Cadarn had returned, and he was angrier than ever. "Hurry up with it, you doltish simpletons! Do you think a great lord has all the time in the world?" Baldred scurried away as Aldus heaved Rowena onto his shoulders. Rowena let out a groan.

"Hurry!" Cadarn shouted, stomping his foot. "I hear footsteps approaching!" He grabbed Rowena and shoved her into a small, dirty closet. Baldred and Aldus quickly took posts guarding Rowena. Anders burst in, splintering the door with a burst of green sparks.

"Fight, villains!" he cried, raising the sword which he had found in the hallway. "Give me the fair damsel whom you took!" Cadarn sneered and raised his rapier. Its narrow steel gleamed in the candlelight, giving off eerie reflections.

"I, Anders, challenge you to a duel!" Anders cried, raising his own sword with much difficulty.

"Prepare to perish, peasant boy!" Cadarn roared. And with that, he thrust his rapier, missing Anders by an inch. Shocked by Cadarn's sudden attack, he fell to the ground. Cadarn advanced towards him, his slit eyes glinting menacingly. Anders jumped up and slashed at Cadarn's thick belt. The belt fell off and hit Anders in the eye with its sharp metal fastening piece. Anders stumbled back, but was not shocked for long. As Cadarn walked towards him, Anders threw his sword directly at Cadarn's chest. With a great shriek, Cadarn fell to the ground. Blood spurted out from his chest. Aldus and Baldred ran for their lives. Just as Rowena emerged from the closet Minivar ran in the room.

"Come, Rowena," he said, ignoring Anders. "I was delayed by some bowmen. Aelfdane wishes for me to take you back."

"I found her, and I shall take her back to Aelfdane," Anders said, smiling as he glanced at Rowena, who was slipping away.

"You dastard!" Minivar cried. Anders ran through the open door, following Rowena. He jumped onto Aurick, shooting a volley of magic fireballs at Minivar as he gave Rowena Minivar's nag.

"Aaaaaah!" Minivar roared, singeing his eyebrows as he fell headfirst into the fire. Suddenly he began to shrink, his skin crackling and withering. As if out of nowhere, a small, ugly dragon hopped out of the fire. Although its glinting black eyes reminded Anders distinctly of Minivar, he saw no other similarities.

"Hurry up, let's get out of here," Rowena whispered, turning back to look at the growing fire. They **marauded** through the castle and out into the chilly breeze, leaving Aeldra (and the Minivar dragon) behind.

Hit the Home Run
Self Revision and Editing

When your child demonstrates interest and ability in revising and editing his/her own writing, you have hit a home run.

Ask any experienced writer and she will tell you that re-writing and editing is absolutely crucial, if not more important than writing itself. Unfortunately, children are not generally taught to edit. Traditionally, students submit work to their teachers and receive corrections. Although this can be helpful, correcting is not the same as explaining. Self-editing is not taught to young students. Students don't get a chance to develop a sense of trust in their own ability to edit, and therefore don't benefit from learning the process of self-improvement.

Just like millions of young students, Adora didn't like to put herself through the tedious process of erasing and re-writing to correct and polish her writing. This was before she learned to type. Because Word automatically underlines spelling and grammar errors, she was immediately able to spot and correct many of her mistakes herself. To teach her how to catch more subtle mistakes, we would sit with her and go over her writing. Instead of correcting after the fact, we were now able to explain why something didn't work as she was writing and ask her to see if she could come up with an alternative. She would type in alternatives until she hit upon one that worked. After months of this type of practice, she now often finds and corrects her mistakes long before anyone else looks at her work. She has even extended this practice to improving sentences that are not technically flawed but that just could sound better.

Thanks to the computer and Microsoft Office/Word software, Adora has discovered the joy and freedom of self-editing. Because the cut-and-paste option makes it so easy for her to play with her organizational structure, she is able to move a sentence around several times until she finds the place it sounds best. It is impressive to see her tiny fingers jumping up and down on the keyboard furiously as she re-arranges sentences, changes what she wrote, or corrects mistakes here and there. Technology has provided tools that are instrumental in her love for writing.

Interview and Tips from Adora

Joyce: How is it different correcting and editing your writing on the computer versus doing it longhand?

Adora: I am normally a very impatient person, particularly with my writing. When you're writing something down by hand, you can't correct as easily as you can on the computer. It's not a push of the Backspace when you write it longhand. It's long minutes of endless rubbing with the eraser.

Joyce: How does typing your story on the computer motivate you to do self-revision and self-editing?

Adora: It's much easier than doing it on paper, and if I'm confused, Microsoft Word can help me. I don't depend on their software now as much as I did when I began typing, because now I'm more experienced in editing myself.

Joyce: What do you learn through self revision and editing?

Adora: I learn to be dependent on myself, not just other editors. It also gives me a chance to practice my editing skills, such as punctuation, grammar, and clarifying sentences.

Joyce: What would you tell other kids who are just starting to write?

Adora: I would say let your ideas flow freely. On the first draft, don't worry about spelling or grammar. Just write down whatever is on your mind.

 ## Tips for Parents and Educators

The appropriate approach to technology has a crucial impact on our children's learning. When we look beyond recreational computer games, and we guide our children to use technology to enhance their learning and nurture their creativity, they benefit from it tremendously. When you can provide your child with a lap-top computer (although she types on both, Adora prefers a lap-top over a desk-top because the keys are so sensitive that it requires little effort) and some typing software, plus Microsoft Word, you have taken the first step to help your child become a competent, skillful and happy writer.

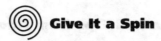 **Give It a Spin**

Children love to have a finished product to present to parents and friends. Pick a story or two from your child's writing and give them an opportunity either to publish online or to print them as a book. Since either format will be viewed by the public, it's important to make it as error free and polished as possible. Encourage your child to revise, re-write and edit their work until they are satisfied with the results. Children are proud to have their work published online or made into a storybook for everybody to enjoy!

Part II

Learning Through Writing

! ABC ⁄

When I just write, the rules come to me. It's natural.

Learning the Fundamentals of Writing

Grammar

Grammar rules are traditionally taught separately from general writing. For many children, learning new rules to obey isn't exactly an exciting prospect. It's not an easy task for children to master grammar rules when the effectiveness of applying the rules has no immediate impact. Grammar only becomes meaningful when children realize that without it, their stories may be misunderstood.

I don't mean to imply that grammar should be a primary focus when you are first encouraging your child to write. Being constantly corrected is what keeps many kids from wanting to write at all. First, show enthusiasm for what your child is writing. Let him/her know that you are excited and interested and want to know more. Enthusiasm is contagious. Most kids have a strong desire for positive attention and approval. When they discover writing is a way to get these desired reactions, it will immediately become something more important in their life.

Only when they have developed a healthy enthusiasm for writing should you begin correcting grammar. When you discover a grammatical mistake, just let your child know that something is confusing you. For example, if it is a discrepancy in tense, say, "In the beginning I thought this story took place in the past, now it seems to be taking place in the present, and here again the past…I'm confused, can you help me?" Thanks to the vast amount of time Adora spends writing, grammar rules have become really easy for her to understand. Long before she was deliberately exposed to the rules of grammar, she was writing. Because we waited until she was already really excited about writing before we began to call her attention to mistakes, her enthusiasm was never dampened by the fear of breaking a few grammatical rules. Once she started to write and realized the need to equip herself with some knowledge of grammar, she was willing to use workbooks to acquaint herself with some basic grammar rules.

She has discovered complex rules on her own through reading and writing, and she has been more than willing to learn when we point out mistakes. She is no longer learning grammar for no apparent reason; she is inspired to learn for the sake of creating stories that her readers can better understand and thus enjoy. Like any child, Adora abhors 'busy work', but she sees clear reasons to learn grammar. She loves to see people getting enjoyment out of her writing and understands that confusing grammatical errors impede this enjoyment. Confused readers stop reading to ask questions. In Adora's way of thinking, time not spent reading is usually wasted time. For her, grammar is no longer a collection of isolated and irrelevant rules, but a tool to become a better writer.

 Interview and Tips from Adora

Joyce: Why is it important to write your story with correct grammar?
Adora: Because I don't want it to be confusing to the readers.

Joyce: How did you acquire so many seemingly complicated and complex grammar rules?
Adora: When I just write, the rules come to me. It's natural.

Joyce: Why would you like to learn your grammar rules through your writing?
Adora: It's easier through writing.

Joyce: How does editing and revising of your stories help you solidify your understanding and knowledge of grammar?
Adora: Once it has been edited, I remember the rules very well so I won't make the same mistakes again.

Joyce: How do you judge if your writing complies with the rules of the grammar?
Adora: I just know through reading many other books.

Spelling

Microsoft Office was invaluable in teaching Adora how to spell. At first I was worried that the tool might make her too dependent on the technology, but as it turned out, the software functions freed her from her fear of making mistakes and reinforced her ability to remember the correct spelling of words. By using the Microsoft Office software, she has become more independent. She consciously forces herself to remember the correct way to spell words so she can take pride when the red line no longer appears beneath the words that she once misspelled. Microsoft Word truly helped her to become a very competent speller.

 ## Interview and Tips from Adora

Joyce: How did you overcome the barriers of spelling?
Adora: After correcting my spelling on Microsoft Word over and over again, I remembered the right way to spell the word and became more confident.

Joyce: What would you say is the best way to become a good speller?
Adora: First, attempt spelling the words. The battle is already lost if you don't try. If you don't think that you spelled it correctly, you check how to spell it on Microsoft Word.

Joyce: Do you feel that being a good speller boosts your confidence when you write? How?
Adora: I believe that it does help a little bit to know that you're spelling everything correctly—you don't have to go up and say, "Mom, did I spell this correctly?" or "Is this right?" etc.

Joyce: Why do you believe it's important for kids to start writing even when they do not spell well yet?
Adora: Once they get used to spelling words in their stories, it will become a habit and they will remember the correct spelling.

Joyce: How did writing itself make you become a good speller?
Adora: When I write, I spell out my words. It helps me to put them in my stories, not just straight-out sentence-writing or word review.

Joyce: Why do you like to spell challenging words?
Adora: It's good practice for spelling and writing alike.

Punctuation and Capitalization

Adora began her writing without the proper use of punctuation. All her words were capitalized. This didn't prevent her from becoming the prolific writer she is today. She learned punctuation rules naturally and intuitively while writing her stories. I asked her to read her writing out loud and punctuate where she discovered natural pauses. First she put a period after each sentence, regardless of whether it needed either a comma or semicolon. She began adding commas intuitively when she realized her thoughts were not finished. Rule by rule, she learned good punctuation. Her ease with quotation marks came when she was writing dialogue. She wasn't aware the quotation mark was required, but once she realized it was necessary to keep her dialog clear, she has always used it correctly. It only took a few seconds to explain the rule, and she applied it right on the spot. I doubt that she would be as fast a learner if the rule was taken out of the context of her own writing. She is now so avid about punctuation that she jumps at the chance to correct the mistakes of others, much to the chagrin of certain teachers who occasionally get sloppy while writing on the board.

 Interview and Tips from Adora

Joyce: Why do you think that you need to use punctuation in your writing?

Adora: It gives you a clear image of how a character is saying a line. It's not the same if you change something like "'You ignorant minion!' the angry lord roared" to "'You ignorant minion,' the angry lord roared."

Joyce: Have you ever wondered what punctuation you should use in your writing?

Adora: Not really. Sometimes I'm stuck between how the character should say something, but that's it.

Joyce: How do you know which letters need to be capitalized?

Adora: It's easy to remember: names, beginning of sentences, official titles…there's really not much I need to think about.

Sentence Structure

Fragmented and choppy sentence structure is one of the major and common signs of childish writing. Once a child loses initial inhibitions about writing and realizes that writing can be fun, it's time to start gently encouraging better form. A teacher's lack of confidence in a child's potential is often the only thing preventing a young writer from writing adult caliber prose. Many adults read listless, poorly written sentences and let it slide because 'He's only eight.' I'm not suggesting that an eight-year-old child should be berated for less than dynamic prose, but kids are often quick to pick up good habits when given examples. Once Adora notices that one way of writing something sounds better than another, she is usually eager to incorporate this new bit of knowledge into the pages that follow. Some children are more sensitive to criticism and require a gentler type of prompting. For sensitive children, avoid correcting their actual stories. Instead, show them how to correct poorly structured sentences you write as a counter example.

A lot of children write stiff, clunky sentences because they associate writing with school busywork. When you do writing activities with your child, emphasize the zany possibilities. Tell your child they can make their sentences about anything in the world as long as they illustrate the guideline in question. For example, when asking your child to combine a series of sentences to eliminate clunky prose, make sure the topic is something memorable. Example:

Before: The armadillo was obese. The armadillo ran at lightening speed. It ran straight towards me.
After: The obese armadillo ran straight towards me at lightening speed.

Teaching children to avoid the passive tense can become an amusing game when you examine a sentence like 'The knight was thrown to the ground.' You can say something like, "Wow, that sounds like he was just standing there and suddenly he hurled to the ground on his own."

If you're feeling spry, you can mime the moment, giving an abstract rule a memorable visual.

These are just a few ideas. Once you begin working with your child you can invent similar exercises that are tailored to their interests and temperament.

Interview and Tips from Adora

Joyce: You used to write pretty "babyish" sentences, as you call them, so what do you think has helped you to become more sophisticated in terms of your sentence structure?

Adora: My tutor helped me a lot, and as I read more complex books I got more used to using complex sentences.

Joyce: What's your method of picking the most dynamic and powerful sentences when you write?

Adora: Usually, I start out with two sentences that essentially have the same meaning and try to decide which one sounds better, or I just make a new sentence entirely.

Joyce: Sometimes you chop off many sentences that you call "empty words." What do you mean by that?

Adora: Empty words are words that have none of my imagination in them. They are empty. I did not imagine them. They were simply words.

Joyce: What are the criteria you use to differentiate a good sentence from a poor sentence?

Adora: I judge good and poor sentences by their descriptiveness and imagination.

Joyce: Why do you prefer writing two types of sentences and then deciding which one is better?

Adora: It gives me some time to ponder on both sentences and even add in a few extra descriptions.

Joyce: What would you say to other children who aim to improve their sentences?

Adora: I would tell them to read high-level books with descriptive sentences and good dialogue. When they get used to these kinds of books, they will write in the same style, thereby creating good sentences.

Joyce: Why is it important for you to read your story line by line to see if each sentence is well written?

Adora: When I come to important parts I usually read line by line. But on other minor sections of my stories I merely scan through.

 ## Tips for Parents and Educators

I have learned a lot from music teachers. The good and experienced music teachers don't correct their students' mistakes and weakness all at once. They space them out so the students are not overwhelmed by their inadequacy. The same method should apply to your child's writing. If your child has just started to write, or lacks interest in writing, go easy on the criticism and suggestions. Start out slow; call attention to your child's greatest strength (either the neatness of the writing, the quantity, the originality of the story, the imaginative descriptions of the scene and characters, the unusual twist and turns in the plot, etc.) and then carefully and sparingly choose something he/she can work on and improve. The following week choose a new skill to focus on. Remember: Love, enthusiasm and an interest in expressing his/her idea through writing are more important than the mechanics of writing. Mistakes in the mechanics of writing can be corrected in minutes; love of writing takes time to nurture. When you foster your child's love for writing, he/she will reap the benefits for the rest of his/her life. With love for writing comes the desire to improve and perfect it.

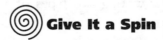 ## Give It a Spin

Children love to look back at their old writing. Take advantage of their enthusiasm. Re-read their writing together and ask them what they think of their old writing. Ask them where they see the need for improvements. If the writing was done by hand, type it for your child to make it easier to work with, or you can have them type it for themselves. You can lay out the possibilities, such as spelling, grammar, sentence structure, or punctuation and let your child choose one or two to work on.

Through active writing, Adora learned the grammar, spelling, and syntax rules she needs to express. Here are just a few examples of her writing.

A note written to Peter Jennings

After reading so many people's postings for Peter Jennings, I further realize how blessed I was to meet Mr. Peter Jennings when I was on the show to write my story live for Good Morning America. My family is a great fan of his television program World News Tonight. When Mr. Jennings discovered that I too have a passion for history, he made sure I received a copy of his history book, *The Century for Young People.* I was touched that he took the time to send me the book, which I enjoyed reading greatly. It is filled with interesting facts, and features interviews with people who have experienced important historical events first-hand. I will cherish meeting the book's author for the rest of my life (I have a long life ahead of me. I am only seven). I even take a great interest in becoming a journalist myself.

I sincerely hope that he will have a speedy recovery and I wish him the best.

Adora Svitak

My Dream Day with Diane Sawyer and Charlie Gibson

I never imagined my writing would take me anywhere, let alone New York. I was just having my own happy thoughts in Redmond. I never imagined my writing good enough to be on T.V., even on the radio or in a newspaper, or a book. I just imagined it would stay on our four computers. And I was content for it to stay that way.

A day after I was on *Komo4 News*, the person on the phone told me that *Good Morning America* wanted me to be on their show. My mom showed me separate pictures of Diane Sawyer and Charlie Gibson on the internet. They both looked very friendly and extremely nice. I was very excited and looked forward to meeting them. I haven't gone on my trip yet, but I am enjoying imagining what it will be like.

One of my dreams is to go to one of New York's biggest bookstores with them and look at all of my favorite books and other books I haven't read yet. I would likely want to go to the Historical

Fiction section, because Historical Fiction captures my interest the most. Maybe they would recommend a book for me to read, an adult's book that I've never heard of before.

I would also like to go to a gigantic museum with a variety of things from ancient times, like a Viking hat, or a Wooly Mammoth's tusk, parts of cave pictures, a cannon from the American Revolution, a pioneer girl's dress, or a wagon's wheel.

Thirdly, we could go into an ice cream shop and look at all of the different kinds of flavors and all the different kinds of cones, and then we could sit down at a table especially reserved for VIPs. It would be quiet all around us.

Then I'd enjoy going to take a peek behind the scenes, to see how they prepare for their show. I would like to see the makeup room and also the office.

After that, we could make brownies and possibly hot chocolate too. I love the smell of brownies, and the sweet taste and warm sensation of hot chocolate. I would hope they do too. When the brownies were finished baking, it would be time to party! I'd also ask for their email addresses so that I could email them from time to time and send them a story I just finished. It would be fun to chat online, too, and see how each person is doing and where they are.

 **Letter to Oprah**

Dear Oprah,

I am Adora Svitak. I am a seven-year-old writer. I have been writing since I was four years old and I started typing when I was six years old. I have written a total of three hundred stories in the past eleven months. The stories contain a total of one hundred and eighty thousand words. I write historical fiction, fantasy, and adventure stories. I have a passion for reading, especially history. I have been featured on five local television shows and on Good Morning America. I would like to be on your show because I want to help other children to learn to appreciate reading and writing more.

I know about you because I enjoy watching your show.

I understand that you value education and you do a great job helping children.

I want to use my writing skills to promote and encourage more children to read and write. I would tell them that reading and writing has taken me on adventures and I have met people I have never imagined I would meet, like Peter Jennings from *World News Tonight*. I want to help your Angel Network by donating my books to children who are less fortunate.

I can type blindfolded—and just as fast as I can type with my eyes open, which is sixty words a minute. I write about three pages or more a day. I also read two or three books a day, at the reading speed of six hundred words per minute.

Sincerely,
Adora Svitak

Part III

Master the Tools
of Learning

Writing made me like math better because I could make fun word problems. Writing gave me a chance to expand my historical knowledge.

Using Writing to Digest and Understand Other Subjects

Writing can be used as a tool to help children learn any subject. Writing helps students sort, digest, and organize information. It helps students discover the limits of their understanding of a subject, and motivates them to search for deeper understanding in order to explain and support their opinions.

In most schools, writing is being taught as a skill, not used as a tool to master other subjects. When it comes to mastering other subjects, writing is Adora's single most effective and powerful tool. She has the most fun using the tool. She takes every opportunity to write in order to continually sharpen the tool. Therefore, her writing gets honed continually.

Although Adora enjoys learning almost every subject, math and science didn't initially excite her at the same level as writing and literature. She complained that math lacked creativity, and that when she was not allowed to make anything up, 'learning' was just memorizing a bunch of boring rules. To help her feel confident in these two important subjects and thus enjoy them, I knew I had to tap into her passion for writing. I began asking her to write word problems for me. I told her she could make the problems about anything she wanted: dancing bears, pirate ships, knights—she just had to follow some basic mathematical guidelines.

This method has proven very effective. She is more willing to solve problems she has made up herself. Using her writing, she spices up mundane multiplication, and turns division into a dispute over pirate plunder.

Her interest in science came a little more naturally. As her interest in science fiction grew, she felt the need to increase her scientific knowledge. Again, she combines her passion for reading and writing to gain a stronger footing in a subject that once intimidated her. She reads on various scientific topics and writes a science journal to sort out the information she unearths in her reading. She can survey math and science from the safety zone of writing.

Writing as a tool for learning can be used both ways. When your child lacks interest in a certain subject, but enjoys writing, you can encourage his/her learning of the subject through writing. When your child is excelling in certain subjects, but not so interested or good at writing, you can have him/her write about the subjects they are passionate about. The more your children share what they know through writing, the better writers they become.

The other day I asked Adora to do her homework. She protested saying,

"Mom! I just got started reading!"

The book in question? A history of the Holocaust—not exactly something most people would consider recreational. The truth of the matter is that Adora has always been interested in history. Her initial interest in history sparked her love for historical fiction, which in turn inspired her to 'fact check' and read even more non-fiction history. Reading historical fiction made her want to write historical fiction, which in turn made her want to do more research into actual history. Although your child may not share Adora's rather morbid desire to read about Dachau during break time, you can still use writing to spark your child's interest in reading history.

If your child is interested in airplanes, challenge him/her to write a story about a World War II fighter pilot. Ask your child what the fighter pilot's planes were like. As she/he uses the internet or the library to research World War II planes, she/he will inevitably absorb other facts about World War II history. Next, challenge your child to find out where the pilots lived, what they ate, etc.

"Mom, Dad, watch what I can do!" Most children love to show off. They seek approval by showing us what they know. 'Showing Off' doesn't have to have negative connotations. By asking your child to tell you about something in writing, you are giving them the opportunity to explore something they are excited about.

Writing is one of the best outlets for children to display their knowledge and skills. Just as you can use an interest in writing to encourage learning in another subjects, you can use an interest in another subject to encourage more writing. If your child is excited about a cartoon, or a field trip, or a movie or a video game, ask him/her to write about it. When you teach your children to use writing to display what they have learned, you have given them a powerful tool that will prove useful in most aspects of life. When they feel comfortable and confident using this tool, their learning becomes purposeful and relevant. They have a dynamic way to communicate their knowledge and ideas. They have an opportunity to showcase their well of knowledge. When they effectively convey what they have learned in writing, they have really gone through all the important stages of learning: recalled facts, digested concepts and ideas, organized the information, and transferred what they have learned into words of their own.

We have included some of Adora's writing here to demonstrate how she is using writing to learn subjects she lacks enthusiasm and passion for. We also include examples of the way she uses writing as a tool to gain deeper understanding of subjects she is immensely interested in.

Our children are facing ever-increasing demands on their intellect and ability to solve problems. In the so-called 'Information Age,' efficient communication is a global obsession. The ability to adapt to new concepts and technology is now prized above actual knowledge. Learning to write well, fast, and with ease is a great way to develop mental agility, and gain a crucial component of success in academics or the workplace. We hope that this book sheds some light on how you can help your children break free from creative inhibition and achieve success in school and in life.

Adora's love for history shines through as she demonstrates her ability to understand and process what she reads. If your children have trouble thinking of what to write, encourage them to write about something they already love. Adora happens to love history, but don't hesitate to encourage your children to write about less academic interests. Even if your goal is to help your children improve their academic writing, their writing progress will be slow if they never discover the inherent joy of writing. Letting your children write about video games or cartoons will pay off more in the long run than forcing them to write about something they find dull.

The Laws of Danaynock
By Expert Danatition

The books of Danaynock are first scanned through an **irksome** and tiresome process and then released, with a special gold seal issued by King Danoclys to indicate that the book has not been illegally printed. Books that disagree with King Danoclys's laws or insult him and the Council of Nobles are strongly prohibited and those who disobey this rule are sentenced to half a year in prison with nothing to eat. If they survive this ordeal they are beheaded by the King Danoclys himself, who strongly enjoys this form of execution.

Schoolbooks are and always were a major jumble of boredom and facts. King Danoclys covered up his many defeats and **censored** out any information he considered "inappropriate for this doltish community I am forced to rule." Like the famed Napoleon Bonaparte, one of his mottos is "it doesn't matter what the truth is, it just matters what the people think." Some, tormented so badly by this, set up secret organizations underground or in secret shelters. Often these remain undetected, but occasionally one or two is broken up and the leaders executed.

> **VOCABULARY LIST**
>
> **irksome** – tedious, irritating
> **censored** – suppressed or deleted information
> **propaganda** – information or publicity (including artwork) designed to convince people to believe in an idea or doctrine.
> **doctrine** – an idea taught as the truth
> **industrial** – related to, used by, or created by industry
> **bestow** – give, donate
> **alms** – charitable donations

King Danoclys rules out books for the mere purpose of entertainment. Like the culture of Danaynock, he thinks these books "soft" and also "of no use to the foolish and lazy peoples whom inhabit this land." If a fictional manuscript is thought to be very well-written, the story will pass to King Danoclys, who scans it and signs his approval or disapproval. A few books, such as *The Prisoners of the Gory Danians* and *The Danians Who Butchered a Lamb (For Children)* pass, but usually it is the unfortunate case that King Danoclys will consider the book trash (with a scornful cry of "Beheaded!").

The influence of **propaganda** heavily affects the **industrial** community—but *only* the industrial community. Posters picture King Danoclys as broad-shouldered with bulging muscles, wearing rich button-up vests of pure gold thread and very fashionable zipper-up blue trousers. Other posters picture him kneeling down to **bestow alms** to the poor. Although Danoclys assuredly never does such things, many *think* he does, and worship him as though he were a god.

The works of great philosophers and scientists are immediately disapproved. King Danoclys strongly believes that if the peasants are educated more than "they need their damn little heads to contain," his throne will be endangered. He desires to remain as their great superior, with them all inferiors in every way possible. Farmers, for instance, are worked from four in the morning to seven in the night, with the harangues of enraged slave drivers ringing in their ears. Young maidens around the age of fifteen are taken from their homes each month as a tribute from the peasants and trained to be maidservants in the king's castle or other nobles' estates. Many of these girls never return.

But here remains the question—*What does the public say about this?*

A: That they're displeased with this and that they'll all commit mass murder in the halls of King Danoclys's castle if the law doesn't change.

B: That they're driven insane with this terrible law and that they're all going to evacuate Danaynock.

C: Nothing. They can't. They're afraid.

Sadly, C. In fear of King Danoclys (who does not prohibit freedom of speech openly but publicly beheads those who try), the populace keeps quiet in hopes that life will change.

History Facts That Will Come in Handy

Ever felt like you can't get enough of history? Need help with your homework? Well, *History Facts That Will Come in Handy* holds the key! Just put on your reading glasses and you're in for the adventure!

Ancient Egypt

Come and explore the tomb of the ancient pharaohs who once ruled the fertile soil of Egypt! Finger the linen that dressed the most divine daughters of the Nile! Would you ever guess that the ladies' hair was scented with bear fat? As the room temperature increased, the fat would melt, drenching the woman in sweet-smelling perfumes. And would you ever think that the tomb robbers would often be the most trusted guards themselves? Can you imagine the curses the pharaohs used to protect their tombs—and the effect? You'll learn this, and much more, in the Ancient Egypt section!

Junior Archaeologist, behold! The wonders of the ancient country of Egypt! In that palace, a pharaoh may have once sat kissing his beloved queen! Cats sacred to the religious order may have strode about, being pampered by servants! Statues of the gods Isis and Osiris may have been bathed in holy water by high priests, while prisoners of war were paraded through the bustling streets with spear points at their backs.

If you wanted to explore farther…then is the great pyramid of King Tut all right?

Memoirs of a Miserable Soldier
Recorded By P. Philippe

Oh, how I rue the day I joined the Grande Army! This march through Russia is pure torture, wearing down my boots till I have nothing more than rags to wear on my bruised feet! Ice grows around men's beards, and even comrades will hide their food and eat in secrecy, if any food is to be found. We eat horseflesh now, and the blood of these animals is most savory. I did see one man in the cavalry scoop out the insides of his dead horse and climb in to keep himself warm. As I scribble these words without a single fire to warm me, my hands are shivering and can barely hold the pen which I use to prevent my hands from growing numb. Others sleep, which is a mistake. Why, I and a few of my fellow privates recently had to shake an officer awake and slap his arms and legs! This is a simple death march. There is not even a warm cup of coffee to keep us awake and to warm our chilled hands. The amount of bodies that lie in the roadside ditches are enormous. Indeed, some are driven crazy by this tormenting place. One of Napoleon's closest friends recently started to go around wearing only his sword. Now he has been found dead with his own sword plunged in his heart. If the smelliest of barns is open, men will run in so fast that others are trampled. One unfortunate man touched the frozen metal of our cannons and escaped leaving bits of his own skin and flesh on the surface. He then tore a piece of his already quite ragged and torn pants and wrapped it around his painful finger. Others will be wise not to follow his example.

When kids get into writing, they love a chance to show off their skills by making actual products. I have always been surprised at how easily most children are able to adopt a journalistic tone. 'Journalism' allows kids to display their natural talent for mimicry; it also gives them a rare chance to sound authoritative. Adora expressed her love for good food by her creating a restaurant menu. While having fun with such projects, they continue to build the very skills they are demonstrating: organization, style range, and the ability to use writing to inform or convince. The following project was not an assignment. It was an enthusiastic playtime activity. To my mind, it beats video games.

SHOWCASE
We Welcome New Readers

This is the first issue of *S.O.L. Showcase*, and we hope that you will enjoy our writing. From crosswords, poems, art, and more, we'll always be your favorite school newspaper!

ABOUT SEEDS OF LEARNING

By Adora Svitak, Editor

It is a warm morning at Seeds of Learning in late June. July is coming, and summer has just recently showed its efforts to warm the shivering students.

"This weather is unbearable. It's *summer*, for heaven's sake!" Adora Svitak, seven, remarks. All pupils heartily agree with *that*. Although summer is the main topic for "What I wish would come," nobody is really that depressed. After all, who could be when there are games like "Marco Polo" or "Monkey in the Middle" to play? Entering the fun-filled recess room of Seeds of Learning, I realize how many games these scholars have scraped up from just one purple ball—and five students.

In the culinary life of S.O.L., the famished pupils gather in the medium-sized kitchen at about twelve or twelve-thirty to chat, exchange news, and most importantly, eat. Occasionally, chips will be exchanged for cake, and sandwiches for dumplings, adding on to the friendly atmosphere of S.O.L.'s kitchen.

Seeds of Learning students come daily, excluding the weekends. They come at various times, some early, some late, and some just right on time. Karen Yao and Joav Gomez are the last to arrive this Thursday, taking their usual places at two of the three tables in the room. Joav sits next to Michael Quinn, who arrived minutes before Joav and Karen. Adrianna Svitak was the earliest to arrive, due to the fact that she lives in the upper section of the house. Adora Svitak, who is Adrianna's younger sister, follows soon after.

BREAKING NEWS

By Adora Svitak

Supreme Court Justice Sandra O'Connor stepped down from her position as Justice at the Supreme Court. She was born in 1930, and nominated to her position by President Ronald Regan in 1981.

A YOUNG MUSICIAN

Edited by Adora Svitak

Adrianna Svitak is only nine years old—and yet, she is already a talented violinist and pianist. With teachers such as James Chen for piano and Christine Dunaway for violin, it's no surprise that she's so good. Of course, talent runs in the family. Adrianna's sister, Adora Svitak, is, after all a prolific writer. Her dad, John Svitak, has a PhD, and her mother, Joyce Svitak, is the founder and president of Seeds of Learning and a successful businesswoman. Adrianna had renowned teachers when she started piano, due to the fact that her parents have excellent taste. Again, it's no surprise Adrianna's a great musician!

BREAKING NEWS:

Adrianna has been cleared of all charges by Judge Joyce Svitak of S.O.L. court! Charged with monkeying around, Adrianna was found to be innocent. Why? The evidence of a pencil was found in Adrianna's back pants pocket. Adrianna was reluctant to let them search her, as the pencil was gold and green striped and a special present from a friend. Again, Adrianna has been cleared of all charges, and although S.O.L. teacher protests that Adrianna was behaving inappropriately by reaching over the table.

"Maybe she was," Adora Svitak, seven, says. "But still, on the charges of monkeying around, I think that you can practically know that everyone is innocent." Adrianna will be giving free autographs away to supporters on July 1, 2005.

CLASSIFIEDS

By Adora Svitak

READ *Dragon*, *Stallion*, and *Tiger*! *Dragon* is a fun-filled magazine for kids ages six to seven, with games, stories, and facts about dragons! Move up one—to *Stallion*, for kids age eight to nine, with the same fun but more mature activities and longer stories! And, last but not least, *Tiger!!!* For kids ten and up! Get a subscription now!!

Dragon Magazine

The dragon is a beautiful mythical creature, peaceful when left alone, fierce when bothered. The only thing that can kill a dragon is an arrow shot straight and true into the dragon's weak spot, which varies with the different breeds. Dragons are almost impossible to tame, and it is extremely dangerous to try. They are extremely cunning and therefore puzzling riddles, temptations, and threats are no use against the great beasts.

Dragons are also unconquerable in battle. They have a strong set of scales protecting the sides of their skin and occasionally some scales on their backs. The rest of their bodies are mostly protected by thick green (or dark red in the case of the Hammerdragons) skin.

The different breeds of dragon are: Hammerdragons, Blue Anvils, Golden-Eyed Dragos, and Narrerdragons. There are many more breeds, but they are closely related or unimportant so I will not list them. Hammerdragons are slow in flying and destructive in landing. Their claws can smash anything with the power of the mightiest hammer.

Blue Anvils are not really blue, but a unique shade of green. No one knows the origin of the name, but there is a hint that the Northern Dwarves named the dragon in honor of their great smiths, who could carve anything into any manner of shape or tool. Blue Anvils are Hammerdragons' tenth cousins, heavy but not nearly so destructive.

Golden-Eyed Dragos have, as you probably guessed, golden eyes. Most dragons have purple, red, or black eyes. Dragos are extremely rare, due to the fact that they have almost no scales to protect them.

Narrerdragons are very special and are never harmed by the rest of the warring dragons. Why? Because Narrerdragons are special in the way that they do not grow except at birth and for the first five years of life. By then they reach their full height and width of six feet, length, and three feet, width.

Well, now you know enough about dragons. Enjoy reading!

The Cavern of the Dragon

Long ago, in the great caverns of Gyraos, which was on the Western side of the Great Forest, there lived a Dragon called Myaat. He was a Narrerdragon, and lived with a young ragged girl who named herself Miriam, having heard the name in The Land of Folk. Miriam had been cast away from The Land of Folk due to her broken arm and supposed ugliness. Myaat loved Miriam and treated her like his own daughter. Miriam loved Myaat like a father. Nobody had ever rumpled her short, crooked red hair lovingly as Myaat did. Nobody had ever smiled like Myaat when Miriam showed him her rabbit-like teeth. Myaat even allowed Miriam to ride him—the rarest thing a dragon ever allowed humans to do. Often Miriam could be seen by the other dragons flying high above the clouds, much to the dismay of the people who lived in The Land of Folk.

"It's unfair," they whined and muttered. "She'll meet a bad end, she will. If only we had kept her to work in the slums! Then she wouldn't have gotten what she hasn't even worked for!"

On the day that Miriam turned twelve years old (although she did not know it herself), Myaat became ill. Sick, in the dragon case, means spurting smoke from nostrils and occasionally a loud cough or so. Miriam stayed at Myaat's side until Myaat shooed her away, quite weakly.

"My last hour has come," Myaat said mournfully (in dragon language, which Miriam understood, of course). "Go, child, and come back when I give a cry." Miriam obeyed Myaat dutifully, although she was in tears as she did so. She was worried that Myaat would be too weak to cry out to her, and therefore she would not have a moment to talk with Myaat. But Myaat scraped up his strength and cried for Miriam, who at once ran to the cavern.

"Child," Myaat said, great drops of dragon tears coming from his misty eyes. "I must leave you now and go to the Land that is far away. But…" and here Myaat breathed smoke from his nostrils, "I fear for your safety. For the dragons who will come to this cavern afterwards have no thought of you, my dear plum. I entrusted the cavern to my friend, Yarghr Golden-Eyes. I have told him about you. But there will be other dragons…rough ones, ones you cannot trust. So take this piece of advice —trust nobody. This land is one of treachery, deception, secret plots, and lies. You will always be in danger. I leave you now." And with that, Myaat rolled over with a groan and breathed smoke from his nostrils one last time.

The Dragon War

Deep in the Great Forest, Hammerdragons and Blue Anvils lived and fought each other for control of the Supreme Empire. The Supreme Empire had been ruled and kept in peace by wise old Hyrkr Hammerdragon. Because the previous Supreme Ruler had been a Hammerdragon, the Hammerdragons insisted that the next Ruler would have to be a Hammerdragon also. They stormed Supreme Palaces, looting ancient treasures and stealing what rightfully belonged to Blue Anvils. The Blue Anvils were angered beyond anger. The Hammerdragons had been gaining too much power, and they were getting terribly conceited.

> ## Dragon cut-outs
>
> Want to make dragons and act out fierce battles? Knights in shining armor and damsels in distress? It's easy. Just get some paper, crayons, and a pencil. Draw what you're imagining! Knights, swords, dragons, princesses...
> Then, get a pair of scissors and cut along the edge of your drawing. If six or younger, ask a parent to help.
> Finally, take some dry and clean Popsicle sticks. Glue your cut-out drawings on the sticks. You have your show!

Why couldn't a Blue Anvil be the next Ruler? In their fury, the Blue Anvils kidnapped Hammerdragon women and children, holding them as hostages in their great fortresses. Despite their great cunning, the Hammerdragons were confused. What should they do next? They had been warned that if they made a single move—a single move that hinted an attack—then their wives and children would be executed. If they submitted to the will of the Blue Anvils, then the hostages would be freed. But Hammerdragons do not give up easily. They collected a group of the smallest Narrerdragons and offered quite a share in the treasure and gold in return for attacking the Blue Anvils. Each of the Narrerdragons was made to swear that if caught, they would not reveal who they had been sent by. The Hammerdragons sent the Narrerdragons off, sure that the plan would work. But it didn't.

To be continued.

Ado's Restaurant

Appetizers

Sourdough Bread $1.00
(With Butter or Cream Cheese)

Beverages

Tea $1.23
(With a choice of Green Tea, Chai Tea, or Blackcurrant Tea)
Juice $1.00
(Orange Juice, Apple Juice, or Grape Juice)

Entrees

Salmon $19.90
Pizza $14.00
Chicken Breast $13.00

Side Dishes

French Fries $3.35
Chowder $4.00

Salads

Caesar Salad $9.00
House Salad $8.90
Garden Salad $8.90
(With a choice of either Ranch or Blue Cheese dressing)

Soups

Pumpkin Soup $6.40

Desserts

Fried Banana $4.00
Chocolate Truffles $10.00
Hot Fudge Sundae $5.00
Vanilla Ice Cream $5.00

Kid's Menu:

Fish and Chips $4.99
Flapjacks and Maple Syrup $5.99
Eggs and Bacon $3.99
(A choice of scrambled or poached eggs)
Pizza $4.99
(Cheese or Pepperoni)
Sandwich Squares $3.99
(All Kid's Meals come with French Fries and Ketchup)
Beverages
Milk $1.99
Juice $1.99
(with a choice of Apple, Grape, or Orange)
Coke $1.59

Come to Ado's Restaurant! Named the Best Restaurant of the Year by the *Washington Favorite!* Get a **50%** discount with this coupon!

Come to Ado's Restaurant! Buy one item from the Kid's Menu and get another **free!**

Adora loves to teach! She has been teaching since age five. She savors any chance she gets to prepare for her lesson, assume active teaching duty and write workbooks or test kits. Even though she is not as eager to learn math as she is writing or history, when she is allowed to use her writing to learn math, her attitude improves. You will find a lesson plan, reading comprehension exercises, and an actual test kit in this section (Adora was a substitute teacher during our summer writing workshop).

To make sure that everyone remembers the meaning of these words, I will have them say or write sentences in which they include the following review vocabulary words.

REVIEW VOCABULARY	NEW VOCABULARY
bombastic	epic
ambivalent	pious
zenith	mortified
vellum	impersonate
insular	rapier
solace	uncouth
insipid	
scrutinize	

We will play a short game of Hitchhiker with both old and new vocabulary words. To make sure they really grasp the meaning of the words, I will have the students write short stories including as many vocabulary words as possible. The pupil with the most vocabulary words included wins...and who knows—I might have a treat for them after Recess. I will have a short story time in which the students present their articles, followed by reading from a history book and a fun pop quiz.

Math Word Problems

1) Adora has a lot of cupcakes!! Adrianna has sixteen, and Daddy has thirty-two. How many times does the number of Adrianna's cupcakes go into Daddy's number of cupcakes?

2) Most distinguished Mr. Garrick Bee has entered the I'm Nothing But Goo store! Garrick wants to rent a purple tuxedo, which costs $10.00. Also, the tuxedo is fifty percent off! Mr. Bee has only has $4.00, however. Will that be enough???? If not, how much money will Mr. Bee have to borrow from Mr. Regal Bee?

3) Mr. Regal Bee is tasting different kinds of honey in the annual honey contest. It is down to three contestants. Miss Bella Fingermidget has three-fourths (75 %) of a jug of honey, Miss Arga Snothog has one-half (50%) of a jug, and Mrs. Anna McLean has one-fourth (25%) of a jug. Mr. Regal Bee was struck by a serious stomach problem known as "Honey-itis" in the middle of drinking Miss Arga Snothog's honey. If Mr. Bee had to stop in the middle of Miss Snothog's honey, what fraction of Miss Snothog's honey did he drink?

Reading Comprehension

The Best Jack's Prep Book

Far, far away in the realm of Phorphae, there lived a king known as the Green King. He was called the Green King because of his long, moss-like hair; also, in Phorphaen the word 'green' meant someone who was disorganized and messy, which was fitting. He had five sons. Now it was the custom for the younger princes to be called jacks, and for them to go fight against the enemy when war arose. The youngest jack was called Cwaren, and for long he had wished for a time to come when he would be able to join his brothers in fighting in the wars. When the War of Social Standard arose, he was most eager.

"O my father," Cwaren had said to the Green King, "I plead of you to give me your blessing, and your permission to join my brethren fighting in the great wars."

"Thou be but a youth!" the Green King exclaimed.

"And so I may be, O my father, but I yearn to join my brethren in these wars," Cwaren had replied.

1.) Who is the main character in this story? Explain. (Answers may vary.)

_____

_____

2.) Who is the youngest jack? Does the story include this information?

_____

_____

3.) What does Cwaren yearn to do in this story? Does the story include this information? _____

_____

_____

4.) Circle one.
The war which was raging between the Blue King and the Green King was called:

The War of Fiery Dreams   The War of Social Standard

Part II

"Go, then, O my son, with my blessing, go, go to join your brethren," the Green King said. And so Cwaren quickly made leave, with his train of attendants, and three squires of honor beside him to ensure his safety.

"And good luck be with thee!" the Green King shouted, his great mane of mossy hair blowing in the wind.

When Cwaren reached the camp, he found his brothers.

"If thou want to join us, thou are not welcome," Hispede, the eldest jack, said coldly.

1.) Who does not welcome Cwaren? Is this information included, and if so, how?_____

_____

_____

2.) Who wishes Cwaren good luck? If yes, how was the information presented in the story?_____

_____

_____

3.) How many squires does Cwaren have with him? _____

4.) Circle one. The squires were with Cwaren to:

Ensure his safety   Bring him to the Blue King

Mathematics

1.) There were twenty-four veils in the box Hispede brought out. Each soldier used two veils, and there were four veils left over in the box. How many soldiers were there?
Answer: _____

2.) Each prisoner was tied with three coils of rope. Twenty-one coils of rope were used. How many prisoners were there?
Answer: _____

3.) The Blue King's army would retreat back to their camp after three hours of fighting had passed. They rested for one hour each time. In one day, how many times would they retreat back to their camp?
Answer: _____

4.) The Kingdom of Green is twenty miles away from the river. The Kingdom of Blue is eighty-five miles away from the river. How many miles is it from the Kingdom of Green to the Kingdom of Blue?
Answer: _____

5.) There were forty gold coins in each part of the chest. Fifty percent of the coins were rusty. How many coins were rusty?
Answer: _____

6.) The Green King had ten pairs of underpants. Nathile decorated ten percent of the pairs with camels. How many did Nathile decorate with camels?
Answer: _____

TEACHERS OR PARENTS ONLY
TOP SECURITY

Cheating is dishonorable—it is what a jack would never do

Answer to:

(1)...10 soldiers

(2)...7 prisoners

(3)...6 retreats

(4)...105 miles

[Adora's Dad adds: This assumes that they are on *opposite* sides of the river (and measuring from the same point and that point and the two kingdoms are on a straight line). The closest they can be (if they're on the same side) is 65 miles.]

(5)...20 rusty coins

(6)...1 pair was decorated with camels

Part IV

Best for Last

> *I believe that women can have different views on politics and religion, and that their voices should be heard!*
>
> *I think wars fit into three categories—they're either religious, political, or merely fought out of greed.*
>
> *I would guess that fulfilling your heart's desire or goal will make one happy. But being with my family brings happiness to me.*

Adora Svitak

Adora on Politics, Media and Society

Joyce: What is the meaning of politics?
Adora: To me, it's a lot of heated discussions and tedious speeches. But politics can also be the root of war and conflict.

Joyce: Would you want to get involved in politics someday?
Adora: Not to the point where I would have to be surrounded by armed guards at every public outing. But I think that it would be harmless if I voted for the president of the United States!

Joyce: In your opinion, what are the causes of war?
Adora: I think wars fit into three categories—they're either religious, political, or merely fought out of greed. I don't believe people seek vengeance and revenge so often anymore, and family feuds just don't last for centuries.

Joyce: If you had the power to choose the members of the Supreme Court, how would you make your choices?
Adora: I would choose three Democrats, three Republicans and three neutral. Three plus three is six, that makes nine, right?

Joyce: Why do you think that media is important?
Adora: It heavily influences the ideas of the people around us. You might never guess that there was propaganda in your daily newspaper or in the everyday news.

Joyce: If you were in charge of making a TV program, what kind of program would you like to produce?
Adora: I would probably make a travel show for the family that focused on historical sites, as well as a talk show featuring young prodigies, educational programs, and everyday subjects.

Joyce: How do you feel about being under the spotlight? What are your concerns of being closely watched by critics and public?
Adora: Being in the spotlight never troubled me that much. I might have got a little bit nervous before shows, but I always felt comfortable once I had "settled in" with the show. As for your second question, I find it amusing reading the words of critics.

Joyce: If one day you become famous, how would you use your fame?
Adora: To donate money to good causes and charities (Plus I might hold a few festivals for every season). I would try to improve the national education system so that the children of America would grow up to be informed, intelligent adults.

Joyce: What's your impression of American society today?
Adora: I believe that we could improve our education system if we were determined to make the children of America grow up into educated, resourceful adults. A great number of the homeless and poor are those who grew up uneducated.

Joyce: What can children contribute to society?
Adora: To let his or her creativeness flow. Adults sometimes appear more restricted about their ideas, not so quick to let them known. Young Children can have natural creativeness, being somewhat less concerned about the events around the world.

Joyce: If you had the power to establish a brand new society, what type of system would you use, such as democracy, anarchy, dictatorship, socialism, oligarchy, communism, or either or a combination of and why?
Adora: I think I would use democracy, because you can actually stand up and voice your opinions!!!!

Joyce: If most people want the same thing, why do we disagree on so many issues?
Adora: Well, we ourselves are different. We might want to achieve the same thing, but we might also think of different ways to achieve that goal. Then an argument might break out.

Joyce: Why is it important for people to understand and accept the way people from different culture think and behave?
Adora: We were all born into different families with different cultures and it's not our fault. Just because you're Catholic or Jewish doesn't mean you're inferior in any way.

Joyce: In what ways do you think that children can contribute to society? Why do you think that it's important to contribute to society when you are still young?
Adora: Try to practice your talents—it's good to use them when you're still a child. Music, writing, drawing, anything! Almost anything

you can do contributes to society. It is important to contribute to society when you're still young so you know what to do when you grow up to be an adult.

 ## Adora on History and Religion

Joyce: You seem to be very interested in what happened during the Civil War. What are the most interesting facts?
Adora: They used women a lot as spies during the Civil war. No one would check their hoop skirts (hoop skirts were these big metal things they put in their skirts to make them stick out. I think they're outlandish myself), so they could stow letters. It's amazing how people found different ways to live.

Joyce: What intrigues you when you read historical books?
Adora: I like reading about ambushes. I put battles in quite a lot of my writing to make it exciting. I'm also very interested in the armor.

Joyce: What's one interesting thing you found in your reading about the American Revolution?
Adora: In the American Revolution it took four men to operate a cannon, so when Molly Pitcher's husband fell down she jumped up and took his place.

Joyce: You have read many biographies of world leaders, who are your favorite historical figures?
Adora: My favorite historical characters are Chairman Mao, Napoleon, Queen Elizabeth, Mary Queen of Scotts, Queen Victoria and Eleanor of Aquitaine (she married this one guy but he was too serious for her, so she divorced him and set up a court of her own that was full of jugglers and musicians and women who wanted to be free).

Joyce: Who are the historical figures you read about who have changed the course of human history the most?
Adora: Adolf Hitler, Napoleon Bonaparte, George Washington, Chairman Mao, Joan of Arc, and Jesus.

Joyce: You seem to favor the feminine movement. Why do you think that it's important that women should have the same power and rights as men in today's society?
Adora: I believe that women can have different views on politics and religion, and that their voices should be heard!

Joyce: Who are some of your favorite female characters in history?

Adora: I find Joan of Arc and Eleanor of Aquitaine very interesting characters, as well as Queen Cleopatra, Queen Elizabeth, Queen Victoria, Anne Boleyn, Mary the Queen of Scots, Marie Antoinette, and Phyllis Wheatley.

Joyce: If you could live in any historical time period, which time periods would you like to experience and why?

Adora: I would like to experience living in the Tudor times to witness the tragic epidemic of the Plague, as well as the Victorian Age for its industrial boom, the Renaissance for its renowned art, medieval times for the code of chivalry, and World War II for the excitement of being in a blackout.

Joyce: Which historical rulers would you like to consider to rule our country today? Why?

Adora: Eleanor of Aquitaine might be a possible candidate because of her independence and intelligence, Queen Victoria for her determination and aggressiveness, Marie Antoinette for her sense of humor, and Queen Cleopatra for her cleverness and willpower.

Joyce: You have read some books on religion. Why do you think that we have so many kinds of seemingly different religion in the world?

Adora: I believe that people find different ways to explain their birth, the creation of the earth, and the afterlife. I do not believe any particular religion, but I respect the beliefs of all humans.

Joyce: Do you have any preference in any religion? Why?

Adora: I might favor Taoism slightly for its "few rules as possible!" law, but Buddhism, Islam, and Christianity are also highly interesting religions.

Joyce: Why are you interested in religion?

Adora: It affects people highly, not to mention an epic holy war could break out and destroy the lives of many people who deserved to live another decade.

Adora on Reading and Writing

Joyce: How did you start to write?
Adora: My mom got me a laptop, which I experimented on. I began typing stories, and that's how it really all began.

Joyce: Please describe your feelings when you write?
Adora: My feelings are just…it seems like I am just in the world of what I am typing.

Joyce: How do you deal with the common 'writer's block'?
Adora: When I do have a writer's block, I usually start another story. Or go back to an old one.

Joyce: How do you come up with all those fantastic names in your stories?
Adora: Most of my names were inspired by books I read. However, I do mix letters together to create names like "Bulrox" and "Crastitoles."

Joyce: Do you make your names fit the time period you are writing about?
Adora: Usually I do make the names fit the time period—for instance, I would not have a wacko name like "Moonunit1" in the age of chivalry.

Joyce: Why is reading important to you?
Adora: It is like fuel for writing and an inspiration. It is like my life.

Joyce: What do you want your readers to get from your stories?
Adora: I want them to be inspired by me to read and write more.

Joyce: Why do you prefer books over TV and video games?
Adora: Books inspire me more. Most TV and video games are nothing but worthless cartoons. Books open up a world of imagination.

Joyce: Can you imagine a society without books? What could happen if people are not reading and writing?
Adora: No, I most certainly could not imagine a society without books. I think I wouldn't have the will to live there.

Adora on Parenting and Childhood

Joyce: What's your idea and image of a good parent?
Adora: Creative, caring, supportive, and loving.

Joyce: What do you think is the cause so many children are obsessed with cartoons and video games instead of spending time reading and writing?
Adora: I believe they're not encouraged or told to read or write until after watching TV and playing video games becomes a habit.

Joyce: What's your concept of a happy childhood?
Adora: Feeling carefree, being happy, reading, writing, drawing, and playing.

Joyce: When you become a parent yourself, how much will you be like your own parents? What would you change?
Adora: I believe I would be almost entirely like my parents, except I wouldn't have my mom's accent or her tendency to brag about her countless accomplishments at every available chance.

Joyce: What would you suggest to parents if they wanted to help their children read and write better?
Adora: To encourage them continually until they developed a sense of self-confidence and begin writing their own stories and reading advanced books.

Joyce: How are you influenced by your parents?
Adora: I think I get my talkative side from my mom and my pessimist side from my dad.

Joyce: What are your favorite family time activities?
Adora: Cranium Turbo Edition, Chess, Scrabble (not to say that I'm that good at it, but never mind), visit to Theno's Dairy (great ice cream place), walk around the block, pick blackberries in the woods, and hike on park trails.

Adora on Education and Kids

Joyce: Why do you think it's important to get other kids more interested in reading and writing?

Adora: If they do not have an interest in reading and writing, they will not be as educated as they could be. Things that would happen if they weren't educated: They wouldn't be able to find decent jobs; they might use drugs not knowing how bad it is for them, and other things.

Joyce: What do you think you can do to get other kids more interested in reading and writing?

Adora: I think that if kids saw somebody (like me) who really enjoyed reading and writing, they might start it too.

Joyce: Are you willing to do workshops with other kids to demonstrate your writing process?

Adora: Yes, I think it would be a good idea.

Joyce: Do you think reading and writing has influence and effect on politics?

Adora: Yes, because you might read something wrong and think that "George Bush believes John Kerry has a pineapple head" was really "John Kerry believes George Bush has a pinhead." If they didn't read well, they might not be able to read the necessary voting information and would make uninformed decisions.

Joyce: Do you think that you have some special skills in writing? What can you teach other children about writing?

Adora: I think I might like it a little bit more than some children, and plus I have the never-ending support of my parents! Also, I like to read, and I learn to write better as I read more advanced books. I would teach them to just be creative—it's their story! You don't necessarily have to write the ideas of your siblings or parents just because you feel like you have to! Sometimes it's nice to have your parents for support, but as you grow older I think you'll develop more ideas of your own.

Joyce: Why is it important to you that children need to read and write more?

Adora: Because nowadays some children are lacking skills in reading and writing, and they are saying things like "I don't like to read" or "I don't want to write." That hurts me very much.

Joyce: What aspects of homeschooling do you enjoy the most? Is there anything about homeschool you wish to change?

Adora: I like homeschooling because it is not so distracting, as is public school, and there is more individual learning. I do not wish to change anything about homeschooling.

Joyce: What aspects of public education do you think that we should improve?

Adora: Not so many students in one class, more one-on-one tutoring, and higher expectations from school staff.

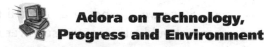 **Adora on Technology, Progress and Environment**

Joyce: What has technology, especially Microsoft Office has done for your writing?

Adora: Microsoft Word boosted my energy to use new vocabulary and not be afraid if I made spelling mistakes. Microsoft Word also has a variety of different fonts which I find useful if the font can reflect the time period I am writing about.

Joyce: What are examples of technology that has improved people's lives?

Adora: It improved mine, and I think that if used correctly, it should improve the lives of others also. Technology helped me learn a list of brand new vocabulary and other things I would never imagine to learn.

Joyce: Do you believe that technology and progress in science can potentially bring harmful results in our lives?

Adora: No, unless suddenly a machine that was supposed to help cure some disease suddenly went haywire and killed the patient instead. I mean, there's quite a lot of things that could happen, but as long as it isn't too serious I think it's fine.

Joyce: In which region of the world do you think we should use more technology?

Adora: If one place is just getting a lot of technology while Africa doesn't even have a computer yet, it's just not fair.

Joyce: You used to stand on the rock in our old neighborhood's park and give passionate speeches on protecting the environment. Why are you so concerned about it?

Adora: We must protect our environment because it gives us fresh air, shade, and natural beauty. If we continue to chop down trees and pollute the air, we will no longer have the natural beauty and fresh air we once had.

Joyce: Do Americans have more responsibility to protect our environment? Why?

Adora: Yes, I believe that Americans should take more responsibility to protect the environment. Since we squander our natural resources more than other countries, we should take care to use fewer resources and be more careful about our use of cars and other things that pollute the environment.

Adora on Travel, Food, Leisure Time and Happiness

Joyce: You are very excited about travel and eating good food. What does each of the activity bring to you?

Adora: Both bring me happiness and nourishment.

Joyce: If you could go to travel to any three places in the world right now, where would you like to travel and why?

Adora: Europe for its many landmarks, China for the famous Great Wall and the Forbidden City, and Alaska for its snowy land.

Joyce: Why do you think that it's important that people have leisure time in their lives?

Adora: I believe it is important for us to have a little rest from our daily routines or else life may seem boring to us—for example, get up, get dressed, eating breakfast, etc. We could add reading before getting dressed and chatting with a sibling or parent before eating breakfast.

Joyce: Is there difference between being fortunate and being happy?

Adora: Definitely. Being fortunate does not necessarily make you happy. For instance, even if you survived Hurricane Katrina, you might be dripping wet from the flood, undernourished from lack of food, and very feverish. I don't know about you, but I would not be happy if I had the fever.

Joyce: Are you an optimist or pessimist? What are the pro and cons of choosing either?

Adora: I am probably a pessimist. When you're a pessimist, you're all the more happier when things go right, and you're not terribly disappointed when things go wrong because you've been expecting it to go like that anyways. But sometimes it can make you grumpy and miserable. Being an optimist (like my mom) will probably make you happy and cheerful most of the time. But if things do not go as you expected them to, your hopes will be dashed and you will be all the more upset.

Joyce: In your opinion what brings happiness to people? What brings happiness to you?

Adora: I would guess that fulfilling your heart's desire or goal will make one happy. But being with my family brings happiness to me.

Selected Poems by Adora

The Philosopher

In his candlelit chamber...
The philosopher works...
Day and night...
Without a rest.

It is great research...
But never credited...
Nothing has worked...
Nobody has paid attention...
But this time they will.

And the philosopher tires...
But he keeps on...
He keeps on through the night.

And on the morrow...
The philosopher wakes...
And studies his books.

A scroll and a stick...
That will tell him...
A ruler made by Merlin...
Will give him success.

And so his work is credited...
Like the philosopher dreamed it would be...
And, his work done, he fell into the
Endless Slumber...
Which he well deserves.

Fairies

One dark night...
In the green of the wood...
Comes young Hazel...
Clad in gold...
Hair shining like pearls...
Gliding across the water.

The fairies surround her...
Their Queen, their ruler...
Hazel stands serenely...
And is gone with the wind.

The fairies go after her...
The wind brings them along...
And they fly and fly...
And the sky becomes clear.

They sprinkle their blessings
On children's windows...
And Hazel rings her bell...
And the sun rises.

And the fairies disappear...
To come back another year.

If I Were a Philosopher

If I were a philosopher,
With a long crooked nose,
Ragged robes, not with bows,
Then I would study my scrolls.

If I were a philosopher,
With the most slender of tapers lighting my way
Then I would write hundreds and hundreds of pages

But I'm not a philosopher
with deep thoughts and ragged robes.

I'm just a poet....
Imagining I'm a philosopher.

Ghost

Under a night with a starry sky,
Under a night with dark blue up high,
Under the night, they sit together,
Anonymous men, as white as a feather.

Quietly they lurk around,
Making not a single sound.
At the stroke of midnight,
They all vanish, leaving their trail shining bright.

In The Land of Darkness

In the land of darkness where the shadows fall
There is a great magic as strong as a stone wall
Where demons and witches and sorcerers roam
For it is their great indestructible home.

In the dark and yet bright middle land
There is no justice, and yet no unkind hand
Both cruel men and kind men wander there,
With many maidens who are sweet and fair.

In the land of light where the sun rays shine bright
There is goodness impossible to fight
Strong noble men defend their lovely castles,
With archers and knights and their ready vassals.

Battle Field

And it was a bright and sunny day,
When he fed his horse some hay,
And mounted the horse, and kicked the spurs,
Speaking to the innkeeper with a slight slur.

On the battlefield it be a solemn sight,
Many men lay dead, although the sun shines bright
Houses destroyed are now black ashes
Their angry owners escaping with great gashes
The cannons are slowly rolled away
Their surviving bearers walked with a sway
On the battlefield it be a solemn sight.

The Princess

In the castle awaits a knight....
Perhaps he's come for me!
The princess awaits...
On her fine steed she rides,
A shining ghost in the midnight.

Oh how she rides!....and they're off...

Against her father's will!
The knight is poor, the princess rich...
And the knight is not nobly born!
And they pass through the streets,
Where nobody can disturb them,
And nobody can tell them to leave!

The King is soundly in bed,
The Queen is almost dead,
The princes are playing,
The horses are a-neighing,
And light begins to shine!

The knight says farewell,
To the sad tears of the princess,
For this is her wedding day!
Her betrothed stands
a-waiting, impatiently
Gazing at the sky.

And many years after,
The knight comes again....
A spirit...
Crying for his love.

The Noblewoman

The noblewoman's dresses rustle as she walks
Her flaxen hair falls into a cascade of a million locks
She has her pick of handmaidens to wait on her
And she wears a red cape trimmed with finest fox fur
Her ladyship is quite skilled at hawking
Men come to her chamber door a-knocking
Just to get a glimpse of that haughty lady.

The noblewoman's servants whisper of her deeds
As they stand in gardens, picking out the weeds
They're quite sure she'll never hear
Even as they loudly jeer
While she peers out from the outside stair
Bathing in cool water her white face fair
Staring at her body in a crystal mirror.

There passes all of us

There pass the horses, with golden saddles bright,
There pass the mermen, holding scepters of light,
There pass the milkmaids, with cheeks so fair and white,
There passes the great king, with his tummy so grand,
There passes his beloved queen, who sits while being fanned,
There pass their noble vassals, clutching precious grants of land,
There pass the weary serfs, with their fair wives,
There pass their hunting dogs, black and eating chives,
There pass the spirits old, with their faces ruined by hives,
There pass the golden priests, praying to the Lord,
There pass the courageous knights, with their noble horde,
There pass the singing minstrels, playing the harpsichord,
There passes all of us, playing, whining, singing, sitting,
working, dining, praying, dying.

In The Darkness of the Night

In the darkness of the night
Stands hidden a tall lady
With her shining rings so bright
She stands there, attired in a green gown tight.

She stands, straight and proud,
Though she be in a web of woe
Stands she with her kinsmen short and loud
Surrounding a burial shroud.

And there approaches the opposing troops—
Lurking in shadows dim,
They leap out, twirling and shooting in great loops,
Only to trip over many hoops.

And the lady's fair face pales
About these men, she was told many tales
As they rise, a dagger she grabs,
And she flees down the greenish dale.

Why is there?

Why is there a roof over my head?
Why is there a pillow and a nice warm bed?
Why am I not out in the cold,
with nothing to eat, too soon growing old?
Why am I rocking in a comfortable chair,
knowing about hunger but not forced to care?
Why is my money not pitifully worn?
Why into this world was I ever born?
Why do I have so many unanswerable musings?
Why, in this world, is there so much confusion?

About the Author

Adora Svitak's literary skills, writing speed, and her commitment to helping other children are dramatically spotlighted by her youth. Her first book, "Flying Fingers" was published when she was seven years old.

Adora envisions a world where all children have the resources to become dynamic readers and writers; where reading and writing help us bridge communication gaps and prevent the misunderstandings and ignorance that lead to conflict. To inspire other children to join her mission, Adora provides her own form of hands-on encouragement: innovative and engaging presentations on how to use writing to entertain, process emotions, and reach a deeper understanding of other subjects.

She is a spokesperson for Verizon's literacy campaign and tours nationally and internationally to teach writing at schools, libraries and bookstores. As a seasoned public speaker, she has given presentations to more than 14,000 students, parents, and professionals. Teacher Felisa Rogers says, "Kids love author visits. Adora's young age and enthusiasm for reading and writing add an exciting element. Kids can really relate to her. When kids meet Adora, being a writer becomes a reachable goal. They have a tangible example of the benefits of concentrating on their writing, and an exciting introduction to the ways writing can be used as a vehicle to explore other subjects. Moreover, they have learned practical tips they will be able to utilize and build upon daily."

In addition to speaking at elementary schools, Adora now conducts writing workshops at high schools, universities, and national educational conferences. To invite Adora to speak at your school or public event, please contact her via her website at www.adorasvitak.com.

Adora lives in Redmond, Washington with her family and studies at the Seeds of Learning school. She has four writing projects currently in the works: two novellas, Yang in Disguise and The Pickpocket Princess; a collection of poetry, Dancing Fingers; and an autobiography.